FLASHBACK GIRL

"*Flashback Girl* is a riveting, compassionately-told story of grit and fortitude. As a childhood burn victim, and now, as a mental health professional (and wife and mother), it's hard to imagine anyone better qualified than Lise Deguire to help teach us lessons in resilience."

—John Hanc, New York Times contributor and co-author of the award-winning memoir, *Your Heart, My Hands* by Arun Singh with John Hanc.

"It may be difficult to imagine how the devastating experience of severe burns could be uplifting, but Lise Deguire has managed to bring light, hope, and strength to her personal story. *Flashback Girl* takes us on her journey from horror to healing, showing us how courage, acceptance, and love guided her every step of the way."

—Barbara Ravage, author of *Burn Unit: Saving Lives After the Flames.*

"*Flashback Girl* is an astounding story of survival and triumph. Deguire's resilience shines as a beacon of hope for anyone who struggles; her self-deprecating humor, wise insights, and astonishing story make for a gripping read. I could not put the book down. A moving tribute to the indomitable human spirit."

— Martha W. Murphy, award-winning author and editor, including co-author of *The Un-Prescription for Autism,* winner of eight national awards and now published in three languages.

Flashback Girl is a unique and inspiring story of resilience in the face of what can only be described as waves of adversity. Yet, as the reader is taken through the choppy waters of Lise's story, we become the recipients of powerful lessons of strength. Flashback Girl, like an agile surfer, finds ways to navigate pain and loss and in the process leaves the reader with a sense of hope and courage.

—Victoria Banyard, clinical psychologist and author of *Toward the Next Generation of Bystander Prevention pf Sexual and Relationship Violence* and numerous articles on resilience; Professor of Social Work at Rutgers University.

"*Flashback Girl* is a story of hope and resilience. Deguire does a beautiful job conveying her pain, both physical and emotional, while leaving the reader inspired by her unwavering courage and strength."

—Beth Schulman, author of *The Gold Mailbox,* a memoir; and *Rosie, The Practically Perfect Puppy,* a children's book.

"To call *Flashback Girl* inspiring is an understatement. Lise Deguire's carefully crafted sentences invite intimacy and pull the reader through this memoir of narrative medicine with momentum. I'd recommend this book to anyone who feels that all hope is lost; Lise Deguire teaches readers how to open and bare their souls, to a place deep beneath our fragile skin."

—Miri Jaffe, Associate Teaching Professor of Writing; Narrative Activist, author of *Spirituality in Mental Health Practice.*

"*Flashback Girl* is Dr. Deguire's deeply personal memoir written to share her personal journey as a burn survivor and the lessons of resilience she learned on her lifelong road to recovery. Told with great urgency and honesty, it is a compelling and affecting story."

—Susan Gregory Johnson, author of *Hey, White Girl!*

FLASHBACK GIRL

Lessons on Resilience From a Burn Survivor

Lise Deguire, Psy.D

DR. LISE DEGUIRE, LLC
114 Straube Center Blvd., Suite 1-7
Pennington, NJ 08534

ISBN 978-1-7349320-0-3 (paperback)
ISBN 978-1-7349320-1-0 (ebook)

Designed by Austin Alphonse

Dedicated to the loving memory of Marc-Emile Deguire.

Contents

This is a true story, as best I can remember. If the story might cause pain for a person, and that person is alive, his/her name has been changed. Other names remain gratefully unchanged, to celebrate the many people who have been kind to me.

Becoming Flashback Girl

I was "Case Number One." I never knew my lawyer presented my sad story to the U.S. Senate. It wasn't until I was 54, trolling the internet, when I discovered my old photo, permanently enshrined in the 1971 Committee on Commerce hearings. These hearings, including my case, eventually led to the landmark creation of the Consumer Product Safety Commission.

I am four years old in this photo, half-naked and burned all over. I am propped up into a sitting position. My hair, which had been honey blonde and bouncy with waves, sprawls in a dark, stringy mess. My chest is completely covered with tight, raw bands of scars. My right arm, also constricted by scars, is attached to my torso by contractures. My left wrist contracts in as well. You can see my tiny right ear and my nose unscarred, still sweet and untouched. The lower half of my face, however, is obliterated. My mouth gapes wide open because I have no lower lip to close it with. Fire has devoured my lip, chin and neck. The remaining skin tightly draws my face down into my chest, like a reverse facelift, preventing any emotional expression.

A black band in the photo covers my eyes to keep me from being recognized. If you could see my eyes, though, I would have been trying to smile as best I could. I was a *Good Girl,* and I aimed to please. Efforts were made to keep my tiny face in profile and to hide my eyes. But burn scarring is as unique as fingerprints; no two burned people get burned exactly the same way. It is clearly me. This was one of several stunning revelations I uncovered as I began to investigate the fire that nearly killed me a half-century ago.

After "the accident" my parents hired an attorney, Edward Swartz. He fought our case against the company National Distillers, manufacturers of Solox, which my mother had poured on the coals while barbecuing during our vacation in New Hampshire. Solox was found to be liable because it did not place a safety valve called a "flashback arrestor" on the Solox can. This half-cent part would have prevented the flames from shooting up the stream of solvent into the can and exploding into a fiery bomb.

This is the story that I was told throughout my childhood and was my explanation to everyone about how I got burned. My parents said that the accident was caused by "lighter fluid" which wasn't canned properly, leading to the explosion which injured my mother and me. The company was negligent and indifferent about their product being packaged unsafely. In this family story, my mother was blameless for the fire. My injuries were entirely due to Solox and its corporate greed.

When I was 54 — the 50th anniversary of the fire — I extricated the yellowed file my father had labeled "the accident" and read it through again. This time, however, something previously unnoticed caught my eye: an article from a local newspaper about my family winning the settlement against Solox. In the article, Solox was described as a "household solvent," not a lighter fluid.

My face furrowed. I stared at this article, which I had read so many times before, wondering for the first time about Solox. Solox had to have been a lighter fluid. It wasn't a household solvent. Who would pour a household solvent on a barbecue? Why would my mother do that?

Solox is no longer manufactured, but it was a product that had been around for decades. I found photos of Solox on the internet, and could read its label: "Solox, Denatured Alcohol Solvent. Shellac thinner, alcohol solvent, cleaning aid" and then: "Warning: Flammable, vapor harmful." The warning was underscored on the back of the Solox can, where it said, in all caps: "CAUTION: FLAMMABLE MIXTURE. DO NOT USE NEAR FIRE OR FLAME."

Given all these warning labels, I don't know how my family even had a case against Solox, let alone won the settlement. According to that small article I read, the warning label about Solox being flammable had been removed. My best guess is that my mother misused the product, and she was at fault for that, but the lack of the flashback-arrestor cap still made the company liable. Also, there were all the devastating photos of this four-year-old girl who was tragically disfigured, which would make a jury sympathetic, regardless of my mother's culpability. So, Solox settled the case with my family and paid us off.

Edward Swartz was a brilliant attorney from Massachusetts. He developed a specialty of cases involving children who had been hurt by toys and defective products. He was one of the leading voices in developing consumer product safety laws, which is how it happened that he testified in front of the U.S. Senate, complete with my half-naked photo. One time, after my case was settled, he visited me in the hospital. He stood tall, with wild, curly hair, his voice enthusiastic and upbeat. He leaned over my bed in the hospital ward, his brown eyes shining with warmth. Because of his efforts, I had money to pay for my school and therapy bills for years to come. I am grateful for this settlement which, while small compared to today's standards, still made my hard life easier.

After I learned about Solox being a household solvent and not a lighter fluid, I tried to call Mr. Swartz. I wanted him to help me understand how we ever won this case at all, given that my mother had misused the product. I learned that Edward Swartz had died. However, I was able to connect with his brother, James, who is also an attorney and works in the same law firm.

I identified myself. "Hi, my name is Lise Deguire and your brother won a case for me from a fire back in 1967. I'm looking for some information."

"Are you the Flashback Girl?" he asked immediately.

"Um, I guess I might be," I said, completely shocked. Flashback Girl? He told me he remembered me well and had lectured many times about my case. He said my case had "changed everything" in the field of product liability and consumer safety.

It moves me to know that my case helped others to be better protected by industry, and led to safer products for other Americans. The Consumer Product Safety Commission, which my case helped inspire, has saved many thousands of lives in our country. Over the decades, the commission has recalled thousands of products that were unsafe and prevented other accidents as bad or much worse than mine. In this way, I guess I have helped more people than I ever have in my psychology practice, even though I never knew anything about it until last year.

Also, I have come to love my new given superhero name: *Flashback Girl*. I have adopted this name; she embodies my quirky survivor identity. In my mind, Flashback Girl wears a bright yellow cape, like Batman's Robin. Her hair flows long, dark and curly in the breeze, and she stands proudly, smiling at the camera. Perhaps her burned lip lays a little crooked. She can hold her arms only halfway above her head, because her arms remain contracted to her sides and require more operations. But no matter. Flashback Girl stands strong, resilient, and smiling. Like the unique scarring pattern lacing her body, she is one of a kind.

With my new name came a new task: it was time to share my true superhero origins. I do have an amazing story to tell, and it only starts with my quirky name. I have endured fire, abandonment, medical torture, negligence, and the death of my entire family. Yet, like Batman and Wolverine, I survived trauma after trauma, strong and resilient. As a psychologist, I now spend my life guiding others toward health and wholeness. How did I get here? Can my superhero life inspire others to keep going? How can we all survive what seems insurmountable?

That is the story of this book.

Prelude

I started writing this memoir three weeks after my mother died. After her funeral ended, and we had emptied her little apartment, I immediately began to work. The book completed itself within a year. The chapters flew out of me, as if writing themselves. I wrote all the time, obsessed. In the middle of the night, chapters marched into my head, unbidden, waking me up. It was as if my unconscious was taking the night shift.

I waited for a half century to tell my story. I waited because I was busy trying to stay alive and to survive. I waited because I was trying to get well, physically and emotionally. I waited because my true story would deeply upset my family, and I am still a Good Girl. So, I waited until my family was dead.

It is said that history is written by the victor. The side that wins gets to say what happened. The North wrote the story of the Civil War. The Allies wrote the story after World War II. History was written by the Europeans who landed in America. History is written by the people who survive.

I stand; I am the lone person left at the end. I am Flashback Girl. I have my own superhero avatar and the scars from my battles, both literal and figurative. I appear now victorious, exuberant and well-loved. I haven't always felt like a superhero though. I have mostly felt small and abandoned.

IN THE HOSPITAL, DRIFTING ALONE

From my earliest hospital days, I have always been afraid that if someone didn't know me, I might die. I would float away into the black universe, a forgotten little burned girl with a crooked lip. Maybe I wouldn't exactly die, but I would be forever lost and no one would even know to look for me.

My own mother seemed to have forgotten me. Where was she?

In the hospital, the staff wore masks and gowns; they were strangers to me and I to them. I lay unknown, perilously untethered to the earth. Still, I knew that my surgeon, Dr. John Constable, knew me. He held me down, clutching my right foot each time I drifted dangerously toward space, anesthesia mask pressed over my nose and mouth. When he held my foot, he staked me to the earth again.

Dr. Constable saw me every day. In the morning, after the dressings were off and before they could be reapplied, I would lie in bed, flayed. All the doctors came to call, visiting at my bed at 5:00 in the morning. They would burst into my curtained bedside, fifteen of them, tall and hovering, like a flock of giant white birds drinking at a morning pond. They were all white feathered, all white male, all in identical white lab coats. They would make their post-pubescent intern stammer out information about my case. The elder white birds would listen to him, and frown at my wounds, pointing.

At four years old, alone in my bed, I listened for clues about myself. How was I doing? Was I getting better? What was going to happen to me? I couldn't tell. They only spoke advanced bird language, and I was just a problem for them, not a little girl. But then, like an oracle, Dr. Constable would speak. His nasal patrician voice would boom out, too loudly for 5:00 in the morning, but never too loudly for me. He would smile at me, and say something that I could understand, no longer in bird-speak. All the doctor birds would listen to him, nodding, respectfully bobbing their heads. The white coated bird-doctors would rustle off, one by one. Dr. Constable would gaze at me, actually seeing this little girl in the bed, and my heart would thump in unison with his. "You can get bandaged and dressed now, Lise. See you later."

I spent years like this, in the hospital, alone.

At home, my mother didn't know me; she only knew herself. More dangerously, she believed she knew me, but it was a self-projection on the screen of her own brain. My mother could not understand anyone apart from her own needs of them. I knew what she expected from me; I should make her feel proud. I should be Phi Beta Kappa, summa cum laude. I should know which fork to use in a four-star Manhattan restaurant. If French were required, I should speak it in a perfect accent. If a singer's pitch began to sag, I should be alert to the quarter-tone fall and nod to my mother, she of the perfect pitch. "I can hear it, Mom, I hear what you hear. That singer sucks. You are so right."

Perhaps I was a gifted actress, the best actress ever, because I could do all those things for my mother. I gave her everything she wanted. I made her feel she was the greatest mother in the world, year after year. I meant it at the time. I was like her dog, cheerfully bringing her my toys, fetching for her, displaying my scarred soft belly for her attention.

My mother had no idea who I was (and I had no idea who she was), but I did know who she wanted me to be, and I brought her that image, holding the illusion in my doggie mouth, looking for her praise. I brought her the cultured daughter, highly educated, well-mannered, independent, worldly.

She would receive this gift from my doggie mouth, slobbery, labored. "Good, Lise," and she would toss it away for me to fetch again. We played this game for 45 years. I didn't even know I was playing a game. But eventually, I came to see the game for what it was.

I am no longer abandoned and alone. After many years of trauma, I sit safely now, cozy in the land of love and plenty. I am here to say, *"I have the most incredible story to tell you."* Along the way, you will meet a cast of characters, some who glitter and gleam with heroism, and some who shrink darkly into the shadows. This motley crew isn't always pretty, myself included. Everyone is scarred, one way or another. Along the way, I have thoughts to share about how one can survive the unsurvivable. As a healer, it is my deepest wish that my story of trauma and resilience can help those who are going through dark times.

For myself though, I want to finally tell my true story.

This is what happened.

ONE

The Fire on the Lake

The Dyers, the Deguires, and the Moffetts. We were a social network group of people intertwined with love and care. We vacationed together and we partied together (often with my dad playing the piano, singing along to the songs of *My Fair Lady, The Sound of Music* or the other big shows of the time).

The axis of our connection was the First Presbyterian Church in Oyster Bay, on the north shore of Long Island. Even though my parents were atheists, they loved their church jobs, which gave them an outlet for their prodigious musical talents. My father conducted the church choir, waving his arms with abandon, while my mother elegantly played the organ. At the time we attended, the church had among its congregation prominent citizens like John Dyer, a Harvard-educated engineer who had helped to pioneer radar technologies during World War II. The Dyers lived in "The Cove" — Oyster Bay Cove — an exclusive enclave just east of the main part of town, noted for being the location of Sagamore Hill, Teddy Roosevelt's home.

In the early 1950s, Mr. Dyer built another home, a vacation cabin on the shores of Lake Winnipesaukee in New Hampshire. This log cabin nestled on a large outcropping, with a six-foot drop-off to the water. It had a small dock as well (although you had to navigate a path through the rocks to reach it), and next to it, a tiny patch of sand that constituted the beach.

Reverend Moffett was just as accomplished in his own right and an important figure in the community; he was the minister. I know that Reverend Moffett must have prayed for me, as did his entire congregation, when the news spread of what had happened to the Deguire girl on the shores of Lake Winnipesaukee.

* * *

In August 1967, Reverend Moffett's son Blair, newly married and a seminary school graduate, was staying at his dad's house on the lake. (His father, Rev. Moffett, had so enjoyed being in the Dyer's cabin, that he had decided to buy his own, next door.) My family, the Deguires, was borrowing the Dyer's house that week, right down the lane.

Suddenly, there came cries for help.

Blair was in the Moffett house, reading. His wife, who was upstairs taking a bath, called to him.

"Blair," she said, alarm in her voice. "Something's going on with the Deguires." Blair stepped outside. He smelled smoke, heard screams, and bolted toward the Dyer cabin.

There were already people there, who lived across the cove, and who had roared across on their motorboat to help. They found my mom half conscious and submerged up to her neck in shallow water. Someone said she'd been burned. Something about the grill exploding when they were about to have a barbecue. Blair grabbed an aluminum lawn chair that was set up on that postage-stamp sized beach. Then he and several other young men waded out in the water, gently seated my mother on the chair, and carried her out.

An ambulance had been called. When it arrived, the attendants took my mother and transferred her onto a gurney. Amidst the chaos, Blair Moffett doesn't remember seeing me.

I, myself, have only one clear memory from that day, August 17, 1967. (I will get to that later.) What I know has been filled in with pieces of other people's memories; some of them, like Blair, peripheral figures in the drama; others — principally my dad — who were caught in the middle. Later, at the behest of lawyers and insurance companies, Dad wrote several detailed recollections of the "Accident" with precise diagrams and a moment-by-moment timeline. It is through these sources that I can reconstruct that day.

While I don't remember the fire, I do remember the lake. It was vast, with huge granite boulders and tall pine trees lining its shores. I remember the scent of the air, a heady blend of pine needles and cedar. To this day, when I catch the scent of cedar trees, I see the lake in my mind, shimmering like a sapphire in the sun.

The Dyer's home, where we stayed, had its own sweet aroma. It was a one-story small cabin with a loft, where my brother liked to sleep, even though a bat had once flown through it, which freaked me out. I had my own room, with actual round log walls, which I thought was cool, as it made me think of Abraham Lincoln in a satisfying way. There was a spacious porch, surrounded by a crisscross railing, which—from the cabin's perch on top of that rocky promontory — afforded a panoramic view of the lake, sparking and peaceful in the sunlight.

It was dinnertime, we were going to have a barbecue. My family of four gathered on the front porch of the cabin, with the clear blue lake stretched before us. My father and nine-year-old brother, Marc, sat reading on one side of the porch. I, four years old, stood next to my mother on the other side, watching as she lit the coals. To get them burning, my mother had gone into the kitchen, rummaged around the shelves for lighter fluid, and found a can of something called Solox Denatured Alcohol Solvent. Commonly used as fuel for alcohol burners and camping stoves, the solvent had apparently been left by either Mr. Dyer or someone in his family.

My mother, with her little girl by her side, poured the Solox on the coals. Nothing happened. She squirted more Solox on the grill, hoping to coax some sparks out of the stubborn coals. Suddenly, the can exploded with a flash and a giant whoosh of flame. My mother and I were instantly engulfed in giant ball of fire. We were also trapped; backed up against the crisscross railing, completely aflame, with more fire blocking any escape off the porch.

In an instant, my mother dashed straight through the fire, off the porch, and threw herself in the lake.

I crouched, trapped in the fire, completely alone. I shrunk away from the flames as much as possible and pressed myself against the porch railing. There was nowhere else to go. I was completely ablaze, trapped and abandoned.

My father leapt over his side of the porch railing, and ran around, standing behind me. Stretching up, he was just able to reach me, and pull me through the rails by my red cotton shorts. Later he would say that if it weren't for those crisscross rails, I would be dead, because he could just barely pull me through the opening. He immediately rolled me on the ground to smother the flames, but the carpet of pine needles wouldn't allow it and they kept flickering back to life.

"Goddamn pine needles!" my father cursed, as he carried me, still ablaze, down to the lake. Running toward the water, he yelled to my mother to take me so he could go back and fight the fire.

"Kathryn, take her! Take her!" my dad screamed.
My mother, standing in the shallow lake waters by the dock, blackened and shaking, protested. "I can't. I can't do it."

"Take her! You have to. She can't swim!"

"Bill! Please!"

"You have to take her!" She nodded reluctantly and dad tossed me, a fiery ball of four-year-old, down into the lake.

The fire was finally extinguished. I huddled next to my mother in the water. In shock, we watched our blackened dead skin float off our bodies.

There was no phone in the cabin, so nine-year-old Marc ran screaming for help down the long dirt road to the Moffett house. Other neighbors saw what was going on and called the fire company as the flames raged visibly from the lake all around. When the ambulance arrived, they took my mother. But there was only one ambulance, so my father drove me to the hospital himself.

I lay crying on the front bench seat of our blue Chevy. My dad drove as fast as he could, honking the horn so that he could pass people and go faster. But every time the horn blared, I cried louder, so he stopped and drove quietly. "What's the point?" my dad thought to himself. "My baby is going to die anyway. Why scare her even more?" My dad drove on, silently, listening to me cry. "My poor girl. What's going to happen to her?"

In that desperate moment, Dad found inspiration, reaching for the one thing he knew that could bring me comfort. "Let's sing, Lise. Come on, sing with me." We had just seen the movie *The Sound of Music* again, which we loved. Dad began singing "My Favorite Things,"

"When the dog bites
When the bee stings
When I'm feeling sad
I simply remember my favorite things
And then I don't feel so bad."

Dad and I sang our mournful song, all the way to the hospital. When we arrived, Reverend Moffett was there, as the doctors triaged my mother and me, somberly and quietly. They could do little for our extensive burns, except call Massachusetts General Hospital in Boston, the best burn hospital in the country and the only place that could give me a chance to survive. Today I would have been helicoptered down there. But in 1967, the medical air transport system didn't exist, so my mother and I were packed up and driven by ambulance one hundred miles south to Mass General.

My sole distinct memory of this day happened there in Wolfeboro Hospital. I was lying by myself on a stretcher in the hospital hallway. There was no one with me, but I knew my mother was nearby. I called out to her. "Mommy, I'm so cold!" A voice replied—flat and almost robotic.

"Yes, I'm cold too."

To be fair, my mother's second- and third-degree burns covered 33 percent of her body. She carried burns on the backs of her arms, the backs of her legs and the bottoms of her feet. For a while, the doctors wondered if she would ever walk again. She worked hard on her rehabilitation and, eventually, she did walk normally again, although her sense of balance was forever affected and she was scarred for the rest of her life. Others likely saw those scars as evidence of her suffering and trauma. But as time went on, I recognized a clear pattern to her injuries. My mother carried burns only on the back of her body, none on her front.

That was because she had turned her back on the fire, the same fire consuming her four-year-old daughter, and she had fled.

If I could have truly understood this situation at this moment, I might have saved myself decades of confusion and disappointment. But I had little ability to judge a person's character at that age. The clues beckoned, but I couldn't yet see them.

* * *

After the fire, the congregation at First Presbyterian rallied around our family. They prayed, wrote letters, made visits and fundraised on our behalf. But how, in the end, did they make sense of this tragedy? A four-year-old disfigured in a fire. What lesson about life, or God, could be learned from that?

Blair Moffett sighs when asked that question today. "The lesson is that you don't spray industrial fuel solvent on a grill," he says.

Of course, on one level, he's right. Yet, for me, the education was only beginning, as was my new life as Flashback Girl.

LESSON ONE:

Tragedies will happen. Do not expect life to be easy; we don't live in a fairytale. Watch to see how people behave in a crisis. People can tell you anything. They might consciously be manipulating you, or it might be unconscious. Behavior is the true clue. Behavior will tell you much more about who people truly are and what you can expect from them.

TWO

The Hospital, Burn Care and Dr. Constable

In 1967, I was lucky enough to be horribly burned in the right locale. My mother and I were whisked to Massachusetts General Hospital, which happened to be the best hospital for burns in the United States, and probably in the world. Even there, in the elite air of the Harvard teaching hospital, it was lucky for a four-year-old, burned third-degree on 65 percent of her body, to survive. When burn care professionals meet me, and find out I was burned in 1967, at the age of four, 65 percent, their eyebrows arch in respect. In the burn world, I am like a black rhinoceros, rarely sighted anymore.

Burn care had only recently made some key medical advances, which significantly improved survival rates. Mass General was on the leading edge of these advancements. There was a famous 1942 fire in Boston, the Cocoanut Grove fire. This fire burned hundreds of people, at the exact time Mass General had received a huge government grant to improve burn care, in advance of the casualties expected from World War II. The Cocoanut Grove fire created a massive study opportunity, allowing physicians to create and compare treatment protocols for burns.

Over the next decades, Mass General became America's center of excellence for burn care. They studied and developed new ways to handle wounds, shock, and to reduce infection. It is not an exaggeration to say that if I had been taken to any other hospital, I probably would have died. But we just happened to be on vacation near the best hospital for burns in the world. So here I am. Regardless of these lifesaving advances, burn care in the 1960s is still referred to as "the dark ages" and indeed, dark times lay ahead.

From the first day, my mother and I were assigned to the brilliant young plastic surgeon, Dr. John Constable. He was 39 years old when he took us on. Originally from England, he spoke in a strong nasal voice, with a posh accent, often just a little too loudly. He stood tall and slim, with thick dark hair, and a handsome face, which somewhat resembled a hawk. He wore gray slacks and a white lab coat, his name embroidered in Harvard crimson on the right breast pocket, "Dr. John Constable." His manner was formal, his speech was sophisticated, and he entered and exited rooms like a king. Years later, I learned that he was distantly related to the great British landscape painter, John Constable.

Plastic surgeons are widely considered to be arrogant, cold people who think of themselves as gods. Dr. Constable might appear to fit this mold on the surface, patrician-accented and ever-formal. If you truly knew him, he was deeply kind beneath this exterior. It wasn't that he necessarily said warm or kind words, but his true caring always shone through. Even when I was four, he would patiently explain every medical procedure, why I needed a particular intervention, and how he could help me. He answered every question. I always felt a part of my care, a key partner in the long arduous task of healing and reshaping my body.

Once, when I was six, returning to Boston for one of my countless surgeries, Dr. Constable presented my case at surgical grand rounds. Before the presentation, he took me into a small waiting area, and we sat on the two chairs that barely fit in the room.

He looked at me, and pronounced, "I want to talk about your case to all the doctors. You have been burned very badly, and we have done a lot of special work to get you better. The doctors here are all young. They learn how to be good doctors by listening to older doctors like me. If you permit me, I can teach them a lot today by presenting your case. However, you would have to take off all your clothes so I can show them. We would drape you with a cloth when possible. Would you do it? You could help them learn how to help other burned children."

"I could help them? OK!" I sat up straight, suddenly feeling much more important. We strolled into the packed amphitheater together, the tall sophisticated surgeon and the tiny, ugly girl. I sat on the stage in front of hundreds of doctors, naked as a jaybird, burned all over, and proud to be Dr. Constable's patient.

In my first hospitalization, I stayed at Massachusetts General Hospital for five months. I was four, wafting in and out of death's door. My father lived in a panic for many reasons, including his worry that our medical bills would bankrupt the family. Desperately, he contemplated that we might have to flee the country to escape the bills. Perhaps, he thought, we could escape to Australia. In a second stroke of incredible luck, the Shriners came to the rescue.

For many years, the Shriners had supported childhood polio as their major charity. By the 1960s, childhood polio had been largely eradicated. The Shriners still had hospitals for kids with polio and spinal cord issues, but they had more to give and they wanted to support a new cause. They decided to support burned children. The first initiative the Shriners undertook was to sponsor the burn care of some children of the Burnham Building, at Massachusetts General. I became one of those first "Shriners Kids." The Shriners assumed all of my medical bills, and my hospital care became entirely free.

In 1968, the Shriners opened up their first children's burn hospital, in Boston, right next door to Mass General. The burn care at Shriners was coordinated with the burn care at Mass General, and the physicians came from Harvard and Mass General. It was the best hospital for childhood burns you could find. I went there for the rest of my surgeries throughout my childhood and adolescence. I have no idea how many surgeries I had there (upwards of 40, I believe). I also have no idea how much any of them cost, because the Shriners never sent a bill. They paid for everything quietly, without fanfare, never once asking for a contribution.

So, despite the incredible misfortune of being seriously burned for the rest of my life, I was fortunate to receive the best burn care in the world, from an extraordinary doctor, completely free of charge, thanks to the Shriners.

It boggles the mind how I could be so unlucky and so lucky simultaneously.

Despite being at the best burn hospital, with the best doctor, my countless hospitalizations were torturously horrific. I cannot verbally convey the physical pain of burns. Words completely fail the task. Burns are widely acknowledged to be the most painful injury in the world, worse than childbirth, worse than kidney stones. Think, for example, of the deep pain of a small burn on your finger, from a toaster or a hot stove. Imagine this pain all over your body, for weeks on end. Even that, I think, cannot convey the profound pain of burns.

When I was first in the hospital, I had bandages wrapped around my entire body, from head to toe. My father told the story of the first day that he could touch a part of my body again, not through bandages, but actually skin to skin. He found a small patch on my right arm that wasn't burned or bandaged. He rubbed his index finger over this little patch, again and again, so glad to be able to touch his little girl's skin again. Another day, as I was beginning to recover, the nurses allowed my father to hold me in his lap. He cuddled me in his arms, and we hugged for the first time in weeks. When he finally lay me back in bed, he looked down in horror to see that he was completely soaked in my blood.

Being bandaged from head to toe wasn't so bad. It felt cozy and warm; protected. But a horror loomed every day: the twice daily dressing changes. Nowadays, newly burned patients are kept in a prolonged coma, to minimize the pain. If a patient is out of the coma, they are often put under twilight anesthesia, each time their dressings get changed. Dressing changes are considered to be so unbearably painful that no one should have to endure them while conscious.

In 1967, this was not the thinking. In 1967, pediatric dressing changes were done without any painkillers at all. I was talking to a burn nurse recently who had worked in the early 1970s. She was there too, back in the day. I talked about how my bandages were changed as a child without any pain medicine, and I said it was "like torture."

Pat, the nurse, interrupted me. "No," she said, appraising me seriously, her light blue eyes intense, "No, Lise, it *was* torture."

In the morning before breakfast, the nurses would wake me up. After getting my medicines, which did not include painkillers, they would come back, and begin to "take down" all the bandages. It would start off OK, with the bandages unwrapping easily in their plastic-gloved hands. Soon, there would be a slight tug, where the dried blood and wound drainage started to make the bandage stick to the deep open wound.

In the beginning, this pain was just a pull, not too painful at all, just a hiccup of pain. But each time the dressing unwound again, the bandage would stick more and more, and the pain began to build. Finally, the long white Kerlix™ bandage would be off, but there would be gauze pads underneath, firmly caked on by dried blood and ooze to completely open flesh and exposed nerve endings. These gauze pads would have to come off too, and the pain was astonishing. Every time, I wound up shrieking my head off, as the nurses ripped the gauze pads off my gaping wounds. My whole body was a wound. Sometimes I would beg the nurses to stop for just a bit, so that I could catch my breath, and get a break from the searing pain. "Please, please stop!"

"Lise, we have to finish your bandage changes. You know we do. This is how you will get better."

"Yes, but just stop for a minute. Please!"

Usually they would stop briefly, and then we would have to get back to it. Sometimes they refused to stop, and they just kept unbandaging me as I writhed and screamed in protest. I'm sure it was horrible for the nurses too. All over the burn ward, you could hear little kids, shouting in agonizing pain. Each one howled the same word, again and again.

"Mommy!"

"Mommy!"

When the dressing change was finally over, I would lie in the bed, bleeding and literally shaking from head to toe from the pain. Relief flooded my chest. One more dressing change had been endured. The nurses would apply new gauze pads, and wrap me back up with white Kerlix bandages, from head to toe like a little mummy. I would feel clean and safe and cozy again. I would never allow myself to think that I would have another dressing change, just as horrific, 12 hours later. That's the only way to get through being burned. Don't think about what's coming next; just survive the moment.

My bed was in the Vincent/Burnham building of Massachusetts General, which was a large hospital, full of many buildings, cobbled together through hallways and tunnels. Although I was four, I was mostly alone. My brother was back in New Jersey, starting fourth grade. My father tirelessly trooped back and forth, teaching his classes at Upsala College from Monday through Thursday, and then flying up to Boston every weekend to visit my mother and me. When he wasn't there, I would listen to the records he had left for me, singing along, waiting for the hours to pass. On Fridays when my dad returned, my bed would often be shifted to a new position on the ward. Still, my dad said he could always find me immediately. He just followed the sound of my little voice, singing along to my portable record player, pretending to be somewhere else.

My mother was in the White Building, also at Massachusetts General. She was also burned, but not as badly as I. She was in terrible pain from her injuries; she suffered greatly. This may partly explain, but not really, why she refused to see me for weeks.

My father tried to get my mother to visit me. She was capable. She could climb onto a stretcher, or into a wheelchair, and be wheeled over to my unit. My mother repeatedly refused. "Poor Lise," my mother would sigh, lying in her bed.

My father would get exasperated with her. "You have to go see Lise. She's all alone every day. She's very sick and she might die. You need to go see your daughter. She's only four years old, for Christ's sake!"

"Poor Lise," my mother would sigh again. "Bill, I can't do it. I just can't. I'm in so much pain. It's so awful, you have no idea. Why can't you just leave me alone?" Truly, my mother lay in pain too. So my father stopped trying to force her to visit me.

Eventually, weeks later, my mother came to visit me. In my mind, I can see myself lying on a stretcher in the hallway. I lie on my back, staring, as always, at the ceiling. But I am staring at the hallway ceiling, lifting up my head when the metal elevator doors open, waiting for my mother to arrive. This is the only memory I have of my mother during that first hospitalization: I remember waiting for her to come. My dad was there, weekend after weekend after weekend. Otherwise I was alone.

These were just the ordinary days of being on a burn unit. The surgeries were another kind of awful event. On a surgery morning, I would wait alone in dread. I was petrified of needles when I was little, and the needles were the first thing to happen on surgery day. The nurses seemed to burst into the room, brandishing three long and painful needles. They moved at stealth speed, somehow getting the three shots into my butt with no cooperation from me.

"Lie still, Lise!"

"No, no, no!" I tried to pull away, but I couldn't go far, stuck in my tiny hospital bed. I remember those shots as being particularly painful. I don't know what was in them, but I assume one of them was a sedative because I would become much more cooperative after the shots. There would be a bit more waiting, as I lay, suddenly languid, in my bed. Then, I would be wheeled down the hallway on a stretcher, watching the ceiling go by, going down the elevator, on my way to the operating room. Sometimes other staff members would stand in the elevator with me, and they would give me a wan smile, always seeming a little sad as they regarded me.

I would be wheeled into the operating room on the stretcher. The OR was a vast white space, with gleaming silver tools and trays. It looked so clean you couldn't imagine a germ contemplating setting foot in it. Everything shined in a white, metallic, sparking way. The people too were spotless. In the OR, everyone was "gowned up" in blue surgical scrubs, hats, booties, gloves and masks over their noses and mouths. It was hard to feel any emotional connection to these sterile blue nurses and doctors, when I couldn't see their faces or bodies. I didn't know any of them, because they only worked in the OR. I was a little girl, all alone without family, skinless, and completely at the mercy of masked strangers.

The surgical team would ask me to transfer over to the operating table from the stretcher. If I were well enough, I could help with the transfer, scooting my little body over. If I were too weak, the team would hoist me over to the table. I would wait, looking up at the ceiling, hearing the bustle of these strange masked people around me. I lay there, full of fear.

Then, like a brilliant ray of sunshine, Dr. Constable would burst into the operating room. "Hello," he would say to the staff in his distinctive voice, striding towards me. He would talk to me, nothing consequential, but his words were always comforting and calm in tone. As soon as he was there, I felt completely safe. I knew that Dr. Constable knew who I was, and because he knew me, he would make sure to bring me back from the death-like anesthesia. That belief was, and actually still is, paramount to me. I didn't trust the masked strangers to care if I lived or died. It seemed to me that my survival wouldn't much matter to them, one way or another. But I knew Dr. Constable cared for me. I felt that he actually loved me, in his own way, and that he would never let anything bad happen to me.

So, he would say his little chatting comments to me, making clear and gentle eye contact. I could see his kind brown eyes, the only part of him visible through his gown, cap and mask. I could hear his nasal English accent, which was so definitively his voice and no other's. Then, he would grab my right foot, and hold my toes firmly in his hand. I'm not sure why it was always my foot. Perhaps it was because neither of my feet are burned, so they were always available for holding. As he held my foot, an oxygen mask would slide over my mouth, and I would go to sleep.

I have always loathed the smell of rubber. The oxygen mask smelled like rubber, and that smell still makes me frantic, especially if it is close to my face. When I was eight, I had a full panic attack in our family Mercedes as we drove cross-country. One day, in the middle of our long expedition, I became convinced that I couldn't breathe.

"I can't breathe I can't breathe I can't breathe!" I exclaimed, sweating and panic stricken.

My parents looked back at me. Marc watched me, puzzled and alert. "You are fine," said my mother, calmly. "You are breathing right now. You are actually breathing. You are OK." The only clue to my sudden panic was the smell of burned rubber that had entered the ventilation system of the car. I associated the smell of rubber to the rubber masks in the OR, which scared me. This fear grew exponentially after one surgery that did not go well.

On this day, I lay in the operating room, waiting for my next surgery. Everything progressed as usual. The masked strangers went about their business, preparing the OR. I lay on the table, staring at the ceiling, waiting for Dr. Constable. This time, though, Dr. Constable didn't come. The staff moved ahead, preparing to put me under anesthesia, presumably knowing that Dr. Constable would arrive any minute. The anesthesiologist stood above my head, and his right arm reached down to clamp the dreaded rubber mask on my face.

I screamed; I was terrified. I didn't think I would survive the surgery if I didn't see Dr. Constable first, and if he didn't hold my right foot. But the nurses and the anesthesiologist went ahead, restraining me, and holding the awful smelling mask on my face. I flailed against the smell for no more than five seconds, but I will never forget it. I was positive I was going to die. Then I fell unconscious. When I woke up hours later, the salt of my dried tears lay stuck all over my face.

After that incident, I made sure to ask Dr. Constable to see me before I went to sleep. Each time before we agreed to a surgery, I plaintively whined, "Please come to the operating room before the surgery starts." He always did, and he never asked me why. Even when I was a grown woman, he would be sure to come to the OR before the procedure, kindly holding my foot as I was put to sleep.

Dr. Constable and I stayed in touch for decades, long after I stopped having surgeries, exchanging yearly letters. Like his OR entrances years ago, his Christmas letters seemed to arrive with their own royal fanfare. Every year, he would describe trips he had taken to India, Vietnam, or Cambodia. Often, he traveled to provide charitable burn care. After he retired, he led Harvard nature tours to far flung corners of the world. Then he would comment humbly on his children, who were inevitably equally impressive. Reading his Christmas letter was vastly entertaining. Here are some excerpts:

> We returned from South East Asia just before Thanksgiving after the second Harvard Museum of Natural History trip, which followed the Mekong River from the borders of Tibet to its delta in Vietnam. The river is not navigable in its upper reaches so we traveled by van and bus as well as a variety of boats. . . . I returned home by way of Bangladesh, where the new burn center is certainly doing good work, but it is sad that their splendidly equipped intensive care center is all set to go but cannot open for lack of nurses. . . . In April/May I took eight botanical enthusiasts back to Bhutan to tour once again

to see even better wild flowers and, fortuitously, to obtain very close up views of the spectacular and rarely seen golden langur monkey. . . . . In terms of future Harvard Museum trips, we are planning one to lesser-known hai parks and to the mountains . . . One has heard of the Japanese catching fish with cormorants but there they apparently use otters in the same way. . . . Grandson John is in his first year at Yale after graduating from Exeter. . . ."

This was Dr. Constable's typical Christmas card. I tore them open eagerly every year, smiling with anticipation.

Years later, when I had a family of my own, we visited Dr. Constable at his elegant estate. We chatted with his gracious wife, Sylvia. We walked on a lovely path of their farm and lunched in their formal dining room. As I walked to my chair, I noticed the artwork on the walls, and inched closer to one of the paintings. "Is that a Monet?" I asked, incredulously.

"Yes," Dr. Constable said quietly, his eyes cast down in modesty. *"Not* a very good one."

This was the last time I saw Dr. Constable face to face. I had just seen another surgeon for a consultation, to see if any more improvements could be made to my appearance. This new surgeon had suggested that he might be able to make my lower lip line better. Until that point, I had never even noticed that my lower lip line was uneven, but he was right, it was. I asked Dr. Constable to take a look at me.

We sat down on his living room couch together. The look in his eyes changed from being my gracious host to being my trusted doctor. We fell back into our roles effortlessly. He appraised me; I sank into the safety of his familiar touch. His strong fingers touched my face, my cheeks, my forehead. He turned my face this way and that.

After some time, he acknowledged that the other physician had a point. The lower lip, the same lower lip that Dr. Constable had built on my face, operation after operation, that he had painstakingly created, was indeed imperfect and could be improved. Quietly, we sat with that surprising proclamation for a moment. I had never contemplated that his work was less than perfect, in all the years that he had taken care of me. There was a moment of silence as we sat on the couch together, pondering the imperfect state of my lip. "But," he declared proudly, in his strong voice, "it's still pretty good!"

In the end, I decided not to have that other surgeon's lip-correction surgery because I just didn't want to work with a different surgeon. My bottom lip is still a little crooked. It is my lip and it is Dr. Constable's lip, too. His work and my body are forever intertwined.

My last Christmas letter from Dr. Constable arrived undated, which was unlike him. His handwriting was changed, and some words were scrawled, indecipherable. Still, he wrote on his usual stationery:

> It gave me great pleasure to be informed of your gift to the S.B. [Shriners Burns Institute] in my 'memory.' You have always been a treasured patient to me. At 84 years it has been time to retire — I have early Parkinson's — walking restricted — at some progressive [illegible] in [illegible] in my hand — so a bit of a wreck. …A Christmas without hearing from you would be very incomplete. Yours, John. P.S. Parkinson's makes handwriting worse than ever!"

That was his last card. But it turns out I was not done with burn care. Nowhere close.

LESSON TWO:
There are excellent professionals who will look after you, assist you, and maybe even save you. Try to connect with experts who seem truly caring and competent. Their humanity can be a healing force in itself. Look for the highest quality professionals you can afford, follow their advice, and let them help you heal.

FLASHBACK GIRL

THREE

Life in the Shriners Burns Institute for Crippled Children

The Shriners built their new burn hospital for children in 1968, next door to Massachusetts General Hospital, the world-famous Harvard-affiliated institution. The new children's burns hospital was a modern brown brick building. The first floor was a busy area, devoted to outpatients coming in for assessments, doctors' offices, and an auditorium. The second floor was devoted to research. It was totally off-limits to visitors and kids. It had a scary, mysterious vibe. The third floor was for patient care, crammed full of burned children.

There were two wings, East and West. Newly burned children went immediately to the East Wing, which was a somber, quiet place. The recently burned kids lay motionless in their beds, with oxygen tents around their heads. Many of them were in quarantine, with plastic sheeting all around, protecting them from infection. The air itself felt anxious, still, foreboding. The stillness whispered that a child could die at any minute.

In contrast, the West Wing buzzed with activity; it was a raucous, happening place. The burn ward was shaped like a U, all beds facing inwards, with a semicircular nurses' station at the front. Everyone there was terribly burned, but we had all survived our initial injury. We returned there, again and again for our countless surgeries. Like sterile sculptors, our doctors were slowly rebuilding necks, arms, hands, feet, noses and mouths. We were injured and bandaged, but none of us lay at death's door anymore. Also, we were all little children, and we were bored out of our minds.

What do burned little kids do with nothing but time on their hands? We played. We couldn't go outside for weeks at a time. We didn't have our own bedrooms or toys. So, we embraced the environment we had, and the hospital itself became our playground. We raced in our wheelchairs, to the endless aggravation of the nurses. We snuck into the kitchen and stole popsicles. We crept into the nurses supplies and swiped masks and gowns. We blew up the surgical gloves into five fingered balloons, and drew tiny faces on each finger. Our imaginative play had one singular theme: playing doctor. In our play, we unconsciously worked through the traumas that were happening to us every day. There were endless reiterations of the doctor game, with kids taking turns being the doctor, the nurse or the patient. We would diagnose each other's fevers and pretend to do surgery. The one thing we did not play at was dressing changes. No one wanted to think about those.

Although I was always a well-behaved child, I rebelled at Shriners. I broke the rules right and left. I stole supplies and snuck into places I wasn't supposed to be. I wandered into the East Wing, where we were forbidden, peering at the gravely ill children behind the plastic sheeting of their isolation tents. I went down to the first floor and snuck around the doctor's areas and into the chapel.

Regularly, I left Shriners altogether, sauntering down into the basement of the hospital. There was an underground tunnel that connected Shriners to Mass General. In my little white hospital gown and blue pants, I padded my way in my green Styrofoam slippers through the tunnel and into Mass General.

For about an hour, I would explore the halls of the big hospital. I walked through the elegant Bullfinch building, the oldest building of the hospital, featuring pictures of the "Ether Dome," where anesthesia was first used for surgery in 1846. I padded past the coffee shop, and the hospital chapel in the Baker building. I made my way over to the White Building lobby, where I rested, watching the cars come and go around the entrance ramp. Eventually, when I had gone everywhere possible, I turned around, climbed down the stairs to the basement, and padded back to the West Wing. No one ever even asked me where I went.

I knew all the hallways of Mass General, thanks to my father. When I was first hospitalized, he loved to take me on "walks." I would get transferred from my hospital bed into a little go-cart. It was like a wooden wheelchair, but the bottom of it extended out so my legs stretched out flat. My dad would tuck a white cotton blanket around my legs and off we would go. We explored the halls of Mass General for hours together, walking and rolling along, the two of us talking. This was our favorite thing to do when he came to visit.

During that first hospitalization, I got in trouble because I wasn't eating enough. I had either lost my appetite, or had lost my energy to keep going. My body became so weak that my life was in danger again. I was four years old and alone in the ward. My mother was in the hospital but she had only recently started visiting me. My father was far away in New Jersey, teaching, coming up every weekend. The nurses bore into me, badgering me into eating. My father came up to feed me but I refused. He tried to feed me little bites of food; I turned my face away. Occasionally, I would take a bite, and then pocket it in my cheek, spitting out the unswallowed food later. My dad grew more and more desperate. The nurses had told him that I would die if I didn't eat soon.

"Lise, let's have some more to eat. There's cottage cheese, you like that."

"No."

"Come on. Just a little bite."

"No I don't want it." I turned my face away from him.

"You need to try! Come on now!"

"No."

My father towered above me. Exasperated, he lobbed his biggest threat. In a deep, stern voice, he said "If you don't eat right now, I'm leaving."

Nothing was worse than my dad leaving. He was the only person I had left. And so, I ate.

During this same time, I had to drink these horrible frappes every day. A "frappe" is the Boston word for milkshake. Every day, I was forced to drink a large chocolate frappe. They tasted horrible and I loathed them. The nurses made me finish the large brown thick drink every day, relentlessly.

"Drink your frappe."

"I hate it. I hate my frappe. It smells so bad!"

"You have to drink it. Have a sip."

Through the straw, I would reluctantly take a sip of the dreaded chocolate frappe, squinting my eyes in dreaded anticipation. They burned my throat, tasting like oil and poison.

At one point, my dad came for another visit, and he got me up in my little go-cart. We went gallivanting around the hospital, barreling down the long metal corridor, past the lobby with the miniature of the hospital on display, past the beautiful chapel. We went into the coffee shop, and my dad offered to buy me something. "Try the chocolate frappe. They are delicious," said the man behind the counter.

"No!" I wailed. "I hate frappes."

The man looked puzzled. "Everybody loves them. They are all the kids' favorite."

My dad looked at the man, cocking his head, quizzically. "Well, let's try one, I guess."

The man made us a chocolate frappe to share. He presented it with a smile. My dad held it out to me and I winced. "Here you go."

Hesitantly, eyes squinting, I took a sip of the chocolate frappe. It was delicious; it tasted like sweet cocoa heaven. "This is a frappe? I love this! This is a frappe?" I gulped the whole thing down.

My dad looked at me puzzled, but then his eyes lit up and he smiled. "I guess they must hide all your medicines in the frappe. That's why they taste so bad, and that's also why they force you to finish them. But yes, this is what a chocolate frappe is supposed to taste like."

I still hate that word "frappe."

Meals at Shriners were served en-masse. Tables would be pulled up, all shoved together to the right of the ward. Some of us pushed our wheelchairs up to the table. Others, further past surgery, would bring a pillow to their plastic chair. We would perch gingerly on our pillows, cautiously avoiding putting weight on our wounds.

The food came out on silver trays, with a plastic dinner plate in the center, divided up into three sections. One section on the plate would hold a thin hamburger, for example. Another section might hold tater tots, everybody's favorite. Then there might be a section of string beans, which we ignored. There would be a carton of milk, and a little round plastic cup of ice cream, divided into half vanilla and half chocolate. We didn't get to choose our meals; we all got the same food.

We were a gruesome crew of kids, all sitting together, wolfing down our tater tots. One girl would have a badly burned hand, her five fingers swollen and webbed together by the pink melted skin, like a duck's foot. Post-surgery, her hand would be spread apart in a large splint, each thickened sausage-like finger surgically separated from the others and now affixed by tight cords, pulling the fingers back into shape. A boy might sit next to her, half of his facial features obliterated by thick scarring, one eye permanently scarred shut, a mass of purple scarring covering what used to be his nose, with only two nostril holes left for breathing. Each face presented a unique devastation. With each new admission to the unit, I would have to get used to everyone's appearance, and they would have to get used to mine. After a minute, and a brief hello, that acclimation time would pass. Then we were all just kids, playing and swiping Dixie cups of ice cream from the freezer.

I rarely saw the same kids again. There were a ton of us, rotating in and out of surgeries. Each hospitalization, I would make friends with new gruesome playmates. We came from all over the country. Shriners Burns Institute provided expert burn care for free. Kids would come from all over, as far away as Puerto Rico. Because we came from far away, parents weren't there often. Parents might visit, but they were not fixtures in the hospital, the way parents are now. We were all mostly on our own.

My father used to say that the other burned kids behaved like little brats. He and my mother decided that I was not going to be spoiled like the other kids. I was not to receive any special treatment whatsoever because I was burned. Absolutely no allowances were to be made, which meant a number of things. My parents did not discuss my scars with me, or how they affected me. We didn't talk about the hospitalizations, surgeries or the pain. They didn't talk about my social problems or help me to cope with them. There was no acknowledgment of the trauma I was going through. They wanted me to be *normal*. I was also expected to be a Good Girl: stoic, obedient, polite, responsible, and above all, God forbid, not a whiner.

I was four when I was first burned, and I was in the hospital for five months. During that time, I lost my toilet training. I started to have accidents now and then. Most people would understand this to be a natural result of physical and mental trauma. My father, however, would have none of it. It wasn't *normal* that a four-year-old would lose her toilet training and have accidents. He declared that I was not allowed to come home and have accidents. So, every time I had an accident, my father spanked me. Somehow, he managed to avoid the freshly healed wounds all around my thighs and my back. He pulled my pants down and spanked me, each time after I wet the bed.

I stopped having accidents.

Perhaps it makes sense that I let loose each time I was at Shriners. My parents weren't there, and no one was demanding that I be a Good Girl, or be *normal,* so I definitely wasn't. I don't think the other kids were brats. Those kids were allowed to complain and whine a bit, but they were not out of control. We didn't fight, and no one teased each other.

Perhaps the nurses even knew that I was stealing popsicles and surgical gloves. Perhaps they saw me wandering off alone and they just didn't say anything. Perhaps the nurses understood that I was a traumatized girl, lucky to be alive, still undergoing horrifically painful procedures, dealing with horrific disfigurement, without much support. Perhaps those nurses were just giving me a break.

The nurses had the hardest job imaginable. On the one hand, they functioned as the temporary parents in our lives: monitoring us, feeding us, putting us to bed, providing us with whatever emotional support they had to give. Some nurses were kind and sweet. They would take the time to chat, sitting by my bed for five minutes, seeming to understand that a friendly word was as vital as the physical care. I would always have one nurse who was my favorite, someone who would chat and joke and help me pass the time.

Other nurses were emotionally detached. One nurse remains frozen in my mind as spectacularly cold. I was about eight, and my father had just left for New Jersey to return to work. Prior to his departure, we went down to the gift shop. It wasn't his way to buy me extra presents (that would be spoiling me), but for some reason, this time he did. He bought me a stuffed black and white panda bear. After he left, I was sitting on my narrow bed in the ward, crying and hugging my new panda bear. The nurse walked by and asked, "What's wrong?"

"My daddy just left. I miss him."

Impassively, the nurse locked eyes with me. Her face was a cold mask, her air was dismissive. "Some of these children never see their parents at all. At least your father was here. You are lucky. Stop crying." Then, she strode away.

I did immediately stop crying, from the shock of her coldness. I hunched over on my bed, suddenly quiet. No one cared how I felt; there was no point in crying. I pulled myself together and put on one of my records. Years later, when I saw *One Flew Over the Cuckoo's Nest,* I felt like I had already met Nurse Ratched. I would know that frozen cold face anywhere.

Although this nasty interaction sticks forever in my mind, I understand this nurse. She had a terrible job. Her job was so horrific that it could kill the warmth in a person's soul. The other job the nurses had to do was to twice daily inflict excruciating pain on every kid. Twice a day, the nurses had to steel themselves, sometimes physically restraining children, and rip their bandages off, while the child screamed and howled in pain. It was torturous and the nurses had to do it, again and again and again. I understand how a nurse could get burned out from these experiences. They were traumatic for us, but I am sure they were traumatic for the nurses as well. It makes sense to me that nurses could become cold and detached. Maybe they almost had to.

* * *

In the late 1960s and 1970s, burn care was usually focused on getting a patient "grafted." Third-degree burned skin can not regenerate itself. The human skin has three main parts: the epidermis, the dermis and the sub-cutaneous layer, or hypodermis. First-degree burns involve injury to the epidermis. They might be caused by a mild sunburn. Second-degree burns involve injuries to the dermis and epidermis. This is a more serious injury and can be very painful. Perhaps you have had a second-degree burn from a cooking accident, or a serious sunburn. Second-degree burns require first aid and sometimes medical attention.

Third-degree burns require extensive medical treatment. Because the skin has been damaged through all the layers (the epidermis, dermis and hypodermis), the skin is permanently unable to regenerate itself. The third-degree burned skin is dead, unable to regrow new layers, and it must be removed. That process is called debriding.

Now, in 2020, debriding is done under general anesthesia, due to the excruciating pain of the procedure. In 1967, when I was a kid, debriding was done in a giant silver bathtub called a tank. I was placed in the tank, sitting up, with warm water swirling all around me. A nurse would come in and scrub the dead tissue off my wounded little body. "Tanking," as it was called, was horrifically painful and done under no pain medication whatsoever. Imagine someone scouring your skin off your body every day.

Once the dead tissue was removed, the next step in treating third-degree burns is to graft the area. Grafting is a surgical procedure. A surgeon will shave off a patch of skin from an unburned area, and suture the patch over a burned, skinless area. The shaved place is called a donor site. The sutured place is called a graft.

I have grafts all over my body. If you were to look closely at my skin, you could see little patches, shaped like rectangles or ovals, marching all up my arms, my neck, my chest. Each patch has a raised border, showing that the skin clearly came from somewhere else, and was sewn into this new place. These are my grafts. If I didn't have them, I would have no skin there at all, and I would have died long ago.

Grafts are not painful, because the skin is so badly burned that the nerve endings are dulled or even non-existent. Donor sites are another story. My donor sites usually came from the back of my thighs or my butt. These non-burned areas saved me, regenerating patch after patch of healthy skin, to be harvested and sewn in elsewhere. Ironically, these non-burned donor sites become the most painful areas. Removing the top layer of the skin leaves a bright red wound, completely skinless and exposed, with all nerve endings intact. This donor site wound now needs to completely regrow itself.

It takes two weeks for a donor site to mostly heal, and four weeks for the site to heal completely. In the meantime, having a donor site is unimaginably painful. The wound would be covered with something called scarlet red. This was a special medicated bandage placed over the large open wound to protect it. However, the scarlet red was stuck directly on the wound after the grafting, and then one would bleed through the scarlet red, onto the bandages. This blood would harden. With each bandage change, the white bandages would have to be removed. They would be stuck hard together, and would be ripped off, sticking to a completely open skinless donor site. These were the bandage changes that we all dreaded, nurses and children alike. Changing the graft site was a painless piece of cake. Changing the donor site could drive a sane person mad. Nowadays, these dressing changes are done under either heavy sedation or anesthesia. Back then, it was just what we did every morning and every night, with no pain relief at all.

Another problem with grafts is that they shrink. If you graft a third-degree burn, you start out initially with a large patch. But scarred skin contracts over time, and the patch will gradually get smaller, sometimes shrinking to half its original size. So, many grafts have to be redone, or revised over the years.

Compounding the problem, grafted kids are still growing and they need even more skin over time. A normal person grows their own skin as they mature. Third-degree burns cannot generate new skin, however. If you graft a burned four-year-old, you have to keep re-grafting as that four-year-old gets taller and wider, and becomes an adult. Thus, Shriners kids were being grafted, grafted and grafted again. I was grafted, repeatedly, on my face, neck, chest, both arms, back, both thighs and my left calf. When I say I was "65 percent third-degree" burned, it means that two thirds of my body was burned and grafted, most of it repeatedly.

In addition to the grafting, there were more delicate surgical procedures. My surgeon had to build a bottom lip for me. He had to graft and construct an entire neck and chin as well. The neck operations were particularly difficult. After the grafting and reconstruction, Dr. Constable worried that my grafts would immediately shrink away. He came up with a solution that would allow my neck to keep stretched all hours of the day. Unfortunately, his solution proved to be ridiculous.

I had a normal hospital bed, with metal sides to keep me from falling out of bed. On top of the mattress, they placed a crib mattress. I was to lie on my back with my body on the crib mattress up to my shoulders. Then, I was to let my head dangle off the edge of the crib bed. Thus, my neck would be fully stretched at all times.

It was impossible to sleep in this position. Each night I would gamely try, lying on my back, with my shoulders on the crib and my head hanging off the mattress, my mouth gaping open for air. But my saliva would pool in the back of my throat, and it felt like I was drowning. Gradually, I would scoot my way down the baby mattress, and curl up on it, sleeping soundly until the morning. I didn't mean to be non-compliant, but it was just too much.

This was not even the worst of the sleeping arrangements I was given. When I was first sent home from the hospital, I was almost five years old. I was fully grafted, in that my skin no longer had completely open areas. But the grafts were tight and shrinking steadily. Dr. Constable was trying to keep my skin as stretched out as possible. It was either he, or a misguided physical therapist, who came up with a solution that involved four Clorox® bleach bottles on rope pulleys.

The Clorox bottles were filled with water and affixed to ropes. The other ends of the ropes were attached to black Velcro® straps, cut to fit my little wrists and ankles. At night, my parents put me to bed. After my story, they attached a Velcro strap to each of my wrists and ankles. The straps stretched all four of my limbs straight out, so I lay flat on my back in bed, spread-eagled. The ropes connected to the bleach bottles, which were heavy with water. I was to spend my night in full traction, completely unable to move. A modern medieval torture.

Alone in the dark, I tried my best to be compliant. I would lie there, heavy weights pulling on all my limbs, and I tried to sleep. Over time, I just couldn't take it. Like a little criminal, I would rub and rub my right wrist against the bed. Slowly, over time, I would rub the Velcro loose. My parents would hear a loud bang downstairs, as the first bleach bottle hit the floor. Then, I would rub my left wrist free. Bang, went bottle two. Eagerly, I would sit up in my bed, reaching in the dark for the two Velcro straps around my ankles. This part was easy. Bang! Bang! Gratefully, I would curl up in my bed, hug my favorite stuffed bunny, and finally go to sleep. Even my parents, strict as they were, did not have the heart to climb upstairs and put those Velcro straps back on.

Going to sleep as a burned kid was no less complicated than waking up as a burned kid. When I would wake up after a surgery, I never knew what to expect. Consciousness crept back slowly, arising out of the dark obliteration of anesthesia. There would be no pain, thanks to the surgical medications, but I was always disoriented. Gradually, I would feel around my body, finding the new grafted area, encased in thick cotton bandages. I could sense my new donor site from the soreness of the area, once I had shifted weight in the bed. I would see my IV in my arm, taped down to a light blue board so I wouldn't accidentally dislodge it. Sometimes, I would wake up and my head would be under a little oxygen tent, plastic sheeting all around me, and I would peer through the clear wall to see if someone were there.

One time in particular, I emerged from anesthesia to find my left arm extended straight up from the bed into the air. My arm was held up perpendicular to my body, mimicking a salute. It was uncomfortable, but designed again to minimize contractures. To my horror, I saw that a thick metal rod, a giant six-inch screw, had been completely drilled through my wrist bone, from one side to the other. This giant screw then was attached on both sides to a silver pole, keeping my wrist up in the air. I looked at the metal rod with terror. Was I always going to have a metal rod in my wrist? Was I going to look like Frankenstein now, with the bolts in his neck? How would they ever get this rod out? I began to wail.

The nurse in charge came over. "What's the matter, Lise? Why are you crying?"

"There's a rod in my wrist! What is that awful big screw there? I have holes in my wrist!"

"It's ok, Lise. It's only for a little while. The doctor can get it right out of you again, don't worry."

"Do I have to go to school like that? It's so ugly. I can't ever go to school now."

"No it's only for a little bit. We will get it out of you before you get discharged."

It was scary when they finally took that rod out, drilling loudly, cutting so close to my skin, but I was relieved. I looked enough like a freak. I didn't need a large metal rod coming out of my wrist too.

Another issue with sleeping arose from the use of silver nitrate. Silver nitrate began to be used in the 1960s for burn care. It is a liquid which drastically decreased infection, always the mortal fear in burn care. Once silver nitrate was developed, burn infections dropped quite a lot. Had I been burned prior to silver nitrate, chances are I would not have survived.

Silver nitrate was a great life saver, but it was a royal pain. Every hour or two, a nurse would come by with a large bottle of the medicine and what looked like a mammoth turkey baster. The nurse would pull down my covers and squirt the liquid all over my wounds, and then tell me to go back to sleep. It's hard to sleep with soggy wet bandages stuck to you, but I tried. Just when I finally went back asleep, the bandages would dry, and along would come the nurse and her turkey baster again. I was never allowed to be dry, and I never was allowed to sleep for long. That's how silver nitrate worked.

The other issue with silver nitrate is that it stained everything it touched dark brown. My skin would look black, and it would take weeks for the stain to go away. Worse for me, my little stuffed animals were blackened too. Even my little animal playmates were permanently scarred by their lives in the hospital.

To this day, I have a little stuffed cat that came with me to Mass General and Shriners. He is a black and white tiger named Kitty. If you look at him carefully, some of his black spots are from his days on my bed, being squirted with silver nitrate. He is still here though. We survived it together. But as it turned out, Kitty spent more nights to come in the hospital than I ever expected.

LESSON THREE:

Even the worst pain can be survived. Take it one day at a time, one hour at a time or even one minute at a time. Pain will pass.

FOUR

The Ugly Girl and Her Friends

WALKING TO KINDERGARTEN

I walked alone to kindergarten when I was five years old. I was short and physically delayed, but I knew the way. It was a half a block up to Midland Avenue, a left turn, and three blocks down that busy street to the school crossway. I liked school. I was in the accelerated class with all the smart kids. Each and every year, we were in the same class together. Once you were in the smart class, you were always in the smart class. (God help any kids who didn't immediately establish their intelligence by five years old.) The smart kids were all a little "different," so over time I managed to fit in with them.

What I didn't like was walking to school. I was hideously disfigured. I had no neck, no chin, and no bottom lip. The fire had burned away all of these body parts, and the grafts over these areas were tight, purple and banded. My scars, which covered two-thirds of my body, were raised purple and red. Frequently, just out of another surgery, I would be strapped into a splint which made me hold my arm permanently perpendicular to my body. These splints were nicknamed "Airplane Splints," because they made a burned kid look like half an airplane. At other times, my arms would be free, but my neck would be splinted up, so I couldn't look down, or eat my food with accuracy. I was truly a remarkable sight and not a pretty one.

I walked alone, in my various splints, with my bright purple scars, down the streets of East Orange, New Jersey. Although kids who knew me were usually nice, the kids who didn't know me were horrible. As I trudged along, kids would run past me, screaming, "Yuck!" "You are ugly!" they would say. "Gross!" Cars would drive past me, their passengers shouting out the window how repulsive I was and pretending to gag. These incidents happened every day. I would cry and cry, walking home alone, one arm aloft in my splint.

"Ugly girl, go away!"

"Yuck!"

I trudged home, trying not to hear the taunts, keeping my tearful eyes on the sidewalk. I tried not to step on the cracks, which was supposed to be bad luck. How much worse could my luck actually get?

My parents were matter-of-fact about these incidents. They showed neither concern nor sympathy and had the attitude of "that's how it is." Perhaps the trauma had exhausted them. Perhaps the trauma had hardened them. Perhaps they were already hard. If he were here, my father would say that he didn't want me to be spoiled. My mother would say that she herself was too traumatized by her own injuries to be able to think about mine. She might even say, voice rising, eyes flashing, that she was so traumatized by her own injuries that she shouldn't *have* to think about mine.

For whatever reasons, I walked alone at five years old, literally and figuratively. I trudged back and forth every day to school, trying to be cheerful and hoping that no one would notice me and my splints. I tried to fit in and be normal, but it was hopeless. I stood out like the ugliest duckling the world had ever seen. By the end of my walk, I was often in tears. But there was someone watching me. A man I didn't know was watching me.

One day, on my lonely walk back from school, an old man stopped me. He lived in a tidy white house with black shutters and a little front porch. He was an older white man, with short gray hair and black glasses. Smiling, the old man said, "Hello there. How are you doing today? Hey, I have something I think you might like. Why don't you come into my backyard for a minute?"

I know: today, a child might fear this man was an abusive creepy pedophile. Back then, in 1968, kids didn't think about strangers with fear. I was also a powerfully lonely five-year-old, and I delighted in anyone who seemed kind. As it turned out, this old man was not an abuser. He had a different agenda.

His small backyard was bordered with a high stockade fence. The yard burst with roses. Roses climbed all three walls of the fence, forming a sea of pink, red, yellow and white. The air itself smelled intensely sweet, like honey and spice and sugar, heated up together. I had never seen or smelled anything like this yard, so surprisingly hidden behind an ordinary fence. It felt like paradise.

The man asked, "Which roses do you like the most? Which ones are the very nicest ones of all?"

"They are all nice." I said politely.

"Well thank you! But which ones do you like the best? I want to make you a little treat."

I peered up at this strange man. He seemed nice enough. I didn't understand why he would want to give me anything at all. My parents didn't give presents unless it was Christmas or my birthday. But this man seemed different. "Well, I like that one. And that one too..." As I pointed to all the prettiest flowers, the old man carefully cut each bud, creating a small, multi-colored nosegay for me. Then, he wrapped the red, pink, yellow and white roses in tin foil, so that the thorns wouldn't cut my little hands. With a surprising flourish, the old man presented me with my own beautiful bouquet and sent me on my way.

I skipped all the way home, holding my sweet-smelling roses, feeling like a princess. No other kids had a nosegay of flowers for their walk home. For the first time in a long time, I felt special, but in a good way. My mother put my roses in a blue vase and I sniffed them every morning before I left for school. They smelled like heaven.

This same man gave me many more bouquets of roses. At the time, I thought he was just a really nice man who liked to give me flowers. Years later, I remembered him, and wept. I recognized that he had probably witnessed my walks of humiliation and rejection, and he had pity on the little burned girl who walked alone, whom everyone called ugly.

This is the thing. Here is my whole story in a nutshell. People can be so awful. They can be so mean and cruel. Life blindsides us with brutality and disappointment. But then there are the strangers who give little burned girls the best roses out of their hidden gardens. There are those people too.

BATMAN AND ROBIN

My world started—and for some time it ended—with my brother Marc. He was my favorite person and best playmate. I was at times his only playmate, even though I was five years younger, because he didn't have many friends. He was a brilliant, sensitive boy, with such thin skin that it barely seemed solid enough to protect his kind heart and his extraordinary brain. His face radiated vulnerability and intensity.

Marc was wiry and thin, with beautiful hazel eyes and thick sandy hair that deepened to brown over the years. Due to early nearsightedness, his thick glasses obscured his direct gaze, stealing his beauty. Once, he took off his ever-present glasses and looked at me. I gazed into his stunning eyes.

"You really should get contacts," I said. "Girls would love your eyes."

He smiled at me. "When they really get to know me, then they will see." But the girls never did see.

Marc's handsome face was scarred with terrible acne, which he never could combat successfully. But he had a stunning smile, with teeth as wide, as straight, and as white as Julia Roberts'. He didn't smile that smile much. He was serious, and he was concerned.

When my brother was an infant, he cried every night. My mother complained for years afterwards, telling me how difficult Marc was as a baby. Every night my brother woke up and shrieked. One night, my father, who had anger problems and who might have been drinking, stormed up in a fury. He and my mother stood blearily in the nursery, listening to Marc howl, as he did every night. My father, in a rage, picked up his infant son and threw him across the room to my mother. I think my mother caught him. I always assumed that she did. Regardless, Marc never cried at night after that incident.

I told you he was smart.

The early photos of my brother show him looking concerned. He peers wanly into the camera, pleasant but unsmiling, always pensive. There are photos of him in a sky-blue jumpsuit, holding a ball with stars on it, looking obligingly into the lens, but not smiling. There is another photo of him, holding a little stuffed dog, again, with no smile.

There is, however, one great photo taken of him and me, when he was six and I was a year old. We are in our grandparents' kitchen. I am sitting on the potty and my brother is crouching in his pajamas on the floor nearby. I am looking at him and he is looking at me, and we are grinning at each other from ear to ear.

I loved my brother with every bit of my little body. He was my favorite person in our family, which I established to myself, every day, with my private rituals. It used to be my job to set the table. There were four different kinds of sharp knives (we had no matching set). In my mind, I had them ordered from my favorite to my least favorite. I would give myself the best, Marc the second best, my mother the third best, and my father the worst. There was also a coaster set which I sometimes had to place. One coaster had grapes on it; my favorite. That one went to me. Then there was the orange, the second best, which went to Marc. My mother got the lemon. My father got the lime. (I wasn't really sure what a lime was but it looked yucky.)

Most of my earliest memories involve my brother. We had a big playroom in back of our house. There was an old dining room table stored there, pushed next to a pillar in the middle of the room. This table transformed into our Batman headquarters in Gotham City. We would reconnoiter there, develop our mission, and then slide down the pillar to the floor below and leap to action. Well, Marc would slide down the pillar and leap into action. I would anxiously cling to the pillar and slink about six inches onto the chair Marc would push there for me, and then scramble off toward our Bat Adventures.

Marc was Batman and he wore a great Batman tool belt with all kinds of play gear on it. To my continual displeasure, I was always Robin. I had a Robin belt with only two tools on it, a fake flashlight and a worthless piece of plastic rope.

"Why can't I be Batman?" I would whine, sticking out my bottom lip. "I never get to be Batman."

"Because I am Batman. You are Robin," he would declare, decisively.

"Can I ever get to be Batman?"

"No." Still, it was ok. We were playing together, Marc and I. Nothing was better than that, even if I always had to be Robin.

I had the very best times with my brother. Almost all of my earliest memories were about him and me, and hardly any involve our parents. He was my world.

Even my parents recognized that Marc had exalted status above them, in my eyes. When I was six, we were on a cross-country trip. We drove across the country three times, when I was little, during my father's summer break from teaching. We camped, stayed in cheap hotels, and visited friends and relatives along the way. One night, we were camping, and I was caught in a lie. I had started to lie, and my parents were concerned. Their unique solution was to defer to Marc, and to ask my eleven-year-old brother to speak to me about morality.

Marc pulled me into the green family tent, and we sat down on the sleeping bags and air mattresses. The air smelled like pine trees and rubber. "Lise, why are you lying all of the sudden?"

"I'm not."

"Yes you are. See you just lied then. Why are you lying? You know it's wrong."

"I don't know." I turned my face away from him and fiddled with the zipper on my sleeping bag.

"Look, Lise, it's a big deal when you lie. People figure it out, and then they don't trust you anymore. If you lie, we will never know whether we can believe you or not. And what if you really need something, and then no one believes you, because you are a liar?"

I sat cross legged on the air mattress, looking at my brother. I was silent.

"Do you remember that story of the *Boy Who Cried Wolf?* He would go around the village, telling everybody he saw a wolf. In the beginning everyone believed him and they ran out to help him. But after a while, they realized the boy was only pretending to see the wolf, just to get attention, so they started to ignore him. Then, one day, the boy really does see a wolf. He calls out "Wolf! Wolf!" but the whole village ignores him. They know he just says that and they don't believe him anymore. Do you remember that story?"

"Yeah."

"Well, I really don't want you to be like that boy and wind up eaten by a wolf, you know what I mean? You have to stop lying. You just have to. It's really important."

"OK. OK. OK," I said. Marc smiled at me. And that was that.

There was nothing I wouldn't do for my brother. He had the highest credibility of anyone I knew. I still think he should have shared that Batman belt. Other than that, he was pretty much perfect.

THE POOL PARTY

East Orange, New Jersey, used to be a wealthier town. We moved there in 1967 when it was a good place to raise two young and bright children. My father taught music history at Upsala College, nearby, and we moved there so Dad could bike to work. The same year, violent riots erupted in Newark, the city next door. Gradually, East Orange changed from a middle-class town to a crime-ridden inner-city zone with a failing school district. By the time we moved away, having struck it big with the Solox lawsuit, East Orange had become a different place. My parents sold our house to a Black family, which was fine with us. But some neighbors on the block refused to speak to us after that, furious that we were enabling the "change."

I don't remember East Orange much. Although we lived there for five years, I spent most of those years in the hospital. I remember our street, Laurel Avenue, lined with old beautiful trees, and houses with welcoming front porches. Laurel Avenue was quiet and we could play in the road, if we found friends to play with. This proved to be daunting for me. Across the street, and down the block, lived the Hannigans.

Judy Hannigan was my first friend/enemy. She was taller, older, and she completely dominated our tenuous relationship. She would play with me, and then she would not. If I didn't do exactly what she wanted me to do, she would literally take her ball and go home. She would abruptly leave my room, head held high in scorn, cross the street, and march down to her yard, three houses down. I desperately wanted to be Judy's friend as she ruled the girls in the neighborhood. Sometimes the girls would play kickball in the street. Unlike every other sport, I wasn't so terrible at kickball. I could, upon occasion, actually kick the ball. I quivered to be a part of this little gang of girls.

One summer day, Judy and I were sitting in my room, playing dolls. "It's my birthday next week. I'm turning eight," she declared with a toss of her head, brown curls bobbing.

"Happy birthday, Judy! I didn't know it was your birthday."

"Yeah. I'm excited because my dad said he has a big present for me. I'm going to get it at my party."

"What party?" I asked. There was a momentary silence. Judy studied her sandals.

"Yeah, well. I'm having a party, a pool party next week."

I looked at Judy, watching her face, waiting for my invitation. More silence.

"I'm not inviting you."

Tears welled up in my eyes. My voice rose, getting higher. "But I want to come to your party. We play all the time. I love swimming. I'm a good swimmer. I can just walk to the party, I live right here."

"I can't invite you. You are all burned. I can't have you at my pool party. You will gross out all my friends. The party will be all yucky if you come. You make people feel . . . sick."

Devastated, I told my family what Judy had said. My father went to speak with Mr. Hannigan about the party, assuming I had misunderstood. Instead, Mr. Hannigan confirmed that it was true. I was not invited to his daughter's party on account of my being burned and ugly.

My brother Marc had always hated Mr. Hannigan, and he hated him even more after the pool party debacle. Marc was a hippie at 11, free spirited, disrespectful, but brilliant. Mr. Hannigan was hostile toward anyone that was different from him. He had short hair and wore white collared shirts; he had a neat, clean house with an ugly metal fence, and a perfect lawn. He also didn't like Black people. Mr. Hannigan owned the sacred above-ground pool in the back, the pool to which I was never invited, even though I dearly loved to swim.

Although he was a lanky, nearsighted boy, Marc could be fierce. He waged a personal war on Mr. Hannigan. My brother began biking down the street, raucously singing, "H -A- double N- I -G -A- N spells Hannigan Hannigan." He would bellow this song over and over again as loudly as possible, daring Mr. Hannigan to protest. Marc would loudly break curfew, and Mr. Hannigan would complain to my father. My father didn't do anything to Marc because he didn't like Mr. Hannigan either. We couldn't stand him. Archie Bunker, the anti-hero from *All in the Family,* could have been modeled on Mr. Hannigan.

Marc made one good friend in our neighborhood, Bobby. Bobby was a kind, handsome young Black boy, just Marc's age. He lived with his single mother across the street from us. Bobby didn't like Mr. Hannigan either and I suspect that Mr. Hannigan didn't like Bobby.

After the pool party non-invitation, Marc and Bobby plotted their revenge. They crept out one night, uncharacteristically quiet, and snuck over to the Hannigans. The night was dark and still; no one saw them. They crept up onto the Hannigan's front lawn, suppressing their giggles, and unzipping their flies. In silent middle school triumph, Marc and Bobby quietly urinated all over the Hannigans' neat walkway, staining it forever, or so they proudly declared the next morning.

"They will never be able to use that sidewalk again," they crowed. "It is going to look like yellow pee forever." The Deguires basked in triumph. No one ever knew it was them. But hey, Mr. Hannigan, if you are still alive, which I doubt, given the meanness of your heart, it was Marc-the-hippie and Bobby-the-Black-kid. My brother and Bobby peed all over your perfect walkway, because you and your daughter were mean to the little burned girl.

LATCHKEY KID

After the fire, and her arduous recovery, my mother went back to college to get her doctorate. Although she was a talented and highly trained musician, she gave up her dream of being a concert pianist. Despite her decades of practice and her studies, she had never developed the classical pianist career that had once seemed her birthright. Now, she decided to be a clinical psychologist. This new goal would entail not only several years in a doctoral program, but she also had to return to college for prerequisite classes. Thus began my career as a latchkey kid.

Perhaps another mother might have devoted herself to helping her four-year-old daughter recover from 65 percent burns. Another mother might have gone back and forth with her daughter to the hospital in Boston, staying nearby, looking after her girl. Another mother might have been concerned that her daughter was enduring painful operations, which she may or may not survive. Another mother might have wanted to sit by her daughter, bringing her comfort, watching over her, for the many years it would take for her child to recover. But this was not my mother. My mother wanted to move on with her own life. So, she went back to school. I went to the hospital a lot, alone for most of the time. When I was home, I became a latchkey kid.

I wore my gold-colored house key around my neck, on a brown leather cord. I walked diligently from school to home, and I let myself in. Then, I would watch our black-and-white TV for the rest of the afternoon, by myself. Sometimes I forgot my key. When that happened, I would anxiously perch on the front porch and hope that someone would come home soon. I would wait alone for an hour or two. Sometimes, I would be able to break in through the front window. I would lift myself up, climb through the window, and crawl into my house. My parents never asked me if I had my key before I left for school. It was my responsibility to remember, and it was my problem if I forgot.

Because of my mother's classes, when I was really little, I walked to Sally's house for lunch. Sally lived with her mom, who was divorced. Their apartment was close to our school, and her mother managed a little side business, making lunches for kids whose moms weren't home. The kitchen was cramped, with fake wood paneling in the den and a white Formica kitchen table where we ate, four kids in all.

I ate my sandwiches at Sally's, along with Mike and John. Mike was two years older than me; he was a bit wild, but there was a sweetness to him, deep down. John was a year older than me, also wild, but he didn't seem to be sweet at all. They sat across from me and delighted in opening their mouths wide like baby birds, displaying their half-masticated ham sandwiches. I would squeeze my eyes shut and try not to see but they played this game daily, enjoying my revulsion. I felt relieved when I didn't have to go to Sally's anymore. I preferred making baloney sandwiches for myself at my own house.

Being a latchkey kid scared me but I tried to be cheerful about it, and I didn't complain. I knew what my parents expected. I had a schedule to keep and I kept it, independently and without supervision. I was supposed to do my homework, practice the piano for 30 minutes, and then go outside to play for 30 minutes. My parents had decided (accurately) that I spent too much time staring open-mouthed at the TV. So, I diligently went outside by myself every afternoon, riding my bike in circles, or walking around our yard, checking my blue Cinderella watch frequently so that I knew when the dreaded 30 minutes were up and I could watch TV again.

I adored TV. As I watched, I would play elaborate pretend games with my Barbies and my brother's discarded GI Joes. I would play Solitaire, waiting tensely until someone came home. The front door would open and slam shut again.

"Hello?" I called out.

"Hi Lise!" answered my brother, and inside my stomach, my muscles instantly relaxed. I always felt better when someone else was in the house. I liked hearing my brother's records and my father's typewriter, the noises of my family in the air around me. My hours of anxiously supervising myself could end and I could rest for a while, safe in my house, belonging to someone again.

MEMERE AND PEPERE

Glens Falls, New York, was voted the Best Small Town in America when my father grew up there. Through my little girl eyes, Glens Falls was all white wooden houses with welcoming front porches, and graceful tall trees. If it had a town center, I never saw it. The town center to me was my Memere and Pepere's house, on Fourth Street. My Pepere, with his big heart, boundless energy and booming friendliness, was the center of everything to me.

Marc and I spent a lot of time with our grandparents when we were little. Memere, French-Canadian for Grandmother, was my father's mother. She was petite and lovely. Her face was delicate and refined, with gorgeous eyes, and hair that curled gently, framing her perfect oval face. It was only later in my adulthood that I realized my face looked quite a bit like hers. She was a true beauty. It is that inherited beauty that has kept my face, burned and all, still in the camp of lovely-faced people. Most facially burned people can't claim that, but I can, thanks to my Memere.

Pepere, French-Canadian for Grandfather, was my hero. He stood tall, handsome and athletic, with a wide smile, vaguely scented by the spicy smell of his cigars. He was friendly and outgoing, able to chat with anyone.

(My father used to talk about the "Deguire Charm." Pepere had it, as did my father, as do I, as do my two daughters. The Deguire Charm is the ability to connect, quickly and effortlessly, with anyone. It is a twinkle in the eye, an easy smile, a ready laugh. It is the ability to notice a person and say something that will make effortless conversation. It is the confident ability to walk into a room, knowing that we will be liked by most people. It is thanks to my Pepere that I have the social skills to make you completely forget that I am burned. Then, once you remember, perhaps you love me extra because of it.)

Marc was Memere and Pepere's only grandson and I their only granddaughter. My parents seemed to need a break from us frequently and Memere and Pepere wanted us around as much as possible. So, we traveled to Glens Falls every month or two, and we would stay there alone quite a lot. We also would visit my mother's family in Minnesota every summer, and my parents would leave us with our Aunt Betty and Uncle John. As Aunt Betty once told me, "I don't know why they always wanted to go on vacation without you, but I was happy to have you."

Besides Marc, Pepere was my other most favorite person. He had the gift of intense social focus. He made me feel like I was the most special person in the whole world. He made everyone feel this way, but I knew he *really* felt this way about me. He played games with me, just him and me. We would play waitress in the basement. He would sit in his favorite rocker, and I would come to take his order. He would rock slowly back and forth, smoking his cigar, and wait for me to bring him "food." I would busily prepare the "food" and eventually bring it to his chair so he could "eat."

"Oh, what a wonderful sandwich you made! And this coffee! So delicious! How do you do it? Please make me more," he would rumble in his deep smoky voice. "I want a piece of pie now."

I would beam with happiness and scurry away to pretend-cut a piece of pie. Giggling with excitement, I would bring the "pie" to him to receive more basking praise. Time stood still with Pepere, and his craggy grinning face, solely focused on mine. The only bad part was when he would tell me we had to go back upstairs.

"OK, Lise, that was a wonderful lunch. Let's go upstairs now to visit with the other family. We have been gone a long time, and they want to see us."

"No, Pepere, please, I want to play some more. I can bring you dinner now!"

Very gently but firmly, he would reply, "No, Lise, we have to visit." I would groan in protest, but up we would go.

Pepere-time twinkled with magic. At 13 Fourth Street, there was an old baby carriage to play with. I would bring my favorite doll, wrapped in a soft pink blanket and lay her gently in the old-fashioned carriage, with big silver wheels. Pepere and I would head out for our walk around the neighborhood, me pushing my "baby" in the black carriage, with the hood up, to protect her from the sun. We would stroll amiably together, just he and I, chattering away.

We would frequently run into other neighbors, about which I was ambivalent. On the one hand, I was proud that seemingly everyone in the world loved my special Pepere, and they all wanted to talk to him. It also made a big impression on me that he could talk to anyone, warmly and cheerfully. I was proud to be seen with my Pepere, hero of the town, as far as I could tell. On the other hand, I was eager to receive his sole attention again. "Come on, let's go!" I would softly hiss. "Come on!"

"Not yet," he would say, "We have to visit." I would sigh, shifting my weight back and forth, waiting as patiently as I could to be my Pepere's sole focus again. I adored him. It seemed like everyone else did too, and I wanted them all to go away, so it could be just us again.

Pepere was a gifted musician. He could read music, although not well. He could, however, play anything by ear. He didn't have a fantastic technique, but he was skilled enough to make the music soar. At night, he would settle down at his upright piano in the front parlor and play. He loved *The Music Man* and *My Fair Lady*. He played songs with an old-fashioned stride piano sound, and Memere and I would sing along.

When it was time for me to go to bed, Pepere would play "Good Night Ladies," from *The Music Man*. I would trudge mournfully up the small bended staircase to the bedroom I shared with my Memere, wishing I could stay up a little longer with Pepere. But, when I got to my bed, there would be a special pack of butter rum lifesavers that Memere had tucked under the pillow, just for me. I could hear my Pepere singing goodnight to me, as I snuggled into the covers.

Memere could not possibly compete with Pepere's wonderfulness, and she never tried. She was a sweet, kind and simple woman. Behind Memere's back, my mother scorned her. My mother commented frequently on Memere's lower intelligence, and how boring she was. Memere did her work with devotion, diligence and kindness. She took care of her family and her house. Everything was neat and tidy.

And she cooked.

My Memere was a notoriously horrible cook. Her cooking was so reliably bad that it was comical. There was seemingly nothing she couldn't ruin. Meats were so dried up they were hard to chew, and you would have to have a little drink just to choke them down. Vegetables were so overcooked that they were a soggy tasteless mush. Even eggs seemed to overwhelm her. Memere did have one dish that she had mastered. She baked a nice chocolate cake with vanilla icing. Somehow, this cake had the singular escape from her cooking woes. We all used to look forward to that cake at the end of each dreadful meal. Memere seemingly never knew that her cooking was atrocious. She served every meal with a confident smile, while we all flinched in anticipation. God bless her.

Every morning, I would arise from my little twin bed in Memere's room. She would wake me up singing, opening up the white lace curtains to let the daylight stream into the room. We would go down the bended staircase into the kitchen in the back of the house. I would sit at the black and white Formica table, and she would make me toast, which she often did not ruin. Memere would chat away, cheerfully. After breakfast, she would go out into her green backyard and feed the birds, singing as she filled the bird-feeders.

Memere and Pepere came to see me in the hospital in Boston after the fire, but I don't remember it. I do remember one visit that Pepere made to me, during my first re-hospitalization. I was five years old, and it was my first time back, after the initial five months in the hospital.

This hospitalization was approached like they all were: matter-of-factly. The hospital was some thing my parents didn't discuss, we just went there, and there I would stay, alone for most of the time.

This time, I was hospitalized for a month. My only clear memory is my Pepere's visit. He stood in front of my bed, tall and strong, and we talked a long time. Then he pulled out a present for me, a Cinderella watch. It had a pale blue band, and Cinderella was on the face of the watch. My parents were not into Disney, so this present was a huge treat. Also, at five years old, it was my very first watch.

There was one problem. Pepere went to fasten the prized watch on my left wrist, but my left wrist was thickly covered with bandages from the operation. I turned my head mournfully. I couldn't wear my pretty new watch like any other girl.

"So, we will put it here!" he said cheerfully, and quickly strapped it onto my right wrist instead. I proudly wore that watch for years. The blue Cinderella tethered me to my Pepere, ticking away time, showing me each second that I was loved. . . loved. . . loved.

To this day, I always wear my watch on my right wrist, never my left, in honor of my Pepere.

Later, I was staying in Glens Falls, alone with Memere and Pepere. In the dining room, they had a record player, and Pepere put on the album of *My Fair Lady*. I guess it's a Deguire thing, this love of show music. We all became more cheerful and upbeat, listening to the beautiful songs. There was one song, "I'm Getting Married in the Morning", that got us all particularly riled up. Somehow we wound up in a three person parade. We began to march in time, me, Pepere and Memere, enthusiastically trooping around the dining room table, again and again. We marched to the beat, grinning wildly, pumping our arms, and singing along to the jaunty tune.

To this day, whenever I hear that song, I will high-step a bit. And if no one is looking, I will even march around the table a time or two, thinking of my Memere and Pepere. I can feel them behind me, moving their arms vigorously, smiling, and singing.

I still feel them there.

DRAMBUIE

At 15, I drifted slowly down the hall of Shriners Burns. I wore my red night-gown, with the white lace insets. It was kind of see-through, but I didn't care. I fantasized that I might look a little sexy. My long brown wavy hair lay loose and flowing and I felt pretty. I limped a bit from my right thigh donor site, which hurt, so I put less weight on that leg and kept moving toward my little room. I hoped that my donor site bandage didn't leak and ruin my pretty red nightgown. The air smelled like disinfectant, sharp and acidic, and the floor tiles gleamed from buffing.

I had a private hospital room now that I was a teenager. For many years I stayed in the U-shaped ward with the other little burned kids. Our beds lay close to each other, with green drawn curtains for what passed as privacy, but were really just curtains. We heard each other at night. We heard each other during the day for the horrific dressing changes. Every single kid yelled for his mother during the dressing changes, but parents weren't allowed. Dressing changes would have been too hard for parents to witness.

Now, I was out of that ward. My small private room lay off the hallway. I had a TV affixed high on the wall, my own bathroom, and one window overlooking a gray Boston rooftop. The little room had white walls, white floors and two white blankets on the hospital bed. Underneath the blankets were green paper sheets. Burned kids got paper sheets that were disposed of after one use. They crackled with stiffness and were completely unsooth-ing. Paper sheets reduced infections and infections could kill burned kids. Without intact skin, germs invade quickly, with sometimes lethal conse-quences. So we lost the simple comfort of soft sheets at night, sometimes the only comfort of the bedridden. All the burned children slumbered, uneasily, on their scratchy paper sheets.

I had a closet in my private room. On the top shelf, behind my army backpack, I hid my new bottle of Drambuie liquor. It was a birthday gift from Ken, my brother's former college roommate. On my birthday, eight

Massachusetts Institute of Technology (MIT) students crammed into my room, bringing presents and blessedly non-institutional food. We caroused (as much as possible in a children's hospital), and I received my first bottle of liquor. I hadn't known these students for more than a year but they had virtually adopted me.

Cindy visited me every day in the hospital, after she was done with her pre-med classes. She was 20. Her round wide face was accented with high cheekbones, greetings from her Native American ancestry. Her long straight dark hair fell halfway down her back. She wore no makeup and dressed in colorful loose cotton blouses with intricate Indian prints. Cindy was the first person in my life to visit me every day in the hospital. Mostly, I had been on my own here, for the last 11 years.

My mother and my father must have called me for my birthday. They didn't forget birthdays. But I don't remember them calling.

I was good though. I felt very cool in my red see-through negligee with my college friends who really loved me. After visiting hours, I sat alone in my hospital room, sipping my secret Drambuie and scribbling in my dreary journal. There was a terrible blizzard one day, and Boston shut down under a foot of snow. The city stopped, and no one could get anywhere, but the Charles River had frozen over, connecting Cambridge to Boston. Cindy and Ken and a couple of other MIT folks trudged across the wide river of ice to visit me. Cindy never missed a day, not even with a blizzard. I felt like a minor celebrity with so much care and attention.

This hospitalization extended past the usual two weeks. For some reason, I had to stay longer. Probably it was yet another infection, despite the forbidding green paper sheets. After my discharge, I went to Cindy's house for another two weeks to recover.

Cindy lived in Cambridge, in a rough area, with three other roommates. They welcomed me at the door and helped me limp up the narrow stairs into their house. I slept on a futon in their tiny living room, covered with dusty Mexican blankets. I was 15 and Cindy was 20. She changed my bandages twice a day, made me tuna and onion sandwiches, and kept me company. Once I was finally well, I heaved up my backpack, caught the train to New York, and went home to my mother.

I was happy at MIT, with my brother's friends, even though he had perished there less than six months earlier. Seeing that tall white MIT building with the round ball on top made my stomach lurch every time. I visited his "grave" there pretty often, crying and picking up the tiny pieces of green glass. I didn't have to go, and it made me sad when I did, but I couldn't help visiting the building, again and again. In a strange way it helped me feel close to him.

Still, I loved MIT. I loved Cindy, I loved Ken, and I loved all these kind MIT students who declared me to be one of them, even though I was just a 15-year-old freshman in high school. Drambuie was only the most tangible of the many gifts they gave me. They took care of me for years, even after the worst tragedy of all happened right in their presence.

LESSON FOUR:

Friends will come from unexpected places. Sometimes the people you think should be your friends won't be there for you. Try not to latch onto them anxiously or resentfully. Notice instead who is truly there for you. They may not be who you think they should be, but pay attention and value them. These people are your true friends.

FLASHBACK GIRL

FIVE

A New Home for the Deguires

GLEN RIDGE

The case against Solox was settled out of court, and both my mother and I won some money. My award was intended to pay for my life-long medical bills. It did not make me a millionaire, but it did give me a financial cushion of safety. My mother was awarded money as well. With this payout, my parents thought they hit the big time. They bought a maroon Mercedes Benz and our first color TV. They sold our little house in East Orange, and we moved to a gorgeous New Jersey town called Glen Ridge.

Glen Ridge is prestigious but tiny, just six miles long and six blocks wide. The main thoroughfare, Ridgewood Avenue, stretches elegantly across the town, lined with stately large homes and leafy grand trees. The signature look of Glen Ridge is its old-fashioned gas lanterns that cast an elegant soft shimmer over the town at night. Glen Ridge bursts with excellent schools and monied families. My parents moved us into a stately three-story home, with an elegantly pillared front porch, generously sized rooms, and five bathrooms. Like a hippie version of *The Beverly Hillbillies,* we had arrived.

We moved to Glen Ridge near the end of the school year, when I was finishing third grade. My parents repeatedly declared that we would move to Glen Ridge to advance my brother's education. Marc's genius required a higher level of attention than East Orange could provide. My educational requirements were not mentioned.

It was true; I was not a genius and Marc definitely was. Still, it would have been a pleasant lie to say we were moving to benefit both children's educations. Perhaps it wouldn't have even been a lie. Although for me, being in the same small class of advanced kids, year after year, had been protective. Those kids knew me; they didn't torment me. Now I would have to start all over again. New kids would have to get used to me, my disfigured face and purple scarred body.

I, the non-genius, made my new walk to Linden Elementary School with trepidation. I was a lonely veteran of my walks to school, with kids yelling "yuck" and pretending to barf at the sight of me. It is never easy to be the new kid, let alone in the middle of the year. It is even harder to be the new kid if you are burned all over. Mysteriously, though, everyone at Linden Elementary was very nice to me. Well, maybe they weren't nice to me, but they pleasantly ignored me. I didn't understand it. I expected kids to be horrible, at least until they got to know me. I walked down the hall and no one stared. To be clear, no one even looked at me. Still, I sighed with relief to be ignored instead of being tormented.

Later I learned that Linden Elementary had had a school assembly before I arrived. They explained to the students that there was a burned girl moving in, and that they should be nice to me. When I finally found out about this assembly, I felt mortified. At the time, I wished the school hadn't talked about me and exposed my story. Later I came to appreciate the wisdom and intended kindness of this assembly, even though it embarrassed me at the time.

Eventually, I made friends at Linden. My brother Marc also made friends, "fitting in" for the first time in his life. His brilliance was not off-putting or weird there, among the wealthy over-achieving Glen Ridgers. He joined the marching band, rising quickly to the top of the percussionists, playing lead snare drum. Soon, he had a large group of friends, roaming in and out of our massive house at all hours. We had the party house, and all were welcome, and nothing was off-limits. My parents were as liberal and laissez-faire as it was possible to be.

THE PAPER CLIP PALACE, "FETALO," AND ONE BEAR

The TV room in the Glen Ridge house became mostly my space. I was nine and watched TV more than anyone, so the room transitioned into my de facto play area as well. It was an odd space. The walls shimmered with shiny metallic wallpaper, bright green and blue, with giant white paper clips, endlessly repeating themselves like a psychedelic office supply parade. It was the kind of wallpaper that you swear you will tear down as soon as you move in but ten years later, the wallpaper is still there, silently mocking your indolence.

My parents overlooked the TV room, rarely spending time there. Even if they had, my parents were not decorators. Our furniture was an uninspired collection of hand me downs and cheap antiques they had acquired along the way. Interior decorating was not their forte; their gift was music.

They fell in love as students at the Eastman School of Music. After my parents married, they moved into their first apartment together. Their landlady watched them unpack. First, they moved in their impressive black Steinway grand piano. Then, they moved in a few suitcases. Then they were done. The landlady looked again: there was no bed, no chairs, no table, nothing. Just a Steinway. For weeks afterwards, my parents would return to their shabby apartment to find something the landlady had left for them: a second-hand mattress; a used kitchen table; two chairs.

Our Glen Ridge house, despite its grandeur, still had this cobbled-together feel. The paper clip TV room held one piece of furniture: a white vinyl loveseat in the shape of a giant cube. Other than that, the room was empty, with only the giant paper clips on display. I filled the shiny metallic space with expansive Barbie townships, GI Joe jeeps, and toy horse ranches. I spread my toys everywhere, with *Sesame Street* playing in the background.

Although I was usually alone, my mother spent time there with me. She would join me during the evening, after dinner, when her work was done. Wearing a tired white bathrobe, held together by a safety pin, she visited my paperclip palace, sitting gamely on the cube couch. I would lean against her, resting my head on her chest, and she would put her right arm around my shoulders. We would watch *The Waltons,* a happy family, and lean together comfortably.

My mother relaxed me. My father excited and scared me. My brother excited and loved me, but my mother relaxed me. She was calm, unruffled, helpful. Her face was neither happy nor sad, just calm. She was steady. She was informative.

After the fire, my little room became overwhelmed with toys. When I was first hospitalized, seemingly everyone in the world sent me a toy. I had so many gifts that my father declared I should only open one a day, to extend the bounty. Toys overtook the space, drowning me. I was instructed that it was time to clean my room. At six years old, I had no idea how to even begin. Panic set in. My toys seemed to be multiplying by themselves, subdividing into more and more toys, come to smother me.

My mother came to my rescue. She sat on my bed, and explained the concept of sorting. "Put all the dolls over here," she said, pointing to a corner. "Now, all the stuffed animals go here," she pointed to another spot. "Games go here," and on she went, breaking down the inchoate mass of presents into a logical system. After that, she dragged up six large cardboard boxes, and labeled each one in big capital letters. My dolls now had a home, as well as each toy, in its own orderly labeled box that fit neatly into my closet.

Another dreaded cleaning day, I sat overwhelmed in my small bedroom, fearfully contemplating my inadequacy at the task. My mother came in, appraising my anxious face. "So, don't try to do it all at once," she said. "Each day, pick one area. One day it could be this chair, another day it would be your dresser. Just choose one area each day, and pick it up. By the end of the week, your room will be all clean."

My mother imparted her skills to me, mostly about practical issues that would make me independent. These skills were useful; some of them still are. She taught me how to balance a checkbook. She inspired me to open an IRA with my first summer job earnings, showing me a graph of how my $2,000 could grow into $60,000 by retirement, if I just left it there. (I still have that IRA; it's looking good.)

My mother, child of her sexually repressed mother, took my sexual education seriously, perhaps too seriously. She bought me a book for girls which explained sexuality and left it on my bed. Afterwards, we discussed eggs and sperm quite thoroughly and I felt "educated." In addition, I perused the copies of *The Joy of Sex*, and *Everything You Ever Wanted To Know About Sex but Were Afraid To Ask* that lay casually around the house. These adult books really plumbed the issue. *The Joy of Sex* even had highly detailed diagrams. I read these books over and over again, fascinated. By ten, I thought myself to be quite the sophisticate about sex, and ready to join the adult conversations my family was having.

One night, we went down to Cape May, New Jersey, for our annual weekend escape. My father was driving, and it was dark. My mother, father, and fifteen-year-old brother were talking about sex. I was never a part of this kind of conversation. This time I was following along quietly, and decided that I could contribute. "Well, what about fetalo?" I piped up.

"What?" they all turned to me. "What are you talking about?" There was a pause, an incredulity in their tone.

"You know, fetalo," I repeated, now confused. My new sexual repartee didn't seem to dazzle the way I imagined it would.

"What is this fetalo you keep saying? That isn't even a word," explained Marc, patiently.

"Yes it is. It's called fetalo." I paused, trying to explain myself better. "You know, when a man takes out his penis, and someone kind of, well, licks it?"

"Fellatio!" declared my family in delighted unison. Their laughter filled the car; my family howled with delight. My dad was literally crying with laughter. He had to pull the Mercedes over to the side of the road just to collect himself. "Fetalo," he repeated, over and over, shaking his shaggy head.

That was me at ten. My parents earnestly wanted me to have a better sexual education than they had had. My mother accomplished that, but perhaps she overdid it a tad.

When I was ten, my mother began her internship to be a psychologist. It was going to be a grueling year for her, commuting into New York City, five days a week. My parents had a plan to divide the workload among the four of us, so that she would not be too overwhelmed. This plan involved dividing the house and yard work into four equal parts, as well as dividing cooking responsibilities. I was to make dinner one night a week.

Ahead of time, my mother instructed me how to make a balanced meal. For the vegetables, I could use either frozen or canned supplies, which was easy enough. I learned how to make a little tossed salad, tearing the iceberg lettuce, and covering it with Thousand Island dressing. The daunting part was cooking the meat. We had an indoor grill in the kitchen, which my mother thought made things easy. "Just put the steak on the grill, salt and pepper it, and cook it for 12 minutes or so, turning it halfway through."

With those instructions, she set me loose, to cook my Wednesday night meal for the family, completely unsupervised. I'm not sure this would be a good idea for any child, but it certainly wasn't good for me, a burned girl, who, literally, had had a barbecue explode in her face. I approached the indoor grill cautiously, turning the knob. The flames flashed underneath, seemingly under control. I slid the slab of uncooked steak onto the grill, and it began to cook. The enticing smell of cooking beef filled the kitchen. Things seemed to be going well. I opened the can of green beans, and put them on the stove to cook.

The juices from the steak dripped down into the flames. I'm not sure what happened or how, but a fire started in the kitchen. The fire was small but spreading, clearly out of control. Panicked, I grabbed the steak and pulled it off the grill. Then, I ran and got a box of baking soda, which I remembered could put a fire out. I dumped the entire box on the grill. Sure enough, the fire extinguished, leaving me with a white sodden mess to clean up.

Somehow, dinner was served, and it was edible. That was my first dinner. I made many more dinners, and set several more fires, which I extinguished myself, going through box after box of baking soda. If not concerned for my welfare, I don't know why my parents weren't concerned that I would burn the house down. But the important thing seemed to be that I was doing my part, cooking my one meal a week so that no one else had to.

Cooking made me panic. I hated it. I still do. I hate the sight of the open flame, the glowing red, the rising heat. I hate the nearness of the flame to my hand, so vulnerable, skin so white and fragile. "How quickly this can all go wrong!" shouts my brain. "Get away, get away!" Both of my husbands cooked. By this I mean, both of my husbands did virtually all of the cooking for the family, night after night, year after year. I microwave, I assemble, I clean. I can still make a nice salad. No open flames for me.

My mother tried to raise me. She taught me about cooking and bills, cleaning and sex, and how to take the subway. She thought I was pretty and she told me she loved me. She taught me how to read music and how to play the piano. She taught me which fork to use in a restaurant, and how to break a roll into small pieces before eating it. She read to me at night before bed when I was little.

I want to say that she gave me what she could, but I can't say it. Any mammal knows how to protect their young. The instinct is burned into our DNA at the deepest level. Dogs, elephants and bears will fight fiercely to protect their babies, to the point of their own death. On the other hand, alligators lay their eggs and just slither away. They spawn their babies, and they move on, hissing "good luck!" on the way out.

My mother was a musician; a child prodigy. Her musical brain operated on a level much higher than the rest of us could hear or understand. She conversed knowledgeably about politics, travel and art. She forged gorgeous stained glass, sparkling with colored lights. Her chocolate cake was so inspired we dubbed it the "oh my God" cake.

And yet.

I barely survived my childhood with my mother. My brother did not survive. My mother sailed on, not even noticing the damage she left in her wake. She birthed us, and she tried to raise us. The mammal in her tried to teach us what we needed to know. The reptile in her repeatedly fled at the first sign of danger. We were left, squirming like hairless blind baby mice, struggling to survive on our own.

The coward in her could never acknowledge the damage she had done.

Here is one more story about my mother. After my parents divorced, my mother became a clinical psychologist, and she practiced for over 30 years. Near the end of her career, she had a home in rural Warren County, New Jersey, with an office overlooking 20 acres of woods. One warm spring day, she was working with a client. She left the back door open, with the screen door in place, so the fresh sweet air could fill the office.

My mother sat in her black leather chair, facing her client, and facing the screen door. The client sat with her back to the door. As the client spoke, my mother spotted a black bear, lumbering through the yard.

The client talked on and on, unaware of the beast in the field behind her. The bear came closer and closer. The client kept talking. The bear came to the house. The bear climbed up the stairs. The bear was at the door.

"John!" screamed my mother, and she fled the room.

The client was left in the room, alone, with a black bear at her back.

My stepfather John burst into the office. He spotted the bear, and he raced to the door. In an instant, John slammed the back door shut, and locked it. The bear was safely behind both the door and the screen door. The client was safe.

Afterwards my mother told me this story, laughing at the event. She never paused to recognize that she had abandoned her client with the bear. She never recognized that she had once again fled a danger zone, turning her back on her dependent, prioritizing only her own safety. To her, it was a funny story. To me, this was the story of my life.

CATHOLICS, LUTHERANS, AND PARTIES

My dad was raised in a strict, but loving, working-class family. His dad, (my Pepere) Emile, supported the family as a linotype operator, setting the type manually for newspapers. His mother, (my Memere)Viola, was a homemaker who didn't graduate high school. The family was 100 percent French-Canadian and devoutly Catholic.

My father was an only child and his parents were warm, ever-present and focused on him. Like Marc and me, Bill was raised to be a Good Child. He went to Mass once a week and endeavored to please his parents and to please God. Alone in the bathroom, little Billy apologized out loud to God whenever he farted. Somewhere along the line, though, he became disengaged from the Church. The teachings about sexuality in particular were upsetting to my father, a closeted gay boy. When he went to college, he began to pull away from Catholicism and he never looked back.

My mother was raised in a strict German Lutheran family. Her mother descended from a long line of strict devout ministers. Their religion was a sober, serious affair, which didn't even allow dancing, let alone any expression of sexuality. My mother, however, was always interested in boys. So, just like my dad, when Kathryn made her way to college, her connection to her faith began to fade.

My parents shared a love of personal and religious freedom, proclaiming themselves to be atheists. They were both scarred by early religious constrictions. My father's Catholic scars are easier to understand, given that he ultimately came out as a gay man. My mother's religious scars never made as much sense to me, but she loathed religion the rest of her life. My parents embraced the freedom of the 1960s and 1970s full throttle, no holds barred. They were particularly passionate about sexual freedom, but they also embraced civil rights, women's liberation, and drug use.

From the outside, this liberal spirit could seem exciting, tolerant, even noble. Guests of the Deguire family had a *Good Time*. There was always wonderful music playing, both on the record player and in live performances, with my dad commanding the piano. The smell of Swedish meatballs filled the air and alcohol flowed abundantly. Although neither of my parents were alcoholic, they liked to drink, and they drank quite a bit. I knew the smell of martinis on my father's breath. I knew my mother's favorite cocktail of bourbon and soda. I particularly hated the smell of Bloody Marys in the morning. That strong tomato smell, mixed with vodka, made me anxious and uneasy, and I loathe the smell of tomato juice to this day.

The heavy sweet smell of marijuana also permeated our house. I don't remember a time when my parents didn't smoke pot. The first time I got high, I was five years old. It was unintentional, but the story illustrates my situation at home well. It was Christmas time, and we were having a big party, full of students from Upsala College. I loved these parties. The students were mostly music or theater majors, so they often wound up singing and performing. My father would accompany them on the piano, grinning wildly and thumping his left foot with exuberance. I stayed up late to watch and to listen, and everyone drank and smoked, and drank and smoked.

At some point, I wound up lying with my head under the Christmas tree. I stared up into the tree, entranced by the colored lights, watching them blink and shine, and following their patterns. Someone finally noticed me there, "Lise, what are you doing under the tree?"

Giggling uncontrollably, I squealed, "I can't stop smiling!" The room erupted in laughter. I had a contact high. My little five-year-old body had spent so many hours in a room filled with so much marijuana smoke that I had gotten high myself. My parents thought my inadvertent high was hilarious. This story was retold affectionately for years to come. They never considered that having a five-year-old daughter get a contact high in her own living room indicated that their parenting might need attention.

The live musical performances at our parties could be breathtaking. My mother and father did a number in which my mother sang "Ich Grolle Nicht," a Schumann song, as if she were a terrible singer with no sense of rhythm or pitch, and my father played her exasperated accompanist. My father would start the introduction on the piano. He would keep playing and playing it, vamping in vain, waiting for my mother to start singing. He would huff and sigh, rolling his eyes at my mother. My mother would ignore him, simpering out to the audience, a vapid, talentless opera singer. Eventually she would start singing, always at the wrong cue. When she did sing, she purposely warbled in a grating, whiny, nasal tone. We howled at each rendition.

My father taught me a piano duet, so that I, too, could have my own signature piece. Because he could play by ear, we didn't need music, and he taught me to play the piece by memory. Rodgers and Hart had a song, "Lover," in which I played the melody with both hands while my dad made the entire piece flow, with beautiful chords and a driving waltz rhythm. At some point at every party, my dad would say, "Do you want to play 'Lover'?" I would proudly sit at the yellow piano bench with him, my feet swinging high above the ground, earnestly executing my part while he did all the real work. Everyone would clap wildly for us.

Thirty years later, when my dad was dying, we made videos of him talking and playing the piano. He was terribly thin, with his red sweater draping off him, and the bones in his face protruding. Toward the end of the tape, he turned to me with a sweet smile.

"Do you want to play 'Lover'?"

We beamed at each other, wistfully, pausing for a moment. Then, I sat down with him on the yellow piano bench, just like so many other times, and we played our piece together, for the last time.

THE MUSIC MAN

My father, Bill Deguire, was the loudest, most jovial and engaging man around. When he laughed, which he did frequently, it rang like a baying shout of HA HA HA! One time my father was laughing so loudly in a movie theater that he was evicted. We four Deguires stood up, my father, mother, Marc and me, and we slunk out, heads hanging and eyes cast downward. This movie banishment also involved my dad drinking too much, which sometimes happened. Bill Deguire caroused like a champ. But truly, my dad did not have to be drinking to laugh too loud. He laughed that same laugh, with full-on gusto, as much as possible, every day of his too-short life.

Bill knew how to have a good time, and he was devoted to having one as much as possible. He flirted and said outrageous things to women of all ages, and to men as well. Friends of mine would murmur, with equal mixtures of discomfort and pleasure, that my father made eyes at them. I am sure that he did, because he flirted with everyone. He also liked to chat with every person he met, no matter how fleetingly. Once, we went shopping and I was trying on a dress. I changed outfits in the dressing room for no more than five minutes. When I came back out, my dad was perched joyfully next to a three-year-old pig-tailed girl, chatting away. They were completely engaged in a pretend tea party, pinkies up, passing the pretend tea kettle back and forth and stirring in the pretend sugar.

My dad earned his doctorate in music and he was a professor at Upsala College. He taught music history and he served as the music director every year for the college musical. He was wildly enthusiastic about the shows and he played the piano for all of them. He was a loud pianist (of course; he was a loud everything). His greatest gift was that he could play any song by ear, in any key, after having only heard the piece once. With this ability, he could adapt any of the musical's songs to a student's vocal range, showcasing their limited talents to their finest. His musicals were amazingly good for a small college. My dad's piano playing was always driving, rhythmic, and engaging. If you came to a rehearsal, you would see him inspiring the students, teaching them, and every now and then, screaming in fury at them. No matter; if you came to a performance, you would be truly entertained, and his students adored him, whether he berated them or not.

Bill Deguire was a handsome man, but he didn't necessarily think so. He was six feet tall, with a head of thick black and gray hair, a bushy mustache, full lips, and striking blue/gray eyes. He had long slim fingers and strong but feminine hands. He had a warm toothy smile and a charming, if too loud, manner. Most people liked him immensely—if they could tolerate his constant outrageousness.

Dad was a charismatic and passionate teacher. He loved his students and fretted when they weren't succeeding. Once, when a promising music major inexplicably failed yet another exam, Bill responded by composing a prayer on her test paper. Instead of criticizing her failing grade, he wrote a prayer, saying "Dear whatever-it-is-that-keeps-this-universe-spinning," imploring the universe to help this talented student achieve her full brilliant potential. Eventually, with his encouragement, she did.

When Bill died, his funeral overflowed with ex-students.

My father loved children and he loved being a father. He was the best of fathers; he was the worst of fathers. I think I would have adored him if he were my uncle. As my father, he scared me. There was something deep in his core that was never at ease. He was restless, self-preoccupied, and he flew quickly into anger.

There was also a kind and patient side to Dad, equally unpredictable. There is a photo of us; I am three years old and we are at a wedding. I sit in a pale blue party dress, lips pursed forward, eyes downward, sulking a serious sulk. My father stands behind me, bending kindly over my shoulder, solicitously offering me a piece of vanilla cake, which I am clearly spurning. My dad looks sweetly concerned that I don't want the cake and I look completely unreasonable. So there was that Dad, too.

Yet, my dad could be ferocious. Something would set him off; we never knew what, and he would scream and scream and scream. He wouldn't make sense when he was in a fury; you could never understand why he was upset or what could be done to make it better. He would pace, blue eyes ablaze, shouting words that were in English but nevertheless sounded like gibberish. We would freeze like rabbits, enduring the rant, keeping mute until he finished. His anger withered me. I rarely felt safe with him, because I never knew when he would explode.

My dad was not a physically violent man, but he did not have control over his anger, and he didn't seem to know this was a problem. He knew he lost his temper, but he inevitably blamed his anger on other people's behavior. He also never apologized for his outbursts. He called me a bitch at least once in the heat of an argument. If I ever tried to talk to him about his harsh words, he would get angry and counterattack. It was impossible to work through problems with him.

He hit me in anger only once, but it was memorable. We took a road trip together when I was 12 years old. My father loved to travel, and so did I. He and I went to the Florida Keys, the Rocky Mountains, Big Sur. We had fun, but again, it could be tense, and the winds could quickly shift.

We stopped along a quiet road to take a quick break. A steep incline led up from the road to a hill, which crested out over a view. The vista was treeless and the sky was gray. My father wanted to see the view from the top of the hill, and he wanted us to climb up the steep embankment. I didn't want to. I was always physically wary, worried about hurting myself, and not confident in my physical strength. (Being seriously burned will do that to you.) My father never liked my cautiousness, and he wanted me to be physically tougher. He probably had a point: it's not good to be weak and wary. But his techniques for intervention were primitive.

My dad insisted, "Let's climb up. Let's climb the hill."

"I really don't want to."

"Come on, let's go!"

"Why don't you just go, and I'll wait here?"

"No, you need to come, too. Let's see what's up there. Come on!"

I submitted, knowing there was no point in resisting him any further. So, we started up the hill. My dad was ahead of me, holding my hand, and pulling me a bit. I trudged along, sullenly. At some point, he exclaimed with tense excitement, "Isn't this fun?"

Staring at the ground, I muttered, "Oh, shut up." In an instant, he smacked me across the face.

Honestly, that wasn't like my father. He was not a violent man. But here's the thing with my dad: you just never knew what he was going to do when he was upset. And he got upset anytime you disagreed with him about something he deemed important. Later on, he told me, without clearly apologizing, that in his family growing up, no child would ever disrespect an adult by saying "shut up" and that he acted without thinking. To some degree, I understood this, and I understand it now. Still, that slap shocked me.

Despite these incidents, my dad and I had one thing in common that bonded us powerfully all our lives: my dad adored musicals, and so did I. My mother sniffed her nose at them, and Marc was pretty apathetic as well. My dad and I, however, were both passionate musical lovers. He wrote two books about the American musical, forever unpublished. He generated an endless source of trivia about musicals and their composers. That trivia now resides in my head. For example, *Showboat* was the first musical to use music to push the plot along. And here is why the song "Singin' in the Rain" works so well: it's in the "doo-dee-doo-doo" ostinato that Roger Edens wrote for the 1952 film arrangement. I have this trivia in my head, and it mostly got there because of my father.

I have been able to pass along our love of musicals to my daughters. When we talk about a show now, I might say, "Your Pepere wants you to know that Oscar Hammerstein always wrote the lyrics first, before Richard Rodgers wrote the music." My daughters will nod gravely in response. Theater connects my daughters solidly to their grandfather, the best pretend-tea-party guest, whom they never knew. He died eight months before Julia, my actress daughter, was born.

Once my dad realized he finally had a fellow musical-lover in the family, he maximized the bond. He took me to Broadway. Thanks to him, I saw the original productions of *Company, Sweeney Todd, A Chorus Line, Annie, Pippin, Into the Woods,* and many others. He also drove me into New York to see film showings of old MGM musicals. We particularly loved *Singin' in the Rain, The Band Wagon* and *Meet Me in St Louis.* We sat together in the vintage movie theaters, eagerly awaiting "The Trolley Song" and swooning over Judy Garland.

Because my dad directed the music for shows, both for his teaching job and for side jobs, I saw his own productions of many shows. I used to accompany my dad to rehearsals at the college. We would drive to Upsala where I would eagerly watch the auditions, the blocking, the rehearsals, the tech rehearsals, the dress rehearsals, and every performance of every show. I started going to rehearsals when I was a five-year-old, and I went every year until our family disintegrated, seven years later.

When I was little, I loved *The Wizard of Oz.* To this day, the opening notes of that movie make my heart soar with excitement and longing. I watched it every year when it was broadcast, on the little black-and-white TV that we had. It was always a highlight of the year for me, although the Wicked

Witch terrified me with her fire torture of the Scarecrow. I would run out into the hallway and frantically shout, "The witch is coming on, she's coming now!" My mother would dutifully walk into the TV room, standing there so I wouldn't have to be alone with the Witch.

When I was about seven years old, my dad took me to a screening of *The Wizard of Oz* in New York City. Just before the movie started, he leaned down and whispered, "There's a BIG surprise!" The movie started, and it was just the same as always, with Dorothy in Kansas, neglected, singing about the rainbow. But, when she opened the door to Oz, and the movie changed from black-and-white Kansas to Technicolor Oz, I was in complete shock. Having only a black-and-white TV, I had no idea that Oz was in vivid color. The yellow brick road was actually yellow; the Emerald City was actually green. The horse of many colors actually changed colors! It WAS a big surprise, just the kind of surprise that he and I alone seemed to love.

My dad and I communicated best through musicals. We were equally thrilled, watching Gene Kelly dance through the rain for the thousandth time. We both turned to musicals when we were deeply unhappy. He said to me once, sadly, "Why can't life be like an MGM musical? Why can't things just turn out OK in the end like they are supposed to?" But even though our lives were increasingly nothing like a musical, the musicals still brought us great comfort. In the hardest times for me, I think my dad helped save my life by providing me with a place to escape to in my mind—the world of song and dance where everything did turn out OK in the end.

After the fire, I was hospitalized for months. For much of that time, I was alone. My dad came to see me on weekends. My mom visited sometimes as well. But, for most of the time, it was just me, lying flat on my back, immobile. In those days, there were no private TVs in hospital rooms, let alone computers or iPads. I had nothing to look at but the white ceiling, no one to talk to, and nothing to do at all. Nothing.

My dad intervened in the most helpful way possible. He bought me a little portable record player, and a small but growing collection of albums, ranging from Disney story albums to show music. I had Rodgers and Hammerstein's *Cinderella,* and Mary Martin in *Peter Pan.* I had *The Jungle Book* and songs from *Winnie the Pooh.* As long as I could convince a nurse to put a record on for me, I was transported, happily singing along to the music. I knew every word, and in my mind, I lived in all the stories. I was Tiger Lily and Marc was Peter Pan. We danced, sang and plotted how to trap Captain Hook. I became Cinderella in "My Own Little Corner", and I hunted on her African safari. I was Pooh, with Piglet in the Hundred Acre Wood, soaring above with my blue balloon, singing a song to the bees so I could steal their honey. I floated in another world, far away.

At the end of the album, the music stopped. The needle of the record player would skip back and forth, making a hissing sound. Suddenly I landed back in the hospital, in my dreary bed. I wasn't in the jungle, or going to meet the Prince, or flying to Never Never Land. I was just a lonely girl, wrapped from head to toe in bandages, staring at the ceiling. I would lay like that for a while, ringing my bell, waiting and waiting for the nurse to come. When the nurse finally walked to my bed, she would ask, "What do you need, Lise? Do you need to go to the bathroom?"

"No. I'm OK. But could you please turn my record over?"

If I were lucky, the nurse wouldn't be annoyed that I didn't have an actual medical problem. If I were lucky, the nurse would remember that I was just a little girl and I was bored and lonely. The nurse would take the time to turn the record over and put the needle back on to play. Then, I could float back to the musical land of make believe for another 20 minutes.

My dad gave me another gift when I was in the hospital that didn't turn out as well as the record player. He observed that I was stuck on my back, with nothing to look at and decided that it would be wonderful for me to have a fish aquarium. He purchased a large glass tank. He installed it in my room and filled it with sea plants and colorful tropical fish, of all sizes. Everyone who came to my bedside marveled at the aquarium, and the beautiful fish.

There was only one problem with the aquarium: I couldn't see it. The fish tank was located to the side of my bed, right near me. I had to lay immobile, on my back, with my neck splinted. So, my aquarium brought joy to a lot of people, but I was not one of them. It was incredibly frustrating to have a gorgeous fish tank bubbling away next to me that I could never see. This fish aquarium story exemplifies my relationship with my dad. He wanted to do whatever he could for me. But he could not understand my point of view. In the case of the aquarium, he *literally* could not understand my point of view.

I wish I could say I was closer with my dad, because he loved me, and he did many thoughtful things for me. But, he scared me. He also often made me uncomfortable. He was a self-absorbed man, preoccupied with his own issues, particularly about his sexuality and attractiveness. When I was little, he used to leave the house a lot by himself. He would spend time in New York City alone. He traveled to South America by himself. Even when we traveled as a family, he would often leave the hotel room or the camping site, to go off and do things alone at night. I never understood where he went or why. He would come back hours later, in the middle of the night, with no explanation.

It was years later when I finally realized what my dad had been doing. He was out cruising for sexual hookups with men. Ironically, I came to this realization in 2015, watching a Broadway musical called Fun Home. There is a scene in which a little girl goes with her closeted father to New York City for the weekend. At night, he leaves her and her brother alone in their hotel room, while he goes off looking for men. As I sat in the theater watching this scene, I came to the startling realization that is what my father had been doing, too. Here again, a musical connected me emotionally to my dad, decades after his death.

My parents separated when I was 12, and my father began dating feverishly. He dated three women at once for a year. He also cruised for men. For some reason, my father felt it important to tell me all about his dating and sex life. He expounded at length about his feelings for all these women, and, later, the men. He shared the details on who were his best lovers. He talked and talked and talked, and he expected me to listen.

I quietly writhed during these conversations, but I tried to listen. There was always a risk in not doing what he wanted. At some point, after I had therapy in college, I told him I didn't want to talk about his sex life anymore. He exploded with fury. Years later, after his death, I read his journal entry where he thought there was something wrong with me psychologically because I didn't want to discuss sex with him anymore.

So my father scared me and he made me uncomfortable. There was one more reason why I wasn't close to him. My mother repeatedly told me all the ways that my father was inadequate. After their separation, my mother talked to me negatively about my father for years, until the very last week of her life. She explained to me about narcissistic personality disorder and that my father had it. (This may have been projection on her part, or perhaps was one of the things they had in common. "It takes one to know one," you might say.) She told me that my father was bad in bed and that he never fulfilled her sexually. She told me that he was incapable of a committed intimate relationship and that he had issues with women. Intentionally or not, she undermined my relationship with my father, filling me with increased negativity toward him. Even in my final visit with my mother before she died, she spoke of him negatively.

My husband Doug and I were visiting with my mother for the last time before her trip to Switzerland. We all knew this would be our last afternoon together. I asked her about a story I had recently been told. Apparently, my dad had once moonlighted as a Broadway show rehearsal pianist. He had a second job at nights, playing for rehearsals, under an assumed name of Michael McGuire, to get around the union rules. I had never heard this story, and I was intrigued. Had my dad worked on Broadway, and never told me? My mother would know, and this was my last chance to ask her before. . . Switzerland.

I asked my mom, "Did Dad ever play for Broadway rehearsals? I never knew. I would think he would have told me, given how obsessed I am with

Broadway. It wouldn't be like him to keep this a secret."

"He had many secrets," she replied. With her aphasia, it came out slowly, and sounded more like "hee-ha ma-nee ee-cress" but I knew what she said.

She was silent. It was hard for her to speak. She stared at me, darkly.

"Oh," I squirmed, realizing what she meant. "You mean he had sexual secrets?"

"Yah," she said. That was all my mother had to say about my dad, in our last conversation together before she died. She had been married to him for 20 years, and he was the father of her children. But she never forgave him for his limitations, and she never let me forget them either.

Regardless of my ambivalence toward my dad, we ended well. I had the chance to take care of him, and to be close to him when he died, skinny and weak, bones protruding. When he was dying, he was gentle. His anger was gone, his sexual inappropriateness was gone, his emotional volatility was gone. My dad became quiet, kind, and vulnerable, like a soft peach. We lay in his hospice bed together, guard rails up, holding hands and listening to Mendelssohn. He didn't talk much. But one time, he cleared his throat and turned to me, his face inches away from my weeping face. "Remember *this*," he whispered, weakly holding up our entwined hands, "remember *this*."

The night my dad died, we played records for him. It was now me bringing music to his hospital room, just as he had done for me years ago. That night, I sang to him. I sang him a song he loved, from one of our beloved musicals, *The Music Man*. I had this cast album since my first hospitalization. It was one of the records that I had sung along to, all alone, when I was four. Now it was my chance to sing to him, in his hospital room, as he lay weak and dying. Choking out the words, I sang him *"Goodnight, My Someone."* I sang him the sweet old-fashioned love song, about longing for connection in the dark night alone.

He died that night, one of the three tragic deaths that happened to my precious family.

LESSON FIVE:

Being a parent is the most important job you will have. Attuned parenting requires us to be as emotionally healthy as possible. Get an excellent therapist, if you can. Work on your emotional limitations as much as possible beforehand, so you can be fully present for your children. Being psychologically healthy is arguably the best gift you can give them.

FLASHBACK GIRL

SIX

My Mother,
Miss Mankato

MISS MANKATO

My mother, Kathryn, was possibly the only woman to ever declare herself the winner of a beauty pageant. She was not beautiful. She had an angular face, thin lips and a markedly long nose, which was bony and prominently red. Her face was not pretty, but it was intelligent, and she had a nice figure. Nothing about her suggested she would even enter a beauty pageant, let alone win one. Still, she possessed an ace in the hole, which she had always been told was the most important thing. She played the piano like a goddess.

My mother descended from a long line of ministers and pianists. Their Lutheran religion was a sober, conservative affair. Their piano tradition was equally disciplined, concentrating vigilantly on proper technique and classical repertoire. Seemingly everyone in the large extended family studied piano; it was an assumption that one should play, just as much as one should learn to read. We could all hold our pianist hands properly, wrists up, fingers curled, spine straight. Once, we had a large family reunion, in a gazebo on a Minnesota lake. There were at least 100 people at the reunion, all told. At one point, my uncle stood up and asked, "How many people here did *not* study piano?" Only five people sheepishly raised their hands. Ninety-five people sat proudly, spines straight, nodding at their own pianistic accomplishments and smiling at each other.

Kathryn started piano when she was two years old. Around that time, her mother, Anna, realized that her toddler daughter had perfect pitch, which is often a sign of superior musical talent. Anna herself was an accomplished pianist, and a renowned piano teacher in the Midwest. Thus, two-year-old Kathryn started piano lessons with her mother in the elegant front parlor of their Minnesota home.

I don't know what these piano lessons were like for little Kathryn. I do know from my own experience what piano lessons were like with Grandma Anna. My refined grandmother scared me. I had a lesson with her myself when I was six. I was also a good pianist, although nowhere near as good as my mother (this was clearly conveyed to me, in not so many words). But I was still good, and my mother wanted her mother to teach me.

I sat with my well-dressed grandmother, who was cool and formal, even with me, her youngest grandchild. I played scales for her, endeavoring to keep my fingers properly curled, and my wrists up. She had me play arpeggios, and she observed my hands. My every move seemed to disappoint her, as she corrected me in her proper, cool voice. She did not compliment me or seem pleased with my skills. My heart thumped with relief when the lesson was over and I could escape her icy disapproval.

So, given my experience, what were those years of piano lessons like for my mother? Kathryn always described her mother as a superb teacher, with whom she shared the love of classical music and piano. According to my mother, Anna was encouraging and skilled, so I cannot claim otherwise. I can say, however, that my grandmother dripped with cool formality. My mother would not initially come across as cold. It might take years before a person picked down far enough to find her inner ice. That same iceberg hid inside my mother, which I can only assume my grandmother unintentionally planted, at the earliest age.

Little Kathryn was quickly embraced by her family as a child prodigy. She gave her first piano recital at the age of four. She practiced, rehearsed and performed her whole childhood. There is a massive scrapbook, compiled years ago, stuffed with local articles on Kathryn's recitals, extolling her gifts. Any extraordinary musician will tell you that this early level of excellence comes with a heavy price. The only way to be that good, that young, is to spend most of your time practicing, alone in a room, hour after hour, day after day. This was my mother's childhood. She emerged from it as an extraordinary musician, but as someone entirely ill-equipped to be a mother.

At the age of 19, Kathryn had completed her first year as a piano performance major at the prestigious Eastman School of Music. In a display of brash confidence, she decided that she would win the Miss Minnesota Beauty Pageant on the strength of her piano playing. She needed the prize money. Her hometown, Mankato, had not selected a Miss Mankato to send to the pageant. Kathryn therefore declared *herself* to be Miss Mankato. She took photos of herself, standing on her parents' staircase, in a one-piece bathing suit and heels, with a homemade Miss Mankato sash draped across her torso. Her dark brown hair is curled neatly around her face. She smiles sweetly into the camera, with eyes that crinkle so much that they become hard to see. She looks young, fit, naive, but not particularly beautiful.

The self-promotion worked. Kathryn went to the Miss Minnesota Beauty Pageant, as the self-appointed Miss Mankato. There, however, she was summarily dismissed in the first round. I'm not sure if she ever got to play piano for the judges. Maybe if they had heard her play, she would have remained in the competition. That was the fantasy; that her piano playing was so extraordinary it would overcome the judges with its beauty, the one true beauty that my mother could offer. But they never heard her play, so her reign as Miss Mankato came to a quick end.

MY MOTHER, KATHRYN

If you met my mother, you would have liked her. She was calm, polite and intelligent. She stood 5'5", thin and nicely figured. Her green eyes weren't warm, but they crinkled engagingly when she smiled. Kathryn had a nice sense of humor, and she laughed easily and often. She read *The New York Times* daily, quickly completing each crossword puzzle in neat print. She appreciated good food and culture and was a reliable liberal vote. She enjoyed walking, hiking, canoeing and birding. I liked all these things about her very much. And for a long time, these great traits were all I could see.

There are the stories that my mother told me about her life, and who she was. Then, decades later, there came to be the stories that I myself witnessed, which changed everything I thought about my mother, irrevocably. One story in particular. Once it happened, I would never be able to see her through the lens of her stories again.

My mother once gave a recital at Carnegie Hall (not the big Hall, just the recital room, but still!). She won a Fulbright Scholarship to study piano in Vienna. My dad said that my mother "played like an angel." I remember her playing when I was little, and she was truly heavenly. By that time, she was no longer performing publicly, so she would be quick to downplay the quality of her performance. Still, she would play Debussy's First Arabesque, right in our living room. She played Chopin and Bach, Mozart and Rachmaninov. She was just playing for herself, but you could have sold tickets to hear it, and no one would have been disappointed.

Despite her strict religious background, my mother left the Lutheran faith in college, and never looked back. Marrying my dad (a Catholic) meant that they both sacrificed their religions, which had come to feel more and more alien to both of them. My mother stayed a professed atheist, even when her aunt told her that the fire was God's punishment for her leaving the church. Her own aunt sent that card to my mother in the hospital, where she lay burned, bleeding and howling in pain.

When my parents married, they shocked their families. Their parents refused to attend the wedding because of religious differences. My Memere literally went into mourning on the day of her only son's wedding. She drew the homemade curtains closed in her small house, which her carpenter father had built by hand. She promised God that she would give up candy for the rest of her life if only this wedding could be cancelled. This was her penance for her son leaving the church, even though she had a bountiful sweet tooth. (A woman of honor, she never did eat candy again. . . kind of. Stealthily, my father found a way around her pledge. Every time he visited, he brought her maple sugar, confidently declaring "Maple sugar isn't candy, it's just sugar!" And then Memere would eat up every bite.)

On the day of the heathen wedding, my Pepere woke up with a start. Although he had said he would never go to the wedding, he changed his mind, declaring "I have one son, and he's about to get married!" By himself, Pepere, who did not own a car, took a bus from Glens Falls, New York, to New York City. Then, he found another bus to take him to Fort Dix, New Jersey. Then, he took a Fort Dix bus to the army chapel.

Pepere arrived unexpectedly right as the wedding began. For perhaps once in his life, this normally warm and jovial man was morose. Pepere stood grim-faced in all the wedding photos. But at least he came, the only family member to witness the heathen marriage of Bill and Kathryn Deguire.

Ultimately, my parent's marriage did not last. They were married for 20 years, and then my mother asked to divorce. My mother felt victimized by her marriage to my father. Bill had a temper. Also, Bill was sexually unfaithful, and incapable of being satisfied in a monogamous marriage to a woman. She was always sexually unhappy with him, which is why she had an affair or two, or three or four. They had an open marriage in the 1970s, but she would have been willing to be monogamous and faithful, if my father were emotionally capable.

Kathryn told me *all* of this when I was 12 years old, explaining their upcoming divorce. The news stunned me. I thought my parents were happy together. My mother sat stiffly on the side of my double bed. On my wall behind us, there were 12 horse posters. They were the "centerfolds" from my horse magazine subscription. The horses, with their sweet black, brown and white faces, all watched serenely as my mother informed me about my father's emotional and sexual limitations. I felt frozen inside, like I was suddenly lost in a blizzard.

As my parents separated, my mother told me more about how my father and his family were inadequate. "You know that Memere is not a smart woman. She never even graduated high school, and she is so boring. I'm really glad I don't have to visit Glens Falls anymore. Those trips were monotonous but your father made us go all the time."

"Dad has narcissistic personality disorder. This is why he has such anger problems and why he can't tolerate any criticism. He's so self-absorbed. And you know, he really hasn't been much of a success in life." Calmly, repeatedly, she poisoned me toward my dad.

After a year of dating, my mother found the great love of her life. She fell passionately in love with John, an attorney that she met through my cousin Mary, who had previously dated him. John was a tall, slim man with black hair and eyebrows, and dark intelligent eyes. He had a thick mustache and long slim fingers. In some ways, he looked like my Dad, to the point where distant acquaintances would confuse them. John was highly intelligent and had a wry sense of humor. He could be quite charming and he could also be very cold. It all depended on his mood, which tended toward depression, and his level of alcohol and marijuana consumption, which tended toward enormity. He was a cheerful substance abuser, however. The more he drank and the more he smoked, the happier he became.

My mother and John started dating when I began eighth grade. She had already made plans that we would move back to Long Island that fall. Our beloved Glen Ridge house, the scene of so many parties, in which my brother had finally been happy, this house was to be sold. The proceeds of the house sale were split. My father bought a tiny historic house along a river in

Annandale, New Jersey, and my mother bought a small house in Oyster Bay, Long Island. She thought it would be a nice community to return to, full of old friends from when we had previously lived there.

At the time, I thought a fresh start sounded like a good plan, seeing as I was the social pariah of school that year. But by the time we were moving to Oyster Bay, kids had started to be nice to me again, and my mother had found John, the Great Love of her life, who lived in New Jersey. Our return to Oyster Bay started to seem like a mistake.

We moved into a modest two-story house, which was a far cry from our elegantly pillared Glen Ridge home. The front door opened directly onto the living room, with a small, poorly lit dining room to the right, and a utilitarian kitchen completing the first floor. Upstairs there were three small bedrooms, one for my mother, one for me, and one for Marc, if he ever came.

Losing his beloved Glen Ridge home, Marc quietly refused to move anywhere in particular. He stayed with Dad, he visited us, he lived with his friends and hung out at our Cousin Mary's house. He was adrift. He didn't unpack any of his belongings at our mother's house, which she noted with a disapproving sniff of her red nose. It was just my mother and me. And then there was John.

My mother and John were desperate to see each other every chance they got. Their eagerness to be together felt more like they were 15-year-olds than two middle aged adults. Every weekend, they had to be together, so they alternated between their two houses. One weekend, John would stay with us, leaving his three teenage daughters unsupervised from Friday to Sunday night. The next weekend, my mother would drive to New Jersey, leaving me completely alone in our house all weekend. I was just 13 years old. This routine, of Mom and John being together, leaving their children to manage on their own, continued every weekend for five years, until their five children either graduated, moved out or died.

But, more on that later.

There were some good things about John's visits. My mother cooked him amazing dinners. Our family meals had mostly gone by the wayside. When my family had been intact, my mother made us wonderful dinners, almost every night. Now that she was divorced, she didn't feel the need to cook much if it were just us. I would have leftovers, or a sandwich, or frozen dinners. But when John was there, we ate like kings.

When John was there, we got high a lot. John and my mother smoked marijuana every weekend, and I was welcome to the party. They would load up my mother's big violet colored bong, and we would smoke away; drinking and laughing, listening to Crosby, Stills & Nash. John and my mother would also drink beer and wine, which I wasn't into, but I would drink too, because, why not? I was thirteen and I thought I was cool to be drinking and smoking with my mother and her handsome new boyfriend. Then, after a while, they would declare with eager smiles that it was time for them to go to bed.

For years, I would hear my mother and John having sex. They could not have been less interested in being discrete. My mother, in particular, whooped it up. She moaned with pleasure loudly at night, to the point of waking me up. There would be loud rhythmic banging, announcing their climaxes. They padded around afterwards in their velour bathrobes, clearly in a state of post-coital bliss. Even if I had friends over, they moaned in delight and banged out their orgasms for all to hear.

Once, after years of hearing them having sex, I got up my nerve to ask my mother a favor. "Mom, I'm sorry to ask. I feel really awkward saying this but, do you think you and John could. . . keep it down?"

"What? What are you talking about?"

"When you have sex. I can hear it. You get really loud. It makes me feel weird."

She considered my request, calmly. "I can try, but I really just can't help myself," she replied, in a superior arch tone. "I am a very sexual person."

As a burned girl, this exposure to my mother's sexuality was destabilizing. Kathryn placed a premium value on her sex life and erotic fulfillment.

She talked about her prodigious sexuality frequently. "John is an amazing lover. I have never had such good sex as I have with him. I'm so happy to make love with him, so much more than I ever was with your father. I never knew I could be this satisfied. It's everything I ever dreamed of."

I writhed with inadequacy. Although I was interested, boys overlooked me. I figured I should try to lose my virginity as soon as possible, given how important sex was to my mother. But really, I couldn't give it away. No boys were interested in a girl who was 65 percent burned, with no natural breasts. It wasn't in the cards for me. I felt unwanted by boys and adrift in my own house, my father and brother gone, left with a mother who, for all intents and purposes, had stopped functioning as a mother in any recognizable way.

At the time, I thought my mother was amazing. She thought she was cool, and so did I. It was the 1970s, a permissive time. The distinction between permissiveness versus child neglect was not so clear in that decade. I had unending freedom to do what I wanted...

Smoke pot every day? OK.

Have unchaperoned parties and serve minors unlimited alcohol? OK.

Go into New York City by yourself when you are ten? Sure.

Travel to Boston by yourself on a train and check yourself in for your own burn surgery when you are 14? Sure.

The more independent I wanted to be, the better. My mother was done being a mother. She enjoyed my company, she loved me, but as a friend, not a parent. Whatever parenting work there was, she was done doing it.

For decades, I truly enjoyed my mother and I felt close to her. She could be fun, and she was an interesting person. I admired her many talents. Everything she touched, she did to perfection (with the glaring exception of parenting in particular, and relationships in general. She was a fabulous cook, and a wonderful baker. She was a talented gardener. She was good with money. She hiked, canoed and birded with the best of them. In addition to the piano, she was a good organist and singer as well. In her later years, she made gorgeous stained-glass pieces, and became a competitive croquet player. She was a superwoman, it seemed. Many people admired her.

I managed to overlook the fire that she set, her abandonment of me, and her neglect of me and Marc for decades. I managed. But my brother. . . he did not fare so well.

LESSON SIX:

Same as Lesson Five. Being an effective parent requires you to prioritize your child's welfare over your own for many years. Parenthood is a demanding job; try not to take it on until you are truly ready to put your child first. Live your life; have fun! But when you have kids, your fun must be secondary to their needs, most of the time, for many years to come.

SEVEN

Four Suicides: the First

I sit, transfixed, looking at these words I just wrote. My brother died 40 years ago, but years are meaningless when it comes to choking grief. Marc's death stands as the single worst thing that has happened to me. Not the fire, him. I feel his loss in my heart, squeezing me, making me gasp a little for the next breath. I feel frozen, trying to write this. There was nothing worse than Marc's death. If remembering could bring a person back to life, Marc would have been resurrected countless times by now. If only.

* * *

My Batman grew into a more distant middle-schooler. He became more somber and serious, and he didn't want to play anymore. I was disappointed to lose my favorite playmate, but I had not lost my favorite person. He spent more time alone in his room, but he would let me in. Our games changed. He carefully taught me how to play chess. "OK, so the pawns are these little pieces, and they can only move one space at a time. But the Queen can move in any direction. She's the most valuable piece."

"Can't we just play checkers? I like checkers better." I preferred to play checkers because it was easier to understand, and sometimes I could win.

"No. Look, chess is much more interesting. There's strategy, not just luck." Marc decided I was old enough to play chess, and he diligently taught me how. I was never any good and I really didn't care, so as usual, Marc would win. My brother was past childish checkers; he was growing up, and serious chess was now the game.

My mother said that Marc was always depressed, ever since he was tiny. There was an oft-repeated story about him sadly proclaiming his hope that the next day would be perfect, but it never was. There was no "perfect day", and that was why he was depressed, or at least that was the story. The story implied that Marc's sadness was lifelong, persistent and also inherently absurd.

I think Marc felt uncared for, and untended — and he was right — which made him sad. I also felt uncared for, and untended. But Marc and I lived different experiences of our plight. I was a naturally sunny person, an optimist, ever hopeful of something good coming from some unexpectedly good person. I also had Marc looking out for me. He had no one.

Marc was serious, appraising, a realist. He wasn't shy, but he wasn't outgoing like me. I think he saw how things truly were in our family, much earlier than I did. He was five years older than me, smarter and more astute. He saw it all, and he didn't have me looking out for him. I wish he had lived long enough, because I would have gladly taken care of him for the rest of his life. I never had the chance to show him that I would always be there for him, like he had been for me. He died when I was 14.

There is a paper my mother saved, which my brother completed in school when he was eleven years old. It is a psychological test, designed to uncover a child's hidden feelings, called a sentence completion test. There are numerous sentence stems, such as "Sometimes I feel___" and the child fills in the blank with whatever he thinks. There are no right or wrong answers. The only object of the test is to expose a child's deeper issues.

I found this paper 48 years later, going through my mother's belongings after her final trip to Switzerland. One sentence stem was, "My father___." and Marc wrote, "is very moody." Another was, "A mother___." Eleven-year-old Marc wrote, "is not a uniform thing at all and can't be treated as such." Another was, "My nerves___." Marc wrote, "are thin."

Another was, "Sometimes___." Marc wrote, "I would kill myself if I could."

So yes, Marc was a serious, somber child, and he knew the score. Somehow, despite his universally acknowledged depression and clear suicidal statements, he did not receive psychological help. The story went that Marc refused to go to therapy. I don't recall my parents dragging him to therapy. It's worth remembering that our mother was a clinical psychologist. But Marc said he didn't want to go to therapy and that was that. No therapy. No medicine. No treatment.

In the middle of his eighth-grade year, we made the move from East Orange to Glen Ridge. Everyone loved Marc in Glen Ridge; he became positively cool. Our beautiful five-bedroom house served as the social hangout for Marc's group of friends. His friends came and went at all hours, entering our grand front foyer, and running up the two flights to Marc's dark blue painted bedroom. There they would lie on his double bed or sit on the floor around an old wooden barrel that Marc had saved, burning candles and incense. He would blast records on his prized stereo, which no one was allowed to touch. Marc was passionate about music. He loved Steppenwolf, his first big rock-and-roll love affair. He loved the Beatles, the Beach Boys, the Who, Jefferson Airplane, King Crimson, Fairport Convention, as well as Stravinsky and Mozart. He shared his music, and his friends would listen with him, smoking pot and talking.

As Marc grew happier and more social, he became more open to me, too. Only an unusual high school boy would invite his fourth-grade sister into his social world, but that's what my brother did. I knew all his friends. I was never made to feel unwelcome. By the time I was in sixth grade, I would join the circle around the wooden barrel, smoking pot and laughing.

Marc didn't seem depressed when he was in high school. He even had a girlfriend he loved for a while. There were some other times, when girls he liked didn't return his affections. He still seemed generally content. He was busy in high school being extraordinary.

My brother was a bit of a genius. Because he only lived to be 19, I can't proudly proclaim all of his impressive life accomplishments. There isn't much to accomplish in life before you even turn 20. But we all knew his test scores. He was in the 99th percentile for all his IOWA test scores, except one, which was 98th percentile. He was a straight A student. He scored a perfect 800 on his math SAT, and a 760 on his verbal. He did all this while graduating high school in three years. When he graduated a year early, he graduated at the very top of his class. He was accepted into MIT and was an excellent student there as well.

Test scores don't really capture Marc's brilliance. Only conversation would capture the facility of his mind, and I can't convey that; he has been gone too long. I can tell you that he also knew how to fix an automobile. And that he was an excellent drummer. And that he was gifted at emotionally reading people. He was offered a job at Upsala College to run their computer center before he graduated high school. The salary offer for my brother, who was 17 at the time, was $30,000. Back in 1976, this was serious money — about $135,000 today. He turned it down. Marc had so much going on in his head. Our Memere used to say that he was "too smart for his own good" and that I was "just smart enough." This used to annoy our mother to no end but I think Memere had a valid point. It's tough to be a genius.

Marc was also a gifted teacher. In sixth grade, I was placed into a group of six girls who were really good at math. I have no idea why I was there, because truth be told, I'm not that great at math. At that age, though, math proclivity seems to have more to do with general intelligence, and I was smart enough to squeeze into the most advanced subset of the advanced math group.

Our little group got introduced early to algebra basics. We sat in a special area of the classroom, with the teacher at the blackboard, writing "X= ? (any number)." This made no sense to me whatsoever. I stared at the blackboard, uncharacteristically lost in a lesson. My young brain could not compute the abstraction.

Day after day our little advanced-advanced math group explored the basics of algebra. One after another, the girls in my group got the abstract concept of X being any number. I was the only one who couldn't grasp it. My anxiety grew like an unweeded garden. What the heck was this? X is a letter, not a number. Why couldn't I understand?

I slumped home one day, crying and hysterical about math. My anxiety sped out of control, taking charge of my cortex, temporarily making me unable to think or reason. I panicked. "I can't do it! I hate algebra, it doesn't make any sense!"

Marc, the family math genius, sat cross legged, listening to the living room stereo. His limp brown hair hung long past his shoulders. He looked at me calmly. "Bring your math book up to my room. I'll help you."

Reluctantly, I trudged up to his blue room, clutching the hated algebra book to my chest. I knelt on his red rug, already on the verge of tears. "I can't do it!" I whined. He gazed at me, serenely, unflustered.

"Open up the first page. Read it out loud."

I put the textbook on Marc's bed, and glumly read the first sentence aloud.

"Stop," he said quickly. I stopped.

"Do you understand that? Do you understand that first sentence?"

I thought for a minute. The first sentence was easy. "Yes. Yes I do."

"OK, great. What's next?"

I read the second sentence.

"Stop," he said again, "do you understand that?"

I thought again. The second sentence also made sense. "Yes."

"OK, great. Let's keep going."

We continued like this, painstakingly slowly, through the entire first chapter. I read each sentence aloud, and Marc would stop me, checking to make sure that I was following the logic of basic algebra, making sure I didn't skip any steps and confuse myself. With Marc's patient and calm approach, my anxiety disappeared. Without the panic, I could pay attention and comprehend what the book was actually saying. By the end of this lesson, I understood how X could hypothetically be any number. My 16-year-old brother had succeeded in teaching me where my teacher had not.

When it came time to apply to college, my brother decided he was going to apply only to MIT, Princeton and Stanford. His academic record was extraordinary, and he was confident. He was so confident that he wrote a self-sabotaging essay. Here is the start of his college essay:

> Probably my worst fault is arrogance. I have a tendency to look down on those who are unable to understand things as well or as rapidly as I can. But this fault by no means overshadows my many others. My temper frequently flares up beyond comfortable limits. Deep down I totally reject the golden rule; if someone is unpleasant to me, I will not hesitate to be the same to him. And I neglect my body. I am far from being a bookworm, but I have not yet managed to bring my body up to the norm. However I am making progress towards eliminating or alleviating most of my problems. Besides, I like to think my good qualities more than make up for my bad. I hope you will agree with me after reading this composition. . . . For years I futilely searched for "the meaning of life." By now, the closest I have come is the arrival at a state of mind where "the meaning of life" as such seems totally irrelevant. At the present I am trying to frequently reach and understand that state. Psychedelic drugs help because they increase one's awareness of one's surroundings and force appreciation of them, but I look upon drugs as a crutch.

It must have been this essay, detailing his personal faults and prolific drug use, that led to Marc's rejection from Stanford, and wait-listing from Princeton. My parents didn't help Marc at all during this process. If they had advised him to revise his work (what parent would let that essay out the door?), I imagine he would have been admitted anywhere in the country. But my parents were not parenting parents. If Marc wanted to do drugs in his room, that was OK. If he didn't want to go to therapy, even though he was suicidal, that was OK. And if he wanted to undermine his brilliant academic career with a snarky essay, that was OK, too.

Around the time Marc was set to go to MIT, our family collapsed. My mother declared she wanted a divorce, and my father was devastated and furious. The plan was for them to separate for a year. My mother stayed half of the week in the house with me, and half the week in a rented room. My dad stayed the other half of the week with me, and half the week in a shared New York City apartment. After a year, the plan was to sell the beloved Glen Ridge house. Marc, 17, was supposed to go to MIT and start being a genius.

I don't think my parents thought about how the divorce would affect Marc. I think their assumption was that he was brilliant, and he was going to college, so the changes at home would not really affect him. This was a fatal error: Marc was affected most of all. He was profoundly unsettled by the dissolution of our parents' marriage. In the beginning, he talked for hours to both Mom and Dad about their feelings, and what was happening. However, after about two months, Marc didn't seem to talk much to our mother anymore. He remained close to Dad, but he became emotionally distant from Mom.

Marc never explained this change to me. I don't know why he got so much closer to Dad, and why he stopped spending much time with Mom. I wish I knew what changed, especially years later, when I had my own crisis with our mother. But Marc was protective of me, and he had more emotional intelligence than anyone in the family. Whatever his reasons were, he would not burden me with them. He also would not undermine my relationship with our mother, regardless of what he now felt, a wise approach that our mother never learned.

Marc matriculated at MIT, earned amazing grades, and then left college after only one semester. The genius of our family transmogrified into a college dropout. It was shocking. He returned to Glen Ridge, and joined me in my odd parental routine, with our parents alternating living in the house.

Back at home, Marc slid into a dark depression. He did not have a job, and he wasn't taking any classes. He stayed alone in his room for days on end, asleep or awake, lying on his bed in the dark. He read a lot and listened to music. He drummed to his records and saw his friends. Other than that, he was completely unproductive. He did a lot of drugs: pot, mushrooms, LSD, and more.

Once again, my parents did nothing to help my brother. My mother complained that Marc wouldn't get a job, but she did not confront him. No one insisted that he go to therapy or get a medical evaluation. He was allowed to drift along, literally lying in the dark on his bed for days on end. He was on his own with his problems. There was no adult help for him. He was 17 years old.

A VERY BAD YEAR

In the meantime, I was having a crisis of my own. I was in 7th grade. The previous year, I had been a member of a tight group of six girls, mostly the same girls in my hated advanced-advanced math class. We played together all the time. We hung out at each other's houses, had birthday parties, rode our bikes and went ice skating.

But in 7th grade, everything changed. One girl, Leslie, who had been on the periphery of our little group, somehow gained social power, in the dark fashion of middle-school-girl power plays. In her first move, she shunned my friend Connie, who had been in the group of six, and who was probably my closest school friend at the time.

To my everlasting shame, I did nothing to protect Connie when she was suddenly thrust from our group. I didn't harm her, I didn't bully her, but I did not help her. I witnessed her exclusion and I let it happen. I sat complicity, witnessing her silent pain.

Karma came for me with stunning efficiency. About a week after Connie's banishment, I was thrust out of the group as well. I don't know how it happened, and I don't know why. One day I had a group of friends, and the next day they all hated me.

Because I had moved so much, I didn't know many other kids in school. I didn't have a deep bank of people I knew to fall back on. Also, it had always been my way to handle people through being ingratiating. I would work and work to get someone to like me. Because of this pattern, and because I didn't know anyone else, every day I worked desperately to get this group of girls to like me again.

For months and months, I tried to be nice. Every day, I would sit with them at the cafeteria lunch table. Leslie in particular would pick at me and say insulting, hurtful things.

"That sandwich is disgusting. How can you eat that?"

"Um, I don't know. I like it."

"Well it makes me sick. You make me sick,"

"I'm sorry."

Leslie would roll her eyes at me and then pretend I wasn't there. The girls talked about parties that they had just attended, parties to which I had not been invited. I would ignore the jabs and taunts, and just keep smiling defensively. I had no skill set for how to handle bullies. I didn't even know I was being bullied. I was just trying with all my might to get these girls to like me again.

At home, I fell silent. I didn't tell anyone that I was profoundly miserable and that I no longer had friends. My parents were focused on their own problems, and neither one of them observed that anything was wrong with me. No one seemed to notice that I never went out anymore. I was embarrassed and humiliated about my social pariah status. Eventually I told my mother and I told Marc what was happening.

One day, for no reason, Leslie threatened to beat me up after school. I don't know what I did to aggravate her, other than continue to exist. I had never been in a fight in my life and I couldn't have been less prepared to defend myself. Terrified, I went home and told my brother that Leslie was going to beat me up.

Marc's jaw tightened as he listened to me. He looked positively fierce. Marc replied, "You tell Leslie that if she beats you up, I am going to come and beat her up."

I don't remember if I ever told Leslie that my brother was going to beat her up. I don't what happened, although I know there was no fight. What I do remember was my astonishment that my depressed pacifist hippie brother, who had also never been in a fight, was 100 percent committed to my defense, to the point of violence if necessary. Despite his months of crippling depression, it was a return of the young Marc, harassing Mr. Hannigan in protest of my social rejection. I felt strengthened.

In March, one day in biology class, we were dissecting a shark. After the dissection, I was sitting at my desk, alone, making notes for my lab report. Hearing giggles, I glanced up to see a huddle of the girls who hated me. They were leaning close together around a desk, writing on a piece of paper, laughing and occasionally glancing at me. I felt chilled. Silently I wrote my biology lab, trying to put them out of my mind.

At the end of school, I walked alone to my locker to get my jacket. I was always alone in the hallways now. No one would be seen with me. A small note fell out of my locker; it had been stuffed through the air vent holes. It was a piece of lined loose-leaf paper, the same paper that the girls had been huddled over in biology. The note read, "Go Away! Can't you see that we hate you?" and it was signed with all of their names. With all my might, I held in my tears, and I fled the school. I hurried along by myself, trudging down stately Ridgewood Avenue, sobbing, all the way home.

When I got home, no one was downstairs. I walked up to the second floor, calling for Marc, wailing. He heard me, and he rushed down the stairs, reaching for the hateful note that I thrust out toward him. We met on the landing, and he held his arms around me as he read the letter. He didn't say anything, but he moaned very softly, "oooh-ooooh," and he rocked me back in forth in his arms. We stood there like that for a long time, me crying, him moaning in deep sympathy, swaying me back and forth.

Eventually, we walked up to his blue room on the third floor. I slumped down on his bed.

"I'm not going to school tomorrow. I'm going to be sick, and I'm staying home. I'm going to be sick for as long as I can. Maybe I can just stay home the rest of the year. I can't go back. I can't see those girls."

Marc looked at me hard. Calmly but firmly he said, "You have to go. You have to go to school. You can't put it off, it will only get worse. You have to go."

"I can't do it. I just can't."

"You have to." I was even more devastated at the thought, but that was it. If Marc said I had to do something, then I would have to do it.

The next day, I did go to school. Having received that hateful letter, I finally accepted that I couldn't make these girls like me anymore. I wasn't going to sit with them at lunch. But where was I going to sit? I really didn't know anyone else.

My panicked solution was to go to the bathroom for lunch. It seemed like the only safe place left. So at lunch time, instead of going to the cafeteria, I slunk into the bathroom. I sat in a stall for a while, and then eventually came out and stood by the sinks. After a couple of days of lunch in the bathroom, I realized that I was not the only girl who was eating there. In fact, there were quite a few girls seeking refuge in the bathroom every day, just like me. Even better, these girls were actually pretty nice. So, my days of miserable school lunches were over. I had new friends. Bathroom friends.

Other sad things were happening the year of the divorce. Our beautiful cat Sylvia, who had suddenly adopted me one day, and who had lived with us for years, had just as suddenly disappeared. We didn't know where she went, and we never saw her again. She was a sweet Siamese cat, very affectionate, and we all loved her. I missed her elegant face, with the black markings around her eyes and ears. I missed her in my room, laying on my bed, purring. But Sylvia had taken off, as if she received the memo that our family was collapsing, and she had better move along.

Worse news was to come. Our beloved Pepere was diagnosed with advanced lung cancer. It was the mid-1970s, and it was a hopeless prognosis. Pepere had been a reliable, steady source of affection for both of us. He had showered us with attention, in a way that our parents did not. His illness and imminent death stunned us.

For my brother, the worst thing about to happen was the sale of the Glen Ridge house. This house, in that town, was the safest, most secure place Marc had ever had. It was only in Glen Ridge that he had made lifelong friends, who were devoted to him. Similarly to me, Marc's friends provided a foundation of love, support, and constancy that our parents could not provide. The sale of the house meant that Marc no longer had a home anywhere near Glen Ridge. Mom and I moved hours away to Oyster Bay, New York, and my father moved an hour away to Annandale, New Jersey.

Our beautiful home, with my room with the horse posters, and Marc's blue room, was sold in November 1976. Marc became a nomad. He would not settle in anywhere. He spurned his bed at my father's house, and his unpacked room at my mother's. He mostly stayed at his friend Stan's house, where he became an unofficial member of their family. Sometimes he stayed with my cousin Mary. Generally, he floated about, not working, not studying and not staying. My brilliant brother, with his lifelong history of despair, was now completely unmoored from any adult who would monitor his well-being. He was 18 years old.

I don't remember anyone talking about how Marc was doing, or whether he was OK. I remember my mother complaining that Marc wouldn't unpack his room, but that's about it. He would occasionally come to visit us. Each time he came, he taught me something.

One time, he taught me how to meditate. Marc had started meditating himself. He was reading The Great Books series, starting with the Greeks, and moving forward. He had also read the *Tibetan Book of the Dead*. He was practicing meditation and declared I should practice, too.

"So, let's sit on the ground. Cross your legs and put your hands on your knees. Are you comfortable? OK, great. Now close your eyes."

"What am I doing? I don't understand why we are doing this."

"We just sit together, quietly. That's all you have to do. Focus on your breath."

We sat on the tan shag carpet in the living room, Marc in full lotus position, me crossing my legs gamely and sitting on a cushion. We breathed in and out in companionable silence. Every now and then, I opened my right eye to sneak a peek at Marc, to see if we were done yet. I had no idea what I was doing. But, if Marc wanted to meditate, and if he thought I should meditate, then I would meditate, too.

Another visit, Marc discovered that I was going on a (pathetic) date with an older boy whom I had met at a Beatles fan convention. The boy was from a distant town, he drove a junky car, and I barely knew him. Marc was suspicious. Later, when I came home, my brother presented me with a pack of condoms. He didn't tell me what to do about the boy. I knew Marc was dubious, and that was enough for me. Most important, though, Marc had decided that if I was going to be interested in older boys, I was not going to get pregnant.

RETURN TO MIT

The spring of 1977, my brother decided to return to college. I'm not sure what made him give MIT another try but he seemed to have a good semester. He lived in a hippie-friendly dorm called Senior House and was assigned a suite-mate, Ken, whom he really liked. He made a new friend, Cindy, who lived across the hall. (These are the same Cindy and Ken who would later visit me every day in the hospital.) He made other friends there, and seemed to fit in well. Marc invited me to come visit him for Pig Roast, which was an annual Senior House event every spring. I was beside myself with delight.

I walked to the train station in Oyster Bay, and took the train into New York City. Then I grabbed the subway across town. Then I took another subway down to Penn Station. Then I bought myself an Amtrak ticket, and took the train to Boston. Then I took the subway from the Boston train station to MIT, and I walked with my green army backpack to Senior House. I did all this travel unsupervised, figuring it out as I went. I was 14, but I was an old hand at getting around New York City by myself. I had been taking buses, trains, and subways alone since I was ten years old. My parents had wanted me to be as independent as possible, as soon as I could. So, by 14, I would get myself anywhere I wanted to go, without help. There were no cell phones, and no one asked me to call "when I got there." Somehow I got where I needed to go, every time.

I arrived safely at MIT, and spent time with Marc and his new friends. One day, my brother brought me to his philosophy class. I listened to the lecture, following it as best I could. Halfway through the class, I raised my 14-year-old hand and earnestly asked the MIT professor a question. The professor looked surprised that I was bold enough to speak. I don't remember my question, but I know it wasn't stupid, because the professor responded to me with a kind and somewhat impressed smile. Marc seemed proud of me at that moment.

Marc was happy at MIT, as far as I could see. He liked his suite, and he had wonderful new friends. He was doing well in school. His main complaint was that there were no women in his life. He wanted a girlfriend desperately. I think this was partly due to the lack of family support we both endured. Marc was adrift and alone. I think he needed a girlfriend to feel grounded and connected. But there weren't many women at MIT in general, and Marc didn't find anyone there to love.

Marc came back to the New Jersey area for his summer break. He lived with Stan and Stan's family again. He stayed with our Dad. He visited me and our mother in Long Island. He drifted around. Nothing seemed different, as far as I could tell. But, on one of his visits, he allowed me to read a 50-page letter, which was more like a journal, which he had been writing for years.

Marc's letter was written on multiple pads of yellow lined paper, in his neat script. He made many entries, most of which documented his profound misery and loneliness. I sat in the upstairs hallway on the brown carpet, reading his most private words for hours. All the while, Marc watched me reading. His long brown wavy hair was messy and loose. He wore his metal-framed eyeglasses, obscuring his beautiful eyes. He sat cross-legged, leaning back against the hallway wall. He watched me carefully.

"You do know that someday I'm going to kill myself?" Marc said to me, gently.

"Yes," I replied, automatically, without question or thought. I never challenged my brother. I never disagreed with him. If he said something was so, then it was. Generally speaking, this had always worked for us. He was older, smarter, and he took care of me. I was deferential to him, and treated him like he was a demigod. We adored each other, and neither of us questioned these roles.

"Yes," I replied. Reading his journal, and his ongoing misery, it made sense to me that my brother wanted to kill himself.

Here is what I should have said. Here is what I wish I said. "No. You cannot kill yourself. I love you too much, and so do many other people, even though our parents suck. You need to go to therapy, and you need to take antidepressants. You should stop doing drugs for a while and get your head clear. If you were to kill yourself, I would never get over it. I would grieve you the rest of my life. My children would never have the chance to learn from you. My children would never know your profound love and kindness like I have. Your friends would never recover from your suicide. You shall do great things in this world, with your brilliance and many gifts. Do not deprive the world, and do not deprive me, your little sister who adores you, of the gift of your presence. You cannot kill yourself. It will get better, with time and with treatment. You must stay alive."

I didn't say any of those things, partly because I would never question my brother, but mostly because I didn't know these things at the time. Another thing I didn't know was that Marc was having similar conversations with his friends. One by one, he was telling people that maybe he would kill himself. With one friend, his ex-girlfriend, he asked if she would join him in a suicide pact. With another friend, they debated the most efficiently lethal way to commit suicide. His friend, to his everlasting regret, proposed that the most efficient way to die would be to jump off a high building.

Marc returned to MIT at the end of August of 1977. He had a single room there and he started his classes. He also voluntarily started therapy for the first time, and he went for a few sessions. He went to the dentist and got his perfect white teeth cleaned. And he made plans.

On September 16, my brother went to the tallest building on the MIT campus, called the Green Building. The building is not green, it is white, rectangular, a giant block in the skyline. He took the elevator up to the roof, intending to jump to his death. But the door to the roof was locked, and Marc couldn't get in. He went back to his lonely single room, and continued on with his classes.

On October 16, my brother went to visit a dear friend who was in the Boston area. He returned to MIT, and he played music, drumming along to his precious records. He wrote a will. He wrote a note. He called my father. Near the end of the conversation, Marc said, "Dad, I think you should be seeing Lise more. Try to take more time to go visit her. It would be good for her." Even at the end, even as he was about to do the worst thing he could do, Marc was still looking out for his little sister.

Around dusk, Marc walked back to the Green Building. He wore his favorite tan corduroy jacket, a hand-me-down from a friend. This time, he went up to the 16th story of the building and wandered down the hallway to a map room. He was able to enter the map room; the door wasn't locked. There was a bank of floor to ceiling windows, but the windows didn't open. Marc found a solid wooden coat stand in the map room, and used it to shatter one of the big windows. Then, he flung himself into the night sky. He plummeted through the air and landed on the pavement below. He died instantly.

Marc's influence on me did not end with his death. In my mind, I have continued to have a relationship with my dead brother. But his death ended this life of his, which was so dear and precious to me. I have truly never recovered from losing him. I have gone on, and I hope I have done him proud. I have done my best to keep going.

Still, on some basic level, I have felt incomplete ever since he died. I feel like a part of me is missing, the part of me that was always defined in relationship to him. A piece of me feels adrift and abandoned, ever since he died. I cannot be at any family function, *ever,* without feeling incomplete. Every time someone talks lovingly about their brother or sister, my heart literally throbs with pain. Marc was my best friend, my playmate, my favorite person, my only childhood protector.

It is my most fervent and profound hope that someday, when I die, Marc will be there to greet me. I will reach toward him, and he will put his arms around me. Just like many years ago, I will cry, and he will moan, "oooh-ooooh" in deep sympathy.

"I have missed you so much. Every day I missed you," I will whisper to him. He will rock me back and forth, and we will stand together, rocking, for a long time.

I almost look forward to dying, just to see him again.

MARC AND HIS VISITATIONS

I have kept Marc alive for decades. He lives in the stories I tell of him. Ask any of my friends; they know all about him. All of my close friends will tell you that they feel they knew him, because I talk so much about him.

I talk to Marc at night when I can't sleep. I lie on my side in bed, and I imagine my pillow is on Marc's lap, and we are driving cross country in our maroon Mercedes. This is just how it was. I sat behind my father, who was in the driver's seat, and Marc sat to my right. When I wanted to nap, he would let me put my pillow in his lap. I slept, stretched out across the backseat, and he would sit perfectly still until I woke up. He never complained.

At night, when I can't sleep, I ride in the backseat of the car, and I put my pillow on Marc's side. I imagine him there, above my head, holding my pillow on his ghostly lap. And we talk. I ask him questions; he answers me.

"Why did you leave me?" I ask him in the silence.

"I left you, and I have never left you. It is the same," says my brother. I woke up with a start the next day and wrote down his answer. It didn't sound like anything I would ever say. But it sure sounded like how my philosopher brother would talk.

"How is our mother?" I asked him, after Kathryn's death.

"She is in transition. She will be there a long time because she has a lot to learn about herself." True enough!

"How does that happen?" I wondered. "If heaven is full of love, but a person needs to learn painful things about themselves, then how is that possible?"

"I will show you," said Marc. "Imagine you are surrounded by love, unending, unconditional love. Can you feel that?"

"Yes," I say, lying in the dark.

"Now, Lise, see that you sometimes use humor as a cover for aggression. Do you remember what you said to Andy's mother last week? You were at the play and everyone was taking photos of their kids. You said, "What kind of a mother are you, that you aren't taking pictures of your son." You said it as a joke, but it wasn't funny. She didn't think it was funny, remember? You did that because you were feeling insecure and competitive. Your aggression slipped in a hostile joke, which you then laughed away. You did that, right?"

"Yes," I say, beginning to feel ashamed.

"But here, feel the love all around you. You are surrounded with love and kindness. Any of your mistakes can be forgiven. You are loved, so loved." I could feel warmth all around me, softness, kindness. I could see my mistake, and the impact that it had on Andy's mother. But I was not awash with shame, but rather with love and care. I knew I would do better next time. I would learn from the lesson and I was grateful for the insight.

"That's how it is here," said my brother.

Another time, I lay in the dark, my head on my pillow on my dead brother's lap. He said, "I'm sorry. I'm sorry. I'm sorry. You were like my child and I left you."

"I wasn't your child. I was your sister. It's wasn't your job to take care of me. You were just a kid yourself."

"But you were my child. You were mine to protect. I was supposed to do that, but I didn't. I will be here for you for the rest of your life. It is my job to look after you. I will always be here."

"OK. Good." I say, snuggling into my pillow. "Stay still until I wake up." And he does. Perfectly still.

I kept the past alive to protect myself and to bring my brother back to life. Now our mother is dead and I don't have to protect myself from her any more. I do, however, need to tell our tale. I need to tell the tale, and I need you to listen.

Here is my family. See us, sitting at our Glen Ridge kitchen table. We are all there, eating the perfectly balanced dinner my mother cooked. We have steak from the indoor grill, canned beans and a side salad. We eat together. We seem happy, don't we? My parents seem to love each other. My brother seems ready to take over the world. Everyone in the family is some kind of genius, except me. But I am a Good Girl, eager to please. My parents seem to take care of us. Look at our elegant house. All is well, right? How did it happen, everything? Everyone is dead, except me. Nothing was what it seemed to be.

LESSON SEVEN:

*If someone you love talks about suicide, do whatever you have to in order to keep that person alive. And **don't kill yourself.** The people who love you will never get over it. Never.*

FLASHBACK GIRL

EIGHT

Four Suicides: the Second and Third

THE SECOND SUICIDE

I met my future stepsister Jackie when I was 13 and she was 11. I liked her OK, but not particularly. Jackie was young and immature and her two older sisters seemed tough. They were pretty girls, all of them, with Jackie the least pretty. Jackie was tall, red haired, freckled and gawky. She had long limbs and not much grace. None of my stepsisters interested me. They didn't seem smart, and they weren't raised with culture. They could be crass and hostile; I could be snobby and judgmental. We had nothing in common, other than the fact that their father and my mother were in love, and we were all completely neglected.

My mother and John dated passionately. After two years in Oyster Bay, apart from the Great Love of her life, my mother decided she'd had enough. "It's time to move. Let's move back to New Jersey."

"I don't want to move. I'm in high school! I love it here. We just moved here so why would we move again?"

"We have to. It's ridiculous that I go back and forth all the time to New Jersey and John has to travel here. It would be so much easier if we just lived near each other."

"It would be easier for you. Not me. I have friends here, really good friends. I don't want to switch schools. Why should I have to do that?" I seethed with outrage. Heretofore, I had always been cheerfully compliant with all of our moves. I had lived in Oyster Bay, Berkeley Heights, East Orange, Glen Ridge, and Oyster Bay again. By now, I was in my third school district. I had attended two different elementary schools, and two different middle schools. Now my mother wanted me to start a second high school and move again. The sole reason for this move was so that my mother could live closer to her boyfriend.

I had lived in Oyster Bay for less than two years, but they were intense ones. I was a happy part of a girl group. My best friend Karen ran to my house the day that Marc died. That night, she slumbered protectively on the floor next to my bed. When I awoke the next morning, shocked to remember my brother was dead, Karen was there, her green eyes sadly peering up at me from the floor below. My new friends banded with me when my brother died, carefully watching over me, their friend who was enduring such a tragedy. These girls watched me more alertly than my parents did. My parents seemed done with that.

Having moved so many times already, I knew what was in store for me. I would face a year of no true friends, people staring at me, sitting alone in the cafeteria, just trying to find my way. I couldn't fathom how she could be so cavalier about my feelings, given that Marc had died that year, and that I was in tenuous recovery from my own depression. But, sure enough, pretty soon I was packing up to move back to New Jersey, heartbroken and spitting mad.

We moved to Fairfield where we settled into yet another house. I started another high school, as a tenth-grader. After I graduated high school,

John and my mother finally got married. They had postponed their wedding until I left for college. My mother said this was because John was sensitive to my needs. I suspected it was more that he didn't feel like dealing with me.

Their wedding in the backyard of our house was a sweet, if strange, affair. It was a small wedding, with some relatives and many friends. On an odder note, Mom and John said their vows high on cocaine. I, the maid of honor, was also high on cocaine. Our newly constituted family had all done cocaine in my sixteen-year-old stepsister's bedroom prior to the ceremony. It was my first time on cocaine and I liked it a lot.

It was the early 1980s. It was that kind of wedding and we were that kind of family.

After the wedding, my new step-sister, Jackie, was wrenched from her beloved high school, and forced to transfer to my school district. She was as miserable as I had been, having to move in her junior year. But, it didn't matter how the moves affected their children; Kathryn and John had to be together. For some time, Jackie refused to go to school at all, necessitating various crisis sessions with therapists. My mother and John were mystified by Jackie's non-compliance, and discussed her school refusal with exasperation. After some time, Jackie adjusted as best she could. She went to classes, made a friend or two, graduated, and went off to Emerson College.

Although we had never bonded earlier, when Jackie moved in, we got along well. We were both surprised to find that we liked each other. I started to think that she was a pretty sweet kid. Jackie was cheerful and bubbly, and she was a hoot. She used to make me laugh, dancing around the living room, making fun of the MTV videos we were always watching. Her long thin body seemed like spaghetti; she could mimic every dance, simultaneously perfectly and comically. My friends embraced her; she was exuberant.

At the same time, Jackie must have decided that I was less of a judgmental snob than I had seemed. I tried to help her get along better with Mom and John. She didn't seem to know how to play the game. I didn't even know I had been playing a game, but I realized then that I was.

"You have to be more. . . subtle, Jackie. Try to talk with them a little before you just. . . ask for stuff. They don't like that. You have to get them to want to help you." Jackie was too blunt, too direct, too entitled in assuming that her childhood needs should be met. Mom and John required clever conversation, subtlety, sophistication. You couldn't just be a kid and expect stuff from them. Parental requests had to be delivered with much more finesse. Getting one's needs met in our household required a fair amount of charm and flattery.

Despite all the difficult school changes, Jackie was a good student, and she was accepted into Emerson College. Initially, she did well there. She liked her roommate and she enjoyed living in Boston. Jackie seemed to be her ebullient funny self. But, over time, everything changed.

I really don't understand what happened to Jackie; it never made sense to me. I was also geographically far away, and it was hard to get accurate information. Jackie seemed to descend quickly into serious mental illness. She developed depression and had to be medicated. Then, somehow she wound up hospitalized for depression. After that, she was never the same.

Perhaps Jackie was on the wrong medication, or perhaps she was on too much of it. She put on a lot of weight. She was sluggish and stopped taking care of herself. She seemed disinterested in everything. The cheerful dancing Jackie vanished, leaving in her place a quiet hulk of misery. She didn't get better. She seemed like an entirely different person.

On March 15, 1985, I got a call from my mother. I was on spring break, driving with my college roommates down to Florida. "Lise, you have to come home."

"What? Why? What's going on?"

"It's Jackie."

"What about her? Is she OK?"

"She's dead."

"What?!"

"She killed herself."

Jackie had taken an overdose of her medication. She was 19 years old and had died alone in her dorm room in Boston. I had only gotten to know her well for the past three years, but she had become my new sister. She had filled a bit of the yawning void that my brother's death had left. We hadn't grown up together, but we had lived together. We shared the same crazy set of parents. We understood what each other was going through. But now Jackie was dead, my second sibling to take their own life near Boston, both at the age of 19.

John never recovered from Jackie's death. He had always been prone to depression and substance abuse. After Jackie's suicide, he drank hard. He and his brother did tequila shots in the kitchen before and after Jackie's morning funeral. Those tequila shots were a harbinger of things to come. John continued to drink, more destructively than he had in the past, until his own suicide, 28 years later.

FOUR SUICIDES: THE THIRD

My stepfather, John Diaz, was a brilliant but troubled man. He grew up in a working-class family in Brooklyn. Brooklyn stayed with him all his life, living in his accent, which he hated. "I practice the lar," he would say, instead of saying "law." He felt his accent branded him as lower class, along with the faded anchor tattoo on his bicep, which he always kept covered. Although ashamed of that tattoo, he was proud of being a Marine. The last words on his suicide note were "Semper Fi."

When John was young, he appeared on the TV show *Quiz Kids*, as he was a really smart little guy. Intelligent as he was, Brooklyn public school bored him, and he dropped out of high school to enlist. After the Marines, John went to City College, and then to New York University for his law degree. When he met my mother, John had built a successful private practice as a divorce attorney. He was tall, slim, and dark. He drove a sexy hunter green Datsun 280Z sports car and was a bit of a player.

John had been married to his childhood sweetheart, and he had three daughters, Sarah, Kerry, and Jackie. He loved his girls but he was not an attentive, intuitive father. He hadn't spent much time with them, and he didn't seem to know how to connect with them. The girls had also been taught to hate him by their mother, who was bitter about their divorce. This dynamic made it even harder for John to connect with his daughters.

John meant well but he couldn't connect with me either. When he and my mother got together, he sat down with me the first day I met him. He wasn't warm; he wasn't cold. His manner was simultaneously well-meaning and aloof. He took a quiet minute alone with me. "It's nice to meet you Lise."

"You, too!"

"I hope that we can be friends. I know you have your own father, and I don't want to be like that. But I hope that we can be friends."

"Oh. OK." In that moment, I felt disappointed and already somehow rejected. I didn't want him to be my father either. But, my family had collapsed, and I didn't have anyone looking out for me. I would have been grateful for a new supportive parental figure. John immediately defined himself as someone not interested in that job. Indeed, he was true to his word. John enjoyed smoking pot and drinking with me. We had a lot of fun parties, hanging around together. He was a friend, kind of.

John said one thing to me that felt parental. It was just a random comment, a joke that he made. The fact that I have remembered it all these years indicates how rarely he made a protective statement to me. Here it is: I was standing in front of the microwave. This is at the time when microwaves were new, and none of us understood or felt comfortable with them.

John saw me standing in front of the microwave. He exclaimed, "Don't stand there or you'll get sterile!" Compliantly, I moved away.

That's it. That's my sole memory of John being parental. To this day, when I find myself standing in front of a microwave, I back away a little.

Now in my fifties, sterility is no longer my concern, but somehow, it still feels safer, and I always think of John with a smile.

When my mother first started dating John, he was a successful attorney, making good money in his law practice. Over time, John's level of functioning decreased. He drank more and more; he worked less and less. His law practice dwindled. After Jackie's suicide, he decided he didn't want to be an attorney. He tried real estate development and lost himself and his investor friends a lot of money. He tried being a Christmas tree farmer. He sold enough trees to justify the farm tax exemption on the property, but not enough to make a profit. He talked about starting a fish farm instead. Then, he went back to school to get his master's degree in history, hoping to become a history professor. After earning his master's, he discovered that it was impossible to be a professor with only a master's. So, he trained to be a truck driver. A tree-growing, truck-driving attorney. . . one of a kind.

John also spent a lot of time not trying anything at all. He drank a lot and he smoked a lot of pot. After many years, he accepted that none of his ideas for other jobs were going to work. He relented and went back to work part-time as an attorney. He was an excellent lawyer. But he hated the work even part-time, and quit the job as quickly as possible.

My mother and John first married in 1981. In the mid-1990s, they divorced. Then, a few years later, they remarried again. This was now my mother's third marriage. She was overjoyed to be back with him, but their problems remained, because they had never solved them. My mother grew increasingly unhappy with John's alcoholism. Eventually, she divorced him, her third divorce, and her second divorce from John.

My mother moved to Bucks County, Pennsylvania, to be closer to me and my family. John was left in their remote country house in the Poconos. He was retired and isolated, with no family and no friends nearby. His health was declining, and he walked in pain due to a bad back.

Although I had offered to keep a connection going, so he could see my daughters, he politely declined. I myself was no longer close to John. I had felt alienated from him for years. He had contact with his daughter Kerry, who lived far away, but no relationship with his older daughter Sarah. My mother had left him. He was completely alone.

John bought himself a revolver. He sent my mother a love note. He found his will and his gun permit and carefully laid both documents on his kitchen table. He remained a lawyer to the end, despite his disinterest, providing careful proof of his intentions. Then he limped out onto his screen porch and shot himself in the head. He lay there dead on his porch for days until his body was found.

By the time John killed himself, I hadn't been close to him for years. I had problems with him, for a long time. I found him cool, aloof, and unsupportive. I resented the financial burden his unemployment and their two divorces had placed on my mother. We had fought, on occasion. Still, his death was sad and tragic; a terrible end for the former Quiz Kid turned brilliant lawyer. John had once been so loved by my mother. He had been everything to her.

No one should ever bleed to death alone on their porch and lie there for days unseen.

John's death wound up being the lynch pin in the final break with my mother.

LESSON EIGHT:

Once again, ***don't kill yourself****. It destroys the people you love.*

FLASHBACK GIRL

NINE

On Psychologists and Superheroes

I never understood why I was still alive when my brother had died. He was the genius, the unspeakably gifted child. I was the ugly burned girl, with a cheerful disposition, whose only remarkable quality was a capacity to survive without complaint. Meeting my brother, you would imagine him getting his doctorate, doing research and teaching at Stanford. Meeting me, you might say, "Well, there's a nice girl. Poor thing."

I once told my father that I thought he would have preferred if I had died and Marc had lived. My father's face filled with red outrage, puffs of smoke blew out of his ears. "What a terrible thing to say! How dare you say that to me!" But I don't remember if he ever said my observation was untrue. I don't think he did.

The mystery of my life is why I am here and my brother is not. Further, after so much trauma, why am I thriving when so many others aren't? This mystery beguiled me into the field of psychology, the study of the human mind. There, I thought I would find the answers about human survival, fortitude and failure. Instead, I learned about statistics, psychoanalytic theory and behaviorism. The classes were interesting, but uninformative as to the central question in my mind.

I became a psychologist to understand myself and my family. My training did not answer these questions, but it did lead to a rewarding career. I stayed a psychologist because helping people in pain sets my heart soaring. When a new client comes to me, weeping and hopeless, calm assurance fills my chest. I sit with their distress, the smoky haze of my own loneliness creeping out toward them. I know they will get better. Even if their suffering is just to be endured, I feel hope for their future. The hope pulls at me, tugging me, like an ocean tide. My client can't feel the hope yet, but I can.

Frequently people ask me if being a psychologist is depressing. No, it is not, not for me. I have treated clients who were instantly quadriplegic, dying of cancer, who just lost their beloved son. To me, these dark places are just where we start. Yes, life couldn't get any worse. That also means it will probably get a lot better. I can guide them to a better place. I whisper, "I see a glimmer of light here, follow me." I lead them through a dark underground cave, a flickering candle in my hand. They follow me, scrambling over the rocky path, jumping over the hidden aquifers. I follow a faint light; they follow me. Eventually, we emerge out of the black cave together, stepping out into the warm rays of sunshine.

Other psychologists are more gifted in technique. I know psychologists who are better read, who do research, who present nationally. I read and I present, but I am a slacker, too. I could work harder. My gift is not academic. I am still the younger sister of the genius. My gift is that I know the way through the dark cave of suffering. I have traveled through this dark cave many times myself, with my own therapists as my guides. I learned the way, back and forth, over the rocky path and the lurking dangers, past the sinkholes and the snakes. Now, I can get a person back and forth safely. That's my job.

I work for myself. It is just me in my sunny office in Pennington, a quiet, affluent town near Princeton, New Jersey. I have practiced here for 20 years and I love my work. I don't mean that I wake up wanting to go to work. I don't mean that I wouldn't often prefer to stay home in my pajamas. But, when I do work, I love it.

In my quiet office, I listen to my clients. The first question of the session is almost always, "How are you doing?" It's a simple question, but I ask it with my whole heart, truly wanting to know. Cell phones are down, computer screens are off. I sit across from my client, with not even a coffee table between us. My heart is open, and my attention is focused. I sit, ready to align myself with my client's feelings, worries and concerns.

It is simple, this alignment, yet it is sacred. Attuned listening is healing. By being heard, we can finally hear ourselves. By being felt, we feel our feelings. When someone reflects us back accurately, getting us, understanding us, we become known.

Much of therapy drifts along, easy talk, catching up. Other moments sneak up, catching me unaware. I might be sitting with my client, as she tells me about her troubled marriage. I listen, she talks. She tells me about her loneliness, her inability to connect in her marriage. I listen, drifting along with the conversation. An image floats into my head. I see a massive stone castle, high on a hill. The castle is surrounded by a moat, and the one drawbridge, the only access to the castle, is drawn up. There is no one in sight.

Although the moments can seem random, I have learned to trust these unbidden images. I say to my client, "I just got this image in my head while you were talking about your marriage and your loneliness. I saw a stone castle, with the drawbridge up and no way to get in. Does it feel like that to you?"

"Yes!" my client exclaims. "That is exactly it. That is exactly how I feel." The relief from the image, the feeling of being truly understood—the solace — stands on her face. She smiles a bit, wrinkles relaxing. We gaze at each other serenely. She is known.

Sometimes the only thing we can do for people is to listen to them and understand them. Sometimes nothing else needs to change because they are now *known*. Maybe being known doesn't change their problems, but it changes their existential experience of their problems. We are all on earth, just living, trying to get along, trying to stay alive.

Another client was telling me about his difficult relationship with his father. His father was critical, difficult, negative. Every idea my client had, his father would question, ferreting out all the potential problems with the idea, drowning my client in pessimism. My client was trying so hard to overcome his depression, but it pained him to be near his father. Another image came to my head. I laughed at the picture. "I just got an image in my head, listening to you. It's like your father keeps throwing hot, wet towels in your face. Every time you have an idea, he throws another heavy wet towel, right in your face."

"That's it!" said my client, chuckling. "That's exactly what it's like." We smiled at each other, sharing both the silly image, and the feeling of being fully connected. Did this session change my client's relationship with his father? No. But, it did help my client feel seen and understood, in a way which his father could not provide. And by feeling seen, he felt better. Stronger. Present.

Everything I have survived helps me with my work. Every life experience, good and bad, informs me and helps me understand the people who come for help. I don't say to my clients, "Yes I have been through that, too." But my listening is attuned and my responses are empathic. Even though I don't explicitly state my common connection with their suffering, that connection is felt.

I love my work because it is my job to sit still and completely focus on a client, without distraction and usually without judgement. It is my job to listen and to care. Sometimes that is all I can do for a person. Sometimes, I can offer suggestions, or help the client marshal her coping skills, or help her handle her feelings better. Whatever happens, I love my work because, always, I am trying to be helpful. The work is not exploitative. The work is true. It is honorable work and in my small way, I help the world be a better place.

When I was little, I wanted to be a pediatrician. Many kids who have been seriously ill want to be a doctor or nurse themselves. I imagined myself working in a hospital like Shriners, saving little kids. But medicine would require lots of science and math, and I wasn't passionate about those subjects. Imagine the amount of Xs being any number! Then, I wanted to be a writer. This was in middle school, when I was writing poems and dreary journals full of pain. Then, when I was in my last high school, I wanted to be an actress.

I arrived at West Essex High School at 15 years old, mad as hell at being forced to move and switch schools for the 4th time. At the new high school, I found myself on my own again, anxiously navigating the school cafeteria, trying not to be caught sitting alone. I eyed the bathroom as a familiar option but managed to find some girls who let me join them. For months, I focused only on my schoolwork, writing pathetic letters to my Oyster Bay friends, and taking the bus, subway and train out to see them as often as possible. Then, I had a bolt of good fortune: I was cast in the school musical.

My new high school was doing a production of *Godspell*. My dad had done *Godspell* the year before, and I had played flute for the show in the Upsala pit band. I knew that I could do a good job if I were cast. But, the casting of the school musical was a highly competitive event, and there were many talented kids. I knew the girl who was considered the best singer in the school; we were in chorus together and we were both altos, so we sat near each other. When I told her I was auditioning for the show, she confidently told me the show was already pre-cast, and she named who would be in it. She was on that list; I was not. No one even knew me. I was not a consideration.

Daunted but undeterred, I auditioned for the show. I figured I should get in, even if no one knew that but me. I sang for the director, and I did the lines I was handed. I think I was helped by the fact that I truly was a hippie,

I dressed as a hippie, and the show is pretty much about hippies and Jesus.

I got "called back" to audition again. This time, I was asked to sing with another girl, Susan. She was a shy, pretty 9th grader, wearing a sweet little white dress and cowboy boots. I was in my favorite blue overalls, with pigtails and pink ribbons in my hair. We were asked to sing a duet from *Godspell* together, to see if we sounded nice and had a good "blend."

I looked at her confidently; she looked at me shyly. We started singing, and we immediately made the most beautiful sound. We had a perfect blend, although we had never laid eyes on each other before. We were both cast in *Godspell*, both of us underdogs, who had not been expected to be cast. In this wonderful moment, I found my new social group, my new after-school passion, and my new best friend for life.

I did theater all through high school. I also played flute in the orchestra and sang in the chorus. I loved music and the performing arts. At the time I was considered to be quite talented, although looking back on it I wonder how talented I was. But, I loved the arts. I wanted to be a professional actress, and I contemplated that direction for a few years. In the end, I concluded that I was not emotionally equipped to handle the life of an actress. I realized that acting would mean lots of auditioning and lots of rejection. I couldn't cope the smallest social rejection, let alone make a living as an unknown actress. I knew I would be too anxious about the auditioning and too despairing about the rejections. I decided to go with my other idea, which was to be a psychologist.

Ironically, my older daughter Julia is now an actress. She is much more talented than I ever was. She also has the emotional fortitude for the life that I did not have. I have seen her preparing with intense focus for her auditions. I have also seen her after auditions, waving away a rejection with a flick of the wrist, eyes focused forward toward her next opportunity. She is built for the life. I was not.

Although my mother rarely provided me guidance, she was able to help me when I decided to pursue psychology, because she was a psychologist herself. Her guidance to me was limited but vital. She told me that I would need to get a doctorate after college, and that doctoral programs were highly selective, even more competitive than medical school. My mother advised me that I would need straight As in college to get into a psychology program.

I went to Tufts University in 1981. After one semester of contemplating a drama major, I declared my psychology major. Following my mother's advice, I earnestly pursued every A I could earn. I was serious in college, with a goal that was clear and important to me. I didn't get straight As in college, but I almost did. I graduated Phi Beta Kappa, summa cum laude. I was flush with pride for those honors; me, the ungifted one of my family.

I did get admitted into a doctoral program in clinical psychology, in Philadelphia. After graduation, I moved to Philly on my own, assuming that I would make a new set of friends, as I had with every previous move. I knew that I would have a lot in common with the other students. I assumed that we would be loving and supportive of each other, as we were all going into a helping profession. Every assumption I had was wrong.

I hated my doctoral program, and I writhed in misery there for the five long years it took to get out. I received excellent training there, and I learned a lot. But the faculty at the time seemed cold, distant and judgmental. Worse, my classmates seemed cold, distant and judgmental. I did not fit there. I was one of the youngest people in my class of 31. Because I came straight from college, I didn't have any work experience and I was single. Most of the other students were at least in their late 20s and many of them had families of their own.

I had moved down from Boston to Philadelphia, where I didn't know a soul. I was 22 and living alone for the first time in a cockroach-infested dorm. I was lonely and needy, desperate for attention and love. I'm sure that the force of my need for connection was off-putting to some classmates. Others were just too busy to want a new friend. I did make some friends but it wasn't the level of closeness that I was used to. No one in Philadelphia wanted to adopt me as a new family member. Also, once again, there were no men who were interested in me. My vision of my new fun life in Philadelphia was a bust.

The doctoral program was grueling. The first year, we had six classes, in addition to a twice weekly clinical placement. The academic work overwhelmed me in its sheer volume. I wondered how I would ever have time to even buy groceries, because I was either in class or studying seemingly every hour of the week. But, I made it through.

Luckily, old friends of mine moved to Philadelphia my second year there. My friend Caryn from Tufts, and her new husband Brad, moved to Philly as he had been accepted to Wharton. They lived nearby for two years, and I was happier with them around. When I was particularly discouraged, which was often, Caryn would call me and tell me to just come over for dinner. I would trudge to their apartment, have a good cry, eat Caryn's amazing dinner, and feel rejuvenated. I never really thought about the fact that Caryn and Brad were just barely making it themselves, on very little money. Every time they had me for dinner, which was practically every week, I think it was a financial sacrifice for them. But they never said a word about it. I was always welcome.

Susan, my high school best friend, my duet partner in *Godspell*, also moved near Philly. She lived a bit outside the city, but I could see her on weekends, and that improved life as well. With my old friends back around me, I was fortified.

My father had his own way of encouraging me. At the end of my first semester there, isolated and exhausted, I opened the door to my dorm room to find a florist box. Inside the box was a single red rose. At the end of my second semester, there was another florist box. This box contained two red roses. For each semester I completed, my father sent me that number of red roses. At the end of my tenth semester, I graduated. My dad said that ordering ten roses was quite the trick. The florist kept saying to my dad, "Don't you just want to send 12 roses? Why would you only send ten?" But my dad insisted, and I received my ten perfect roses, one for each daunting semester that I had completed, until my doctorate was done.

It is not easy to become a psychologist, but I think it shouldn't be easy. In order to be a psychologist, you compete for very few spots in doctoral programs, you complete five more years of grueling education, you write and defend a dissertation, and in my program, you do a three-hour oral defense of your clinical work. Even once you have a doctorate, you must work another two years of post-doctoral work in order to qualify for state licensure. Licensure requires another long national-level exam, and in my case, yet another demanding oral presentation.

Any doctoral level psychologist you meet has completed this high level of training. Therefore, most psychologists are intelligent people, because you have to be smart to make it. What you don't know, when you meet a psychologist, is whether they are kind and emotionally healthy. The training does not screen for emotional health, which is unfortunate, because it is hard to cure other people if you are not well yourself.

I was in therapy, many times and with quite a few people. Psychology training does not usually require that a psychology student be in therapy themselves. I think it should but it doesn't. I credit some of my therapists with saving my health and improving my ability to function well. I have benefited greatly from the kindness, understanding and skillful intervention of six therapists over the course of 25 years. They helped me become the person I am.

I started therapy when I was 14, after Marc had killed himself. Immediately after his death, I became suicidal myself. Flooded with sadness, I desperately wanted to follow my brother into death, to be with him again. My mother found me a psychologist in Manhattan.

For my first session, my mother took me into New York. We walked to the Long Island Railroad. We took the train into Penn Station. Then we took another subway uptown. Then we walked to Dr. Mann's office. After that first trip, it was up to me to get back and forth to the office once a week for my therapy sessions. I did this long, complicated trip to New York City, both ways, by myself for the next four years.

I don't remember Dr. Mann much. She was smart and reserved. I don't remember finding her particularly kind or supportive. I do remember one interaction clearly; it was about punctuality.

When I was little, I used to be late. I would show up late for dinner, and make the family wait for me. I wouldn't be ready on time to go to the movies, and we would have to scramble to get there. My mother and father were both highly punctual people, and my tardiness annoyed them.

One day, we were about to depart on a family cross-country trip. We would leave New Jersey and drive all the way to California and back again. I was seven years old and excited for the vacation. The night before our departure, my father said to me, "You have to be outside, bags packed, ready to go by 7:00 AM or we will leave without you."

"Yes, Daddy," I said, and scampered off to bed. In the morning, I stood in my room, packing my toothbrush and pajamas into my suitcase. I glanced at the clock. I was a few minutes late, but no big deal. I sped downstairs and out the back door.

My mother, father and brother sat in the Mercedes, doors closed, looking at me. I huffed down the stairs to the curb, lugging my suitcase behind me. Impassively, my father looked away. He started the car, and they drove off down the driveway. I stood there, holding my bags, aghast. I watched as the car took off down the street and drove away from view. "My god," I thought, "what am I going to do? My whole family just left and they won't be back for a month. What am I going to do?" My heart thumped with panic.

One minute later, the Mercedes re-emerged. "Get in," snarled my dad. "No more being late." I slunk into the car, catching my breath.

From that day on, I became the most punctual girl ever known. To this day, I am highly punctual. But there was one time, with my first psychologist, Dr. Mann, that I was late for the appointment. My train was delayed, and the subway came late. Despite my careful planning, I arrived at Dr. Mann's office ten minutes late, completely distraught.

"I'm so sorry I'm late! The train was late and then the subway was all messed up. I ran all the way but I'm still so late."

"It's OK. Sometimes that happens."

"But I'm late! I shouldn't be late! I really tried. I ran as fast as I could."

"It's all right."

"But it's my fault I kept you waiting. I'm so sorry!"

Dr. Mann looked at me carefully. She was never one to criticize my family, and she was usually quite neutral in her reactions to me. This time, though, she let more feeling show. "Lise. Listen to me. It's only human to be late sometimes. Everyone is occasionally late. You are fine."

I found my second therapist at Tufts University, during my junior year there. I had developed anxiety when I was studying abroad in Vienna the term before. Somehow, being so far away from home caused me distress. I developed hives; my period stopped; I worried a lot. So, when I came back to Tufts, I went for help. Carol was an amazing therapist, and she helped me immensely. She had a perfect balance of professionalism and warmth that gave me the structure and courage to start to face my past. One day, in particular, devastated me.

I had been in therapy with Carol for about a year. That summer day, we were sitting facing each other in her home office. She had a lovely home in Belmont, with a dark small private office in the back of the house. Carol had asked me to tell her more about the fire. I explained to her about the cabin in New Hampshire, the barbecue on the porch, the "lighter fluid." I told her how my mother and I had caught fire, and how my mother had run through the fire, and my father saved me. I said all this automatically, repeating the same story I had told my whole life. Then, I stopped talking. I froze like a rabbit, my mouth hanging open, completely alert, silent.

"What?" she asked me. "What is it?"

"That means she left me. That means my mother. . . left me there in the fire."

"What do you mean?"

"That means my mother left me, her four-year-old, standing right next to her. She just. . .forgot all about me. She ran off and left me to fend for myself, without even trying to save me. She could have picked me up or dragged me. But she just. . . saved herself."

"Yes."

"But that isn't how my parents ever tell the story. They never said that part. They just said that my father rescued me. They never admit that my mother abandoned me there."

"Yes?"

"And then. . ." Now I am beside myself with grief. I am crying, trying to speak. "Then she didn't see me at the hospital for a long time. We were in the same hospital for months. My father said he had to force my mother come and see me. She wouldn't come for weeks; she would just say 'Poor Lise,' and refuse to go. I almost died twice after the fire. She left me in the hospital all alone, and she could have come to see me every day."

I was shattered to realize the extent of my mother's abandonment. The family story of the fire had either glossed over, or completely minimized her neglect of me. What I began to realize for myself, at the age of 21, was only the beginning of what I needed to understand about my mother. But I had begun the journey of understanding the mother I had, versus the kind of mother she told me she was, or the kind I hoped she would be.

When I moved away to Philadelphia, I had to start with a new therapist. I continued in therapy for about ten years, on and off, with different people. Every one of my therapists helped me get through difficulties. Some of them were better than others at helping me understand myself and my family.

The best therapists helped me understand my own weaknesses and shortcomings. I learned about ways I protected myself that inadvertently hurt other people. Those lessons were hard. I didn't like facing my shortcomings, and my snobby, judgmental, rigidified knife edge that caused others pain. The best of my therapists combined a warm, caring approach with the ability to point out my shortcomings. I would not be the person I am, and I would not have the healthy relationships I have, without their skillful help.

I still mess up sometimes. I still cause pain, judging people harshly, taut in my righteousness. I still wail in helpless despair, calling on people to save me, needing someone to read me the algebra book that really, I should just read myself. But, I function better than I used to, and I can catch my errors now. I can take a minute, look inward, see my mistakes and right my course.

Now, I provide this same help to others. It is usually easy to connect with a client, and to help them feel supported and understood. The real trick is to provide this support, while also helping them see their own dark side, their mistakes that are contributing to the pain they are experiencing. Those are hard lessons for clients, but they are ultimately the most important lessons. If you can't see what you yourself are doing to make your life hard, then you will never stop doing it, and your life will always be hard. Still, a person needs a lot of support to be able to tolerate seeing their own imperfections.

If you were to see me in my little office, you would never know the long journey it took me to get there. Being a psychologist means that I did four years of college, five years of graduate school, and two years of post-doctoral work. It means that I took countless exams to prove my competence. Yet, that was just the academic part.

For me, being a good psychologist means that I, too, have suffered. I have been through my own journeys of sadness, loss, disappointment and struggle. I have worked through my traumas, and learned the good and bad ways I coped with pain. I worked a long time to get healthy. That emotional work was just as hard as the academic work, and probably harder.

I don't discuss my struggles or my own therapy with my clients. That would be inappropriate, distracting, and burdensome for them. Still, my scars are always there in the room with us. Although I rarely mention them, my burn scars whisper to my clients silently. They murmur, "Life is hard. Life is hard for all of us. I survived something ghastly, and here I am. I am here to help you now. You can make it through something bad too. We will do it together. You can do it."

SUPERHEROES

My husband loves superhero movies. Although he is a scholar, with a doctorate, in charge of a large program at a major university, a little boy lives inside him. This boy loves video games, silly jokes, *Lost in Space,* and superhero movies. This little boy yearns to be noticed and cherished and has his own story to tell of neglect and oversight. I live with this boy in surprise. I didn't know the boy was part of the package that was Doug. This boy did not wear the handsome blue suit and exchange wedding rings with me. Just the same, this boy is part of our family.

Residing inside my thickened scarred skin is a little girl. This girl is all feelings. She maintains no connection to my intellect or my reasoning. This girl crouches in defense, smiling, saying "Please like me. Please. I am here, do you like me?" She pleads this with everyone, trying to stay safe and hoping to be loved. This little girl surprised my husband, who was expecting the independent, intelligent, sophisticated woman he had met at work. He tries to accommodate her, sometimes out of kindness, sometimes because he has to. She is here to stay.

I accept my own inner little girl. I know she is there and I give her room. I feel sensitive about her, and I understand her vulnerability. I can do all of this because I have been in years and years of therapy. When my inner little girl starts to take over, I usually know what to do. I let her speak, if it's safe. I let her speak her fears, her needs, her vulnerability. As she speaks, my adult brain begins to contribute to the conversation. My adult brain modulates what I am saying, takes perspective on my feelings, and tries to understand the other people's points of view. Also, my adult brain is learning, over time, that I am able to take care of this little shattered girl myself. I don't need to keep asking for help. Sometimes, I can calm myself down. I can whisper to the girl, "I am here for you. We are together. You are safe and it is OK. I am in my fifties now, and I can watch out for you."

All that took years of psychological work. I worked in depth with Carola, Carol, Fred, Dr. Slap, Maya, Megan, and Cecily as therapists. So many! What kind of a nut job psychologist has seen seven therapists? I shrink to admit it here, fearing the judgment. But I moved a lot, and I went through many different life traumas, I needed every one of those therapists. I have been through psychoanalysis, psychodynamic therapy, Imago therapy, EMDR (eye movement desensitization and reprocessing) and family therapy. Every technique was useful and also not useful. What stands out for me are the therapists themselves. I remember the moments of profound empathic connection.

A movie came out in 1980 called *Ordinary People,* about a teenage boy who survives an accident, but his older brother does not. His older brother is the favorite child, a gifted athlete with a bright future. Their mother is cold, seemingly unfeeling and unavailable for her surviving son, Conrad. Their father is kind-hearted but ineffective. Conrad tries to kill himself.

Perhaps I identified with this movie just a bit.

A psychologist, played by Judd Hirsch, steps in to treat Conrad. Dr. Berger is good natured, a bit rumpled, and warm. He forges a connection with the boy, who had no interest in therapy. Week after week, he is there, listening to him, caring for him, protecting him as painful truths start to emerge. He loves his client and sees the best in him. He stands there for Conrad, kindly witnessing, putting the pieces together until his shattered client feels whole again.

That's therapy.

Why is a superhero a superhero? I don't watch the movies; I find them silly. Doug would say this is because I am snobby. Maybe I am, but I still find them silly. (How ironic that I am now writing about superheroes.) I find them silly because superhero movies are fantasies. There is nothing real about them and they bore me. But, I am riveted by real superheroes.

In the movies, a superhero possesses an extraordinary, superhuman strength of some kind, and uses it to battle against evil. Often, the superhero has gotten his or her special strength from enduring a trauma. Spiderman walks on walls because he was bitten by a mutant spider. Wolverine has special powers because he endured evil experiments. OK. But show me the real superheroes.

I was reconstructed from the ashes of a fire I was not expected to survive. I was abandoned and neglected by my family. I was horribly disfigured and endured torturous medical procedures. I was shunned and rejected. My family is dead, all due to their own folly. But, thanks to whatever gave me superhuman strength, I stand here, stronger than ever. I use my painful past to protect others as they go through life's vicissitudes. The evils I fight are loneliness, self-hatred, and cruelty. My bright yellow cape waves behind me, rippling in the wind. My pain has transformed into the superhuman strength that now helps others. My superhero belt is more powerful than Batman's, equipped with acceptance, attunement and empathy.

My childhood attorney's son gave me the name Flashback Girl. It is a quirky name for a superhero, but I'm going with it. A flashback arrestor is a tiny device that keeps flames or gas from shooting back up a container and igniting it. A flashback arrestor is also a psychologist who helps clients stop torturing themselves with traumatic memories. The girl is the little girl who crouches inside me still, eyes blinking up, smiling defensively, looking to see if it safe to come out.

SUFFERING, LONELINESS AND
HOW THAT HELPS TO BE A THERAPIST

I understand other people's lonely suffering because I too have endured lonely suffering. Despite my best efforts, burn care cannot be described. I cannot convey what I have lived through in words, and no one alive was there to see. I suffered in the hospital for years. Process that. Years. Day after day, month after month of isolation, howling in pain, enduring terrifying treatments; these were my ballet classes and Girl Scout meetings. Burn treatments stretch on in eternity. I finish them when I am exhausted, not because they end. I could be cut open, sewn, patched, or lasered for the rest of my life, there is always work to be done. It's a marathon that ends when I groan in weariness and cry, "Enough."

Just the same, a weird peace settles on me when I am in the hospital. Despite my anxiety and my fear, I also feel unexpected peace. I feel known in the hospital. The burn nurses and the doctors understand my life; my body sings them the song of what I have survived. We have a wordless understanding about my life, and I don't have to explain it. They already know.

For a recent procedure, I had to have an IV installed. This routine insertion always terrifies me, because my veins stand in rebellion. My veins have seen too many battles; they have been assaulted for more than 50 years. My veins loathe the sight of a needle and they have a stealthy plan of attack. My veins wave beguilingly, saying "I'm here, no problem, come on in!" As soon as the nurse inserts the needle, my veins roll away, softly, hissing, "Gotcha."

At the most recent procedure, the doctor displayed ninja vein skills. He took his time, slowly assessing the battlefield that is my right arm. He patiently chose his weapon, a catheter small enough to slip in, large enough for my operation. He numbed my hand ahead of time, and he slipped the catheter right into my yielding vein. I sighed in relief. The doctor explained how important it was to use the right sized needle. In gratitude, I played show and tell with him, showing him all the "cutdown" scars I have, on my arms and legs.

A cutdown tells a war-weary doctor everything he needs to know. Cutdowns are an emergency procedure in which a vein is surgically completely exposed, as a desperate ploy to gain vital IV access, because the other veins have collapsed. Nowadays, central lines are installed when a patient needs needle after incessant needle. Back in my day, they sliced my skin open repeatedly just to get the IV in. Multiple cutdown scars slice the interior of both of my arms and both of my ankles. There have been many emergencies, and many collapsed veins. I showed the doctor all my cutdowns wordlessly. Equally wordlessly, he sighed.

No one else understands, or perhaps wants to understand. I sit desolate in isolation, even though I am surrounded by love. I feel like a soldier who survived foreign imprisonment. I have been isolated and tortured in a strange land for years on end. To be honest, I don't think anyone wants to know about it. So, like a soldier, I smile bravely and I tell you that I am fine, that it was so long ago.

Sometimes, I try to talk about my suffering. Here is what happens when I do. I talk about the fire, the hospital, my childhood. If I have a good listener, she tunes in for a while. I feel awkward going on and on, even though I am only at the beginning of the tale. I don't want to dominate the conversation; I don't want to complain. So, I ask her, my listener, something about herself. Usually the listener takes the bait. She begins to talk about herself, and my tale is over. I have not begun to fully disclose the extent of my trauma, but she thinks I am done.

Sometimes when I talk, I feel an energetic withdrawal. My listener has had enough. She can't take the pain of listening. I know when this happens and I change the subject.

Once, in my third round of psychotherapy, I spoke about the hospital at length. I described the children's ward, the bandage changes, the screaming. The words poured out of me, laying it all out. Although I was crying, I felt giddy with the joy of unburdening. I went on and on. My therapist listened kindly. Then, his expression changed. My therapist leaned back in his chair, and something closed in his face.

"What happened?" I asked quickly. I stopped talking. Silence grew in the room, which had just then been buzzing with my gruesome tales.

"What do you mean? Nothing happened; I am listening. Keep going."

"No, something happened. It's like you were here and then you weren't. You went away, somehow."

He looked at me calmly. We paused. He thought a bit, looking down. "OK. I think I couldn't take it anymore. That's what happened. I just couldn't listen to it anymore."

That moment shattered me. I was relishing sharing my story and having someone fully there. The sting of being suddenly alone sucker punched me. Still, I appreciated my therapist's honesty. He didn't make me feel crazy. I knew in my gut when he was with me, and when he wasn't. I also appreciated his acknowledgment that he was overwhelmed by my story, and had unconsciously protected himself.

But, here's the thing. If my own therapist can't handle what I have lived through, how many other people can?

My loneliness hovers around me like a smoky haze. It follows me around the house, when I walk the dog, when I call a friend. It whispers, "No one understands you. Not really. Not now. Not ever. No one wants to know."

Once, I started going to a burn support group. Everyone there had a family member with them. I came on my own. I sat in the circle, introducing myself. When you sit with burned people, you have to make adjustments to each face. "Oh, that face has one eye. That face has a crooked nose. That face isn't scarred at all, no wait, there it is, right on the forehead." I adjusted to their faces and they adjusted to mine. But then a young man walked by, offering snacks. He couldn't have been older than 15, but it was hard to tell because his face was obliterated. A mass of raised scars lay where his nose, mouth and forehead should have been. He was non-verbal.

I cried through the entire meeting, ninety minutes in all. I cried because I came alone. I cried because I had to adjust to everyone's face, which meant that everyone had to adjust to mine. I cried for the young man with no discernible face at all. I cried to be in a room of burned people. I cried for everything I had been through.

Even there, in a room full of kind-hearted burned people, I felt alone. Because my fire wasn't just a fire; my own mother set that fire and left me in it. Their burn treatments, anesthetized with modern pain medicine, were nothing like my burn treatments, scrubbing the skin off my writhing body while I screamed. And although we didn't discuss it, I don't think anyone there had also lived through four family suicides.

The smoky haze of loneliness settles down the most for me when I am working. The haze lowers to the ground, and is barely visible. How ironic; when I am working with clients, I rarely talk about myself. So, it is not because I am sharing that I feel less lonely. Perhaps there is a relief in knowing that I can't share, therefore I don't feel rejected that no one wants to know. But it's more than that.

When I see clients, my loneliness is put to work. It lies in the office, swirling around me like a cloud on a low-lying mountain. The smoky loneliness beckons silently to my clients. "I know. I'm here. I understand. Talk to me."

I used to work in a rehabilitation hospital, years ago. There was an old woman I treated there once, in recovery for a hip replacement. She had anxiety and needed extra support to get through the physical therapy process. I liked this woman, Hildie. She was 90 years old, petite, polite, white-haired. She had emigrated from Austria many years ago, when she was only 16. She spoke with a charming German accent.

I worked with Hildie for the three weeks she was in the hospital, giving her psychological support to endure rehab. One day, we began to talk about how she came to America. "You came when you were 16, right? Your family immigrated?"

"No. They didn't. I came alone." She looked at me sideways and glanced away.

"You came alone? You came here alone when you were 16?" I said, astonished, reconsidering this frail old lady, sitting with me. "Why would you choose to come to America all alone at the age of 16? That is so young to move to another country without any support. What strength that must have taken. Why did you do this?"

She looked at me carefully. There was silence as we regarded each other. I sat patiently, my smoky swirl of loneliness sifting around me, calling to her as well.

After some moments of silence, she answered me. In her soft German accent, she answered quietly, "I was raped."

"You were raped?"

"I was raped. I have never told anyone. Never."

"You were raped, 75 years ago, and you have never told anyone?"

"I have never told anyone, until you."

After 75 years of silence, why did Hildie tell me about her trauma?

To be sure, I asked. But further, I asked in a way that let her know I truly wanted to know. That is the key to trauma. We survivors know who wants to know, and who doesn't. We can feel it in our guts, the level of interest, the genuineness of the concern. Our smoky haze of loneliness calls out to each other, "Hello? Hello? Shall we talk? Shall we?"

LESSON NINE A:

Listening to someone's pain with an open heart is a tremendous gift. Sometimes, an attuned presence is all a person needs to feel great relief from suffering.

LESSON NINE B:

Do whatever you can to utilize your strengths. Go to school and put effort into education. The joys of rewarding work will live inside you every day, filling your life with meaning and purpose.

TEN

Two Husbands

"Are you positive?" Mike gave me a hesitant look as he set the bag of groceries on the counter in our small kitchen.

"The strip turned blue," I said. "I'll see the doctor next week but I'm pretty sure... I think I'm pregnant!"

Mike stepped toward me quickly, wrapping his arms around my waist as he lifted me off the floor and spun me around. Giddy with excitement, we laughed as I locked my legs around him and he carried me to the bedroom. The groceries could wait.

Young and carefree, we were euphoric at our accomplishment. Spontaneous sex in the afternoon? Why not? We were like young playful animals, oblivious to the changes that lay ahead when middle of the night feedings, diapers, trips to the pediatrician, and the nonstop demands of parenthood would change everything.

That afternoon, we were on the golden cusp of creating our own family, a miracle in many ways and one that would enrich our lives like nothing else before. But making the shift from young couple to parents would also irrevocably change our relationship, forcing cracks in our marriage, our trust in each other, and our intimacy.

* * *

I still don't know how I, of all people, wound up married. And not once, but twice. The odds were that I would never have one husband, never mind two. I couldn't get a date to a school dance until I was 18. Boys liked hanging out with me—we would laugh, and talk about music and theater and stuff, but nothing would *happen*. While they just wanted to be pals, I hoped they were interested in dating me.

They were not. Boys weren't into me that way.

Who could blame them? I had terrible scars over 65 percent of my body, scars that had stolen my breasts and my bottom lip. Reconstructive surgery had helped—I had transitioned from hideous to actually pretty, if you could overlook the scars. But that's a tough sell for a teenage boy. And seriously, what boy wants to overlook breasts?

Which is why it was hard to imagine that I would one day find someone to love me. That I'd marry. That I'd have a family of my own.

At age 14, I began keeping journals. I had at least 15 volumes by the time I was 37, when I heaved them into the trash in a fit of disgust. You might think my journals would be fascinating because, as the survivor of horrific burns, I had lived through so many unique experiences. But my journal musings focused on boys — inane desperate ruminations about boy after boy after boy, none of whom ever returned my interest. The endless dreary documentation of my wasted affections horrified me.

I can still remember the names and faces of some of those boys. There was Darren, Danny, Mark, Joe, David, Ken, Ben. Even now, as a happily married woman, my heart sinks to remember the long string of boys (and, later, men) who were indifferent to my romantic interest in them. But I kept at it. I even dated Jimmy. I knew he wasn't right for me—I got good grades, had nice friends; he was a druggie, and barely able to graduate high school. But, I could at last tell myself I had a "boyfriend." Eventually (actually, it was only one week after our first date), he broke up with me. "It's your scars," he said in a flat voice. "I'm just not into you." I will give him points for honesty. No other boy had ever been so truthful.

Friends would say, "No, you are beautiful, Lise!" They would say that my spirit was so warm and lively, ". . .you can't even see the scars once someone gets to know you." Or, "Even with the scars, you're pretty." I do have a sweet, oval-shaped face, thanks to my Memere, and an easy smile. And a cute figure. I'm funny and engaging. I have a clever wit. I can be flirty. My Deguire charm, passed down from my Pepere to my father to me, serves me well.

All of this is why more than a few boys and men were almost into me. I could feel their interest, and my hopes would rise. But at some point, there would be a pull back and withdrawal. Perhaps it was because, as my mother explained, I was "smart and strong." But I noticed that my smart, strong girlfriends managed to get boyfriends. I figured it really had to do with my third-degree burned skin, ruined breasts and crooked lip.

Still, I was not alone or unpopular during my teenage years. Most of the time I had a lot of friends. In fact, from high school on, my friends functioned more or less as my family. My mother was done being a mother, and my father lived far away. My beloved brother was dead. So, friends became my source of love and stability. This worked well for many years. As much as I missed having my own family, I was grateful that friends took me in as part of theirs. When I was little, my best friend Melissa and her family became my first pseudo-family. Then, in eighth grade, after we moved, I was instantly adopted by my friend Karen. When I moved again in tenth grade, Susan's family adopted me, inviting me over every year on Christmas day. In college, I acquired yet another group of friends and their families. I was never without a family; it just wasn't my own.

In my twenties, my family of friends began to fade. It's not that anyone stopped being my *friend;* it was the natural shift that occurred when couples pair up, eventually starting families of their own. Still, it took me by surprise. Slowly, I descended into the deepest, darkest depression of my life. I had been through much worse: the loss of my family, the death of my brother, the fire. But I had always had the love and support of friends, and I had rarely felt completely alone. Now, it seemed as though there was no one to call family. My parents were busy with their own lives. My friends were busy with their new loves. And no man wanted me.

I was so depressed that I contemplated suicide, repeatedly. In graduate school, I eyed the Tylenol™ bottle that was under a government recall (possibly laced with cyanide), wondering if it would kill me. I took two pills, just to see, but I didn't die——they were just Tylenol.

I was relieved. I was disappointed.

And so, who would have imagined that I would end up married not once but twice? That I would have two daughters of my own? That I would wind up living in a beautiful home, in a lovely town, sending out Christmas photos of my family every year?

Before all that would come to pass, I was in psychoanalysis with a kind, classically trained psychoanalyst named Dr. Slap. (I'm not making that up.) Although his name was aggressive, he was a gentle, witty man. I worked with him for three years, lying on the couch as Dr. Slap sat behind me, pleasantly cracking an un-analytic joke or two. We explored my history, my relationships, my parents, my lost brother. I told him about my friends and all the men who weren't interested in me. I cried and cried and cried. My depression seemed to know no bounds, although I managed to function and do what I needed to do.

Dr. Slap helped me enormously, yet I remained terribly sad.

One day, lying on the couch, I mentioned a new thought. "I keep reading about that new antidepressant, Prozac™."

"Yes?" His low voice rumbled from where he sat behind me.

"They say it works surprisingly well and that there are hardly any side effects. I've been wondering. . . do you think it could help me?"

"Hmm. You know, we don't usually *medicate* depressions like yours. Your depression comes from your life circumstances, from being alone, from all the losses. We use medication for biological depressions, not ones like yours," he explained. "Your depression comes from your life itself."

"I know. I know that. But, just the same, do you think we could try it?" Dr. Slap didn't answer right away. I had been in therapy with him for years; he knew how miserable I was. "Yes. OK. Let's try it."

One day after starting Prozac, I felt a little better. I knew that such an immediate response must be a placebo effect; Prozac normally takes at least three weeks to work. Dr. Slap and I agreed on this, however, that placebo effect never went away. I just felt better and better the longer I took the medicine.

For the first time, I felt hopeful about my life. I no longer faced my future with dread, sure that no one would ever love me and that I would always be sad and alone. I began to consider that I might have a happy life on my own as a single woman. I started to think about adopting a baby by myself in my 30s, if I never married. I took a jazz dance class, leaping about unselfconsciously in my blue leotard. I decided to audition for theater again, something I hadn't done for years.

MIKE — MY FIRST REAL LOVE

Anyone will tell you that when you no longer care about meeting someone, you will meet someone. I met Mike during auditions for *Godspell*. He was slim and well-built, with beautiful blue eyes and a military-style crew cut that showed the strands of silver in his black hair. He was charming, slyly flattering, with a wide, sweet grin. My heart beat faster every time I saw that smile. And, he sang beautifully.

The director cast the show a few days later and I was in. Susan, my best friend, was also cast. She and I would be performing in *Godspell* together again. Mike, however, was not cast. I couldn't believe it; it made no sense. Disappointed, I assumed I would never see him again, but I couldn't stop thinking about him. After a couple of days, I asked the show's producer for Mike's number. I dialed, telling myself it was fine that I was making the first move.

"Hello, Mike?"

"Yes?"

"This is Lise, from the *Godspell* auditions?"

"Oh yeah, hi!" He seemed truly happy to hear from me.

"I was so sorry that you didn't get in the show. . . ."

"Me too, Lise. It's nice that you called though. Hey, do you want to get together sometime? I have tickets to see *The Crucible* next Saturday. Want to go?"

Mike picked me up, and we chatted non-stop on the way to the play. My heart sang with excitement. At intermission, I practically skipped out of the bathroom, unknowingly trailing a long piece of toilet paper that was stuck to my boots. Silently, Mike moved behind me and stepped on the toilet paper, freeing me from mortification. I could feel my face turn red, but he smiled widely at me and I knew I was with a gentleman, a gentleman who also loved theater.

Still, looking back, it was easy to see hints of what would go wrong in our marriage right from the get-go. For starters, Mike later told me that he hadn't known who I was when I called that first time. He just pretended to. Although I had been completely smitten with him, he had been flirting with me and two other women at the audition. When I called him, he had trouble placing my name with a face. So, when he came to pick me up at my house, he literally didn't know who would open the door. Grinning, he later confided, "It could have been any one of you. That dancer, your friend Susan, you. I liked all of you."

Did he say he was glad it was me? I don't remember.

There were other signs too, but none of that mattered at the time. I was wild about Mike and, miracle of miracles, he felt the same about me. We were very different people who, improbably, seemed compatible. I thought he was funny and charming. He made me laugh hard. He was physically affectionate, which was soothing and thrilling after all my years of loneliness. We both loved theater and music, and we loved to travel. We drove through the Austrian Alps once, singing every song from *The Sound of Music*, in order, reenacting every line. We managed to cover all the parts and sing every word. Our undoing was "The Lonely Goatherd." A low alto, I began to warble Maria's soprano *oh ho ho ho, lady o-de-le-ho. . .* and we lost it, laughing uncontrollably as we drove through the mountains under a brilliant blue sky.

Mike seemed to know me. My heart felt snug and safe when I was with him. We moved together at a matching speed. He came home to me every night, warm and affectionate. We loved to cuddle. We were like two kittens, curled up together, sharing our body heat to keep alive. He helped me heal and made me know love was possible.

Mike proposed on Christmas Eve, at my mother's house. I knew he was proposing then, because we had already discussed it. He felt bad that he couldn't afford a ring for me, although he did have an old ring from a previous engagement gone awry. I thought for a minute. I really wanted to get engaged. "It's OK," I offered, "I don't mind. You can use that same ring."

"Are you sure? You don't mind?"

"No, I'm so happy. It doesn't matter to me."

And it didn't matter, not at the time.

But later, it mattered. I got engaged to Mike with a ring that he had left over from his last engagement, a used ring, because he didn't have money for a new one. At the time, I was thrilled to be getting engaged at all, and I loved him. Later on, though, that same scene seemed tawdry and sad. So, who changed? Me, not Mike. I'm the one who changed.

HAVING BABIES

When I was a child, Dr. Constable examined me countless times, but one visit was so surprising that I remember it vividly. I was ten years old, standing naked in front of him. He assessed me carefully, from many angles, looking at the patterns of the scars up and down my torso.

"You will be able to have children, Lise," he pronounced, in his patrician accent.

I peered up at him, quizzically. It had never occurred to me that I couldn't have children.

"Your tummy will be able to expand enough that you will be able to carry a baby to term."

I did carry two babies to term, my daughters, Julia and Anna. But growing babies inside my scarred torso was torturous. I don't have a body like other women. Only the lower half of my torso expanded with pregnancy. The upper half of me stayed taut, requiring the lower half of my belly to balloon out massively, stretching and stretching to accommodate the baby inside. My inner organs were crushed from all sides, making digestion extremely uncomfortable.

My body is *not* normal; I suppose it is now time to explain how. Isn't this what you have wanted to know all along? Reading about me, haven't you been wondering, "But what does she really look like? What is that body like? How bad is it?"

It is everyone's unasked question.

OK, then, I will fully expose myself. I am used to it. I have been naked in front of more doctors and nurses than you can imagine. All burn patients wind up being reluctant strippers, shedding their clothes again and again for medical experts, hoping to be healed.

Let me take you back over fifty years, to when I was a patient on morning rounds led by Dr. Constable. I lie on my hospital bed, naked. The newly minted doctors under his charge push the flimsy curtain aside and burst into the small space, ready to evaluate me. Here I am.

My body is two-thirds more scar than skin. The burn scars are tough and hardened. They are shot through with little lines from surgeries, where I was sutured back together. The scar might be smooth or rough, too red or too white, raised or depressed. Sometimes the scar degenerates into whirls of uneven tissue, chaotic looking. The texture is uneven. It is skin-madness; no order, no symmetry. Skin entropy. Because scar tissue is thicker than regular skin, you can't see my bone structure under the skin, nor can you see muscle definition. So, despite the fact that I am thin and I work out, my scars obscure my efforts. The scars sit on top of all my efforts, proclaiming themselves to be the most important feature of my body.

Scars live on 65 percent of my body. Scars march up and down my left arm. My right forearm stayed mostly untouched but my upper arm is completely scarred. Scars sweep across both of my thighs as well as the back of my left calf. My abdomen, buttocks and genitals remain blessedly untouched, which is how I was able to deliver my babies. When the fire ignited, I was wearing exactly one piece of clothing, a pair of red cotton shorts. (It was summer and I was a free spirit, and not wearing a shirt.) The shorts protected my most vulnerable areas from harm. Looking closely, you can still follow the shape of those toddler shorts on my body, outlined in unsullied white flesh. Because I was shirtless, my chest, back, and waist are the worst; they are "circumferentially scarred." This means that I am banded 100 percent by tight, thick scar, front to back and front again, from my waist up to my neck. I do not have normal breasts. Scars snarl their way down my neck. The lower half of my face is scarred. I have a chin implant. My lower lip is reconstructed.

How I wish I had worn a shirt.

Had I worn a shirt, my chest and shoulders would be outlined in white, unmarked flesh. My middle-aged breasts would sag now but still be dignified. I long to have breasts. Where normal breasts should be, I have hard pouches, bulging from saline implants. They look like bumps on my bony chest. Stuffed inside a bra and then inside a shirt, my shape is fine, attractive even. But shirtless, my chest consists of a mass of scars, bumpy and hard. I admire other women's breasts as if I were a man. Breasts beckon to me as something exotic and attractive that I have never had.

Breasts are so beautiful.

My beleaguered breasts did stage their own miracle, twice. I have virtually no regular breast tissue; it was almost all eviscerated in the fire. When I gave birth to Julia, I knew I would not be breastfeeding, yet a lactation consultant marched into my hospital room after Julia was born. I could have strangled her for her insensitivity. Irritated, impatient, and self-righteous, I hissed, "I can't breast feed because I don't have breasts. Surely that is obvious to you! Seriously, please leave. I just need to get some sleep."

"OK, if you're sure I can't help. . ."

"Obviously not!"

"Well, here's my card, just in case."

Four days later, at home with my newborn, I bent to lift her from the bassinet when she began to cry. I felt something wet fall on my foot. I peered up at the ceiling, thinking there was a leak in the roof. But there was no leak. Confused, I looked around the room. I noticed that my shirt was wet. Opening my blouse, I found that my right breast was oozing droplets of milk.

I dug out the lactation consultant's card, mortified that I had been so dismissive of her help. I called and explained my odd situation. She couldn't have been kinder. She told me how to reduce the milk in my breasts but she also suggested that I try to get whatever drops I could into Julia's tiny mouth. "It's gold for her," she said. Two year later, when Anna was born, the milk returned, oozing out of my skin like white lava.

You might assume, given this body that I live in, that I am physically inhibited, that I avoid touch, that I hide myself. I do not. I only cringe with shame when someone rejects me. Inside my own head, I accept my body. I think my parents gave me this gift. They were both physically affectionate. And because I was raised with little parental recognition of my injury, I was also raised to be physically unselfconscious. In this one way, their minimization of my injury worked to my benefit. Because they treated me like nothing was wrong, I learned to think about my body like nothing was wrong. I paid a heavy price for this emotionally, but physically it has worked for me. I like to hug; I love to be touched. My body is scarred but responsive. I am surprisingly uninhibited. If you like me and my body, I am good to go. I am rarely focused on what my body is not. I think this is one of the positive things about being burned young: I don't remember having a different body. This body is what I have. I don't need the lights out when I undress. It is only when I see disappointment in another's face that shame washes in on me. Mike did not make me feel shame.

Neither does my second husband.

* * *

Doug was my boss. He had been one of the people to interview me for my job as staff psychologist two years earlier. From the day I met him I found him tremendously attractive. He was six feet tall, slim and lanky, with thick, wavy brown hair, a beard, and round glasses. Anyone who knew me would have spotted him as my type immediately. I was hired for the job and settled into my work. As is the norm for the staff of a mental health clinic, we all worked closely together, sharing clinical information as well as the emotional burdens of doing therapy.

I tried not to fall in love with Doug but, over time, I fell. Two years after I started my job at the hospital, he became my direct supervisor. This meant we would have an hour-long meeting every week to discuss my cases. This hour became the highlight of my week. We were not flirtatious, nor even the slightest bit inappropriate. But I loved talking to Doug. I loved his intense blue eyes. We shared stories about cases, finding the humor in the sadness around us. My feelings for him grew and my heart ached to act on them.

One day, completely unplanned, Doug came into my office to discuss a work issue. Our conversation suddenly shifted to personal matters and gradually, the conversation deepened and deepened. I don't know how we went from discussing computer support for a database to a frank reveal, but somehow we got there.

"Lise, I'm not sure how to say this. I love how you smile. I think about you a lot." He took a deep breath. "I think you. . . you are the kind of woman that I could soar with."

Silence filled the air. I stared at Doug. He had said the words I had been hoping, and fearing, to hear. That day was both the happiest and most wrenching one of my adult life. I knew that conversation meant the end of my marriage and the start of my new life, all wrapped into the same breath-taking, bittersweet moment.

"I feel that way, too, Doug."

"You do?" He was incredulous. I couldn't believe how surprised he was. I figured that my adoration for him had been perfectly clear, as much as I had tried to hide it.

"Oh, yes. I do."

We gazed at each other. Doug kept muttering, "You mean, I'm not alone in this?"

I whispered, "No, I feel the same way."

Over the next five days we discussed our feelings and our fears about our situation. We were overjoyed that our feelings were mutual and overwhelmed with the implications of being in love. During those conversations, Doug said many things to me, but the most precious was, "I will treat your girls like they were my own." Given my experiences with John (my reluctant and ambivalent stepfather who had never embraced his role), Doug's promise meant the world to me. I had known Doug for two years, and I believed him.

Mike and I separated in 1999, five days after that life-changing discussion with Doug. We divorced two years later; the divorce was my fault. While there were difficulties in our marriage, I was the one who ended it. I broke Mike's heart. I never meant to hurt him and, when we married, I never thought I would. Still, life had played an ironic joke on me. After decades of no boys being interested in me, I had fallen out of love with my husband, and fallen in love with another man. Most surprising, this other man loved me, too.

Instead of no one ever wanting me, suddenly two men wanted me, at the same time.

MARRIAGE AND MY SKIN

Doug and I have been married now for almost two decades. We paid a heavy price — emotionally, financially and ethically — to be together. It has been years since the days we were madly in love, breathless to be alone with one another, when my body would throb in anticipation of his touch. We are now a typical middle-aged couple, hanging out, paying bills, traveling, teasing each other. You wouldn't guess that we had had such a turbulent start. It's been worth it. We are good companions. We understand each other. We make each other laugh. We have each other's backs. We take care of each other. We have built a fine life together.

Doug is married to a burned woman. To meet me now, you might think my scars are not so bad. But my scars under my clothes are another thing entirely. My dear friend Joe, who is an architect, once said that my scars are like marble, swirling with different colors and patterns. He said this with warmth in his voice, his deep brown eyes smiling at me. I think he truly sees me that way. But he has known me for 40 years, and we love each other dearly. He sees the best in me.

There was a boy I hurt once, back in college. To my surprise, we dated for a bit. I desperately wanted to make it work, because he liked me, but I wasn't into him. In the heat of the rejection, he stared hard at me, his face contorted with rage. This boy spit out, "I like another girl at school anyway. She's beautiful. She doesn't have scar tissue for tits." There was nothing he could have said that would have wounded me more. He struck at my greatest shame with vengeful precision.

None of this body feels beautiful. It doesn't matter how many people have tried to tell me that I am beautiful just the way I am, because it just isn't true. *Nothing truly beautiful to the eye requires an adjustment period to get used to the sight.* Although I am accustomed to myself, I can cry to think of how beautiful I might have been. I was a gorgeous little girl. My daughters glow with beauty, much of it from my ancestral lineage. Sometimes when I look at them, I am reminded that I was robbed of the life of a beautiful woman. I freeze writing these words. This is my body. The body I have. I want to be beautiful, desirable, lovely.

I cannot say that Doug doesn't notice my scars, but I can say that he completely accepts them. Partly that is because he finds me physically beautiful in other ways; partly that is because we are connected in ways beyond the physical. We share similar professional training and respect each other's talents and skills. We root for each other, taking fierce pride in each other's joys and accomplishments. We laugh. Our values align.

One thing that Doug has given me, that no one ever has, is a feeling of complete security. He is a man of his word, and he is steadfastly protective of his family. He works hard and is 100 percent reliable. Given my neglectful, abandoning mother, my rage-filled father, and my brother who left me, Doug's complete stability heals me. I never worry if he will be there to help me — he always is. I never worry if he will do his best to protect me — he always does. He is stable, functional, hard-working and solid. He is therapy personified for me.

I will always feel bad that my first marriage ended, and that I was the one who ended it. I believe in keeping promises; and I am sorry for the hurt I caused Mike. For some chapters of my life, I feel heroic — the

Flashback Girl, yellow cape flying. This chapter of my life, when I ended my first marriage, is not one of those. In my mind's eye, I see my cape drooping desolately about me.

When I was deciding whether I could end my first marriage, I thought about my life up until Mike, when I was on my own. My dear brother was dead. My father, erratic, was now deceased. My mother had repeatedly neglected me. Mike meant well but he was unreliable, and my life had come to revolve around supporting him. I had two daughters to raise, daughters who needed me to be the parent that I had never had.

I looked at Doug and I saw someone who would actually look after *me*. I knew he was stable and capable, and that he would take care of me, as much as I would take care of him. I thought of the first four decades of my life, which were about me fending for myself. I decided that I was entitled to have a life in which I myself would be taken care of, too.

At the same time that I gave myself permission to leave Mike, I made a promise. I knew that a divorce would do damage to my daughters, deep damage. I promised that I would do everything I could to give the girls what they needed. I would stay in the same town; I would keep them in the same daycare; I would not move, then or ever, away from their school; I would work hard to keep a productive relationship with their father, despite his anger toward me; I would do every single thing I could think of for them. But I needed to be with Doug.

Doug has kept his first promise to me: He has, indeed, raised the girls as his own. From day one, he was an involved stepfather, watching, feeding, playing. He did everything a father would do, and more. He is a model of male stability—competent, generous, reliable and sturdy. As much as the divorce has hurt the girls, I know they have gained from having Doug and his family in their lives.

Regardless of the pain of our divorce, I will always be grateful to Mike, because without him there would be no Julia and no Anna, our two amazing daughters. And I am grateful to Doug, my dear life partner, who has given me the love and stability I needed to finally have a happy life.

THE LONELINESS THAT LIVES INSIDE

Despite this happy ending, inside me lives an emptiness. After my decades of loneliness, perhaps I don't know how to not feel alone. Perhaps it's just who I am now. Perhaps I have lived a life of such extremity, so many bizarre circumstances, that no one can fully understand me—or perhaps that is just what I tell myself.

I do not always feel known by my husband. He can be too busy, too independent, too overwhelmed. Sometimes I have to tell him, "I've been crying. I'm upset."

"Really? Why? What's the matter?"

"You didn't hear me crying in the other room?"

"No, I need to get this project done." He sighs loudly through his nose. I watch him wrestle between his need to get his work done, and his emotional commitment to me. I stand, shifting my weight. He sighs again, but softer now.

"OK, tell me. What's the matter?"

My needs can be inconvenient for Doug. His mother was a very independent person, and he would like that from me, too. I am self-sufficient in many ways, running my own business, capable, but not as much as he would like. We disappoint each other in this way. He would like me to be more independent, so he doesn't have to worry about me. I would like him to be more tuned into me, so I can feel known. It's a tightrope that we walk together, balancing, accommodating, tipping over now and then.

Maybe nobody knows who I am, or ever will. What tethers me, now that Dr. Constable, my beloved surgeon, is dead? Do I still float dangerously off the ground, drifting out toward the moon, no one there to hold my foot? And yet. . . .

Here is what Doug inscribed in my wedding ring: In tiny letters on the inside of my gold band are the words, *"I see you."* Doug keeps me on the ground. He tethers me with love, care and commitment, healing my deep wounds, pulling me into health. In the end, I am here, floating away no longer. Doug and I are here, together, and thank goodness. It turns out that I would need his support more than I ever thought.

LESSON TEN:

You never know when love will finally come for you. Stay open and be hopeful. This is a cliché, and is very hard to do. But love comes when it comes; it can't be forced. In the meantime, work on yourself. Get strong and healthy so you are ready for the love when it arrives.

ELEVEN

Sex, Danger and Goodnight

LIONEL, A SEXUAL PROLOGUE

My dad worked hard to keep his friends. He kept in touch with the people he loved, over many years and many miles. He had Glens Falls friends, college friends, Oyster Bay friends, Upsala friends, theater friends, and so on. He earnestly kept in touch, bristling with righteous indignation if people didn't return his efforts in kind. He kept all of his friends, for as long as possible. Most of them were delighted to be in his favor. At his last birthday, his 66th, he threw himself a massive party. Scores of friends spilled out of his house, drinking, laughing, and celebrating him.

When I was little, we frequently visited Dad's old friend, Beth. She had been a college friend of both my parents, back at Eastman School of Music. She was a pleasant blond woman, friendly and warm and bland. Her husband, Lionel, however, was most memorable.

Lionel was a tall man, hunched over due to childhood polio. He walked with a black cane in his right hand, limping along. His left arm was twisted and weakened from the polio as well. He was balding and plain, but friendly. I liked him, because he was nice to me in particular, always wanting to spend time with me. I was lonely, and hungry for attention.

Given that I was unsupervised for much of my childhood, I have often thought it was a miracle that I was not targeted and abused by men. I would have been an easy mark for a sexual predator, as I was needy and often alone. I think my scars made adults feel sorry for me, though. I have no other explanation for how I traveled so much of the world, without protection or guidance, and was never hurt. No one robbed me, touched me, or hurt me. I was left alone.

Lionel was the exception. I think because Lionel himself was physically disabled, my scars did not move him. So, ironically, although I walked alone through New York City hundreds of times as a young girl unharmed, I was molested in my own living room when I was six years old.

On that day, my mother was in the kitchen. I don't know where my father, Beth and my brother were. Lionel was friendly, and he wanted to spend time playing with me alone. I was delighted to have his attention. My family was busy, and Judy Hannigan and the other girls were swimming without me again. We sat together in the small living room, sharing the blue tweed couch and chatting away.

As always, I was fresh off a surgery. With Dr. Constable's expert help, I now had a reconstructed neck and chin. He had even rebuilt a new bottom lip for me. My new lip was red and swollen and it stuck out too much, but I had a lip again. I was glad to be able to talk normally, and I chattered away.

"Would you like to play a game?" Lionel inquired, innocently, eyes wide.

"Sure, what kind of game?"

"Well here, let me show you how to do it," said Lionel. He smiled at me encouragingly. I smiled back, with my new lip. He leaned his hulking body closer and started kissing me. I kissed him too. That seemed OK. People kissed all the time.

"Now we do this," Lionel muttered, and he opened his mouth and pushed his tongue into mine. I thought this felt funny, but it seemed like an interesting game to play. I'm not sure how long we played this special new tongue game. No one stopped us. No one came in.

Later on, I hopped excitedly into the kitchen. My mother was sitting alone at the small Formica table. "Lionel taught me a new game!" I squealed to her.

"Oh? What was it?" she said, without much interest, but listening.

"It doesn't have a name, I guess, but it's a tongue game," I earnestly explained, and told her all about it. My mother's face turned pale and frozen. I got the clear impression that she did not like this tongue game, and that I shouldn't do it anymore. So I knew that part was bad somehow, even though she didn't explain why.

Beth and Lionel stayed for the rest of the afternoon. We continued to socialize with them for years. I was not warned to stay away from Lionel, nor do I think he was spoken to. I was not supervised when Lionel was in the house. My father was committed to his friendship with Beth which seemed important to him. As I got older, we didn't see them as often, but they were still friends.

After my parents' divorce, I saw Lionel one more time. My dad and I had gone into New York City to see a show, and Beth and Lionel were there, too. I was 15 years old. Scars aside, by this time I was a fairly pretty girl. I had long thick wavy brown hair, and soulful green eyes. I wore loose colorful Indian dresses, and I had a certain style that people were drawn to. Lionel was drawn to it, too.

At the intermission of the show, Beth, Lionel, my dad, and I gathered into a chattering circle of people. Lionel spotted me, and he crossed through the circle of friends to say hello. He limped toward me, cane in his weak-ened arm, and he extended his strong right arm to embrace me. He held me strongly, remarkably forceful with his one good arm. He pushed his face into mine, and forced his old tongue into my mouth again, holding my head so I couldn't escape. He kissed me right in front of his wife and my father. I submitted, waiting for it to end.

When he let me go, I looked to my father for help. Somehow, my father hadn't witnessed what happened. He was chatting away to Beth, cheerfully. Somehow Beth didn't see either, or perhaps she pretended not to. I stood there, shaken, waiting to get away. When intermission was over, my dad and I went back to our seats.

"Didn't you see that?" I hissed at him.

"What?"

"Lionel forced me to kiss him. He did it right in front of you."

"What? No, come on, you are exaggerating."

"Yes, he did, right in front of you. He held my head and put his tongue in my mouth."

"Oh, come on. If he did, Lise, just let it go. Don't make a big fuss. He's my friend."

I was stunned. My dad didn't seem to care what Lionel had done to me. When I was six, and Lionel kissed me, I thought it was a new game, and it didn't upset me. This time, however, I was 15, and I knew very well that I had just been assaulted. What's worse, my own father was minimizing it.

I sat through the rest of the show, shaken. I can't even tell you what show we saw, which is a major indicator of how upset I was. But, I was barely present. At the end, Lionel and Beth came up to my father and me to say goodbye. Lionel's brown eyes were gleaming. He limped directly toward me, leaning in to kiss me again.

"NO!" I bellowed, as loudly as I possibly could. "NO!" and I held my right hand up in front of me, like an indignant police officer. "NO!"

Lionel stopped short. He looked at me. Beth looked at me too, curiously uncurious about why I was speaking to her husband so abrasively. My father quickly said his goodbyes to his friends, and we fled.

It was dark out, and my father had to take me from New York City to Oyster Bay. It would be a long night for him, as he would then have to drive home to New Jersey. We sat in his little red Volkswagen Rabbit together. It was quiet. The overhead lights flashed on us as we sped on the expressway.

I thought a long time. "I am never going to see that man again," I finally said.

My father was upset, but not with Lionel. He was upset with me. "These are my friends. They have been my friends for a really long time. When I have parties, they always come. You come to my parties too. I can't not invite them, just because you don't want to see Lionel. Be reasonable, Lise."

I looked out the car window into the dark. I was calm and firm and fearless. For once, I didn't care if my father got mad or yelled at me. I was resolute. I was done. "If you invite him, then I am not coming. You invite him if you want to, but I won't be there. I am never going to see that man again. Never."

That is where we left it. That is how we left it for 20 years. We would discuss it one more time, my dad and I. But I never did see Lionel, ever again.

"I AM WHAT I AM" *LA CAGE AUX FOLLES*

I was eight years old when I first learned what "gay" meant. It was the early 1970s, and homosexuality was not an everyday concept for a kid, not even in my family. Somehow the word had come up in conversation, but I didn't know what it meant, beyond the "happy" meaning in my musicals like "Glitter and Be Gay," from *Candide*. My father carefully explained to me that gay people were people who loved and had sex with someone of the same gender. "Yuck!" I said. "That's gross!"

My father regarded me with calm intention. "You mean like Frank? Frank is gay. Is he gross?" Surprised, I thought of our beloved friend Frank, who was a frequent house guest. He was tall, with blond curly hair and a sweet smile. He taught me how to waltz, teaching me the steps as we glided along to the overture of *A Little Night Music*. We stepped together, one-two-three, one-two-three, and he whirled me around the living room. I glided, holding his hand, pressing my face against his strong chest.

"No," I said to my father, "Frank isn't gross at all."

"OK, then. You mean like Holly? Holly is gay too. Is she gross?" I thought of my dear cousin, Holly, who had come to stay with us the summer after the fire. Recently burned skin itches terribly. Because my back was burned, I couldn't reach it myself, so I hounded my family to scratch me. My dad would say, "Don't keep scratching Lise's back, Holly, or she will never stop asking." Holly didn't care. She scratched my back anyway, surreptitiously scratching me against my parent's wishes.

Every day, Holly played with me. Once, when I took a bath, she read *Winnie he Pooh* aloud, while I listened transfixed in the tub. Holly enacted the Hundred Acre Woods characters, giving them each of them their own little character voice. Piglet sounded tiny, sweet and anxious. Eeyore sounded deep and mournful. I had never had so much fun taking a bath in my life.

"No, Holly isn't gross either."

"There are a lot more people you love who are gay. Do you still think it's gross?"

"No," I concluded with a smile of my crooked mouth. "I guess it isn't." My dad and I looked pleasantly at each other.

"Right," said my dad.

That was the end of my prejudice against gay people. It was a good thing too, because there were a lot of gay people in my life at that time, and there always would be. If you love show tunes, singing, theater, and tap, then you love gay people, even if you don't know it.

My third grade best friend was a gay boy, unbeknownst to both of us. Michael and I both loved theater and movies. He liked to direct his own productions, and he would often cast me in the starring role, which was thrilling. When we weren't putting on plays, we liked to pretend we were in *I Dream of Jeannie*. Unfortunately, we both coveted the part of Jeannie so we had to take turns.

My mother had given me a bunch of dress-up clothes, which, in retrospect, consisted of a weird assortment of her cast-off negligees. There was one bright pink polyester baby-doll nightie that Michael and I both loved. He would don the nightie, and we would wrap a bright scarf around his head. There was a bit of rouge involved, which brought out his high cheekbones. He didn't really look like Jeannie, but he did look pretty and we were pleased with the effort.

Someone else important in my life was gay too, but I didn't know it yet. I'm not sure when is the best time to tell your daughter that you are secretly bisexual. It isn't an easy conversation to have, for anyone. I am fairly sure, however, that my father picked one of the worst possible times.

(To give my dad his due, what follows may not have been his worst conversational gaffe. He had the art of saying exactly the wrong thing at the wrong time to the wrong person. He once cheerfully congratulated a female colleague on her pregnancy, only to be grimly informed that she was not pregnant. Then there was the time that he was standing with a fellow professor, watching a woman walk down the college pathway. "That has got to be the homeliest woman I have even seen," said my father.

"That's my new girlfriend," said the fellow professor.

So, let's be clear, my dad really knew how to stick his foot in it.)

I was 13 years old and experiencing one of the most terrible years of my life. My parents were separated, my beloved Pepere was dying, my Siamese cat had run away, and my brilliant brother was a college drop-out. Our beautiful Glen Ridge House was about to be sold. Awful as all this was, in my self-absorbed way, nothing was as tragic as being the social pariah of seventh grade. I had been rejected and shunned by my group of friends, and no one else would get near me. Although I had hid my situation from my family for months, I reluctantly told Marc, and then my mother, what was happening to me. I hadn't yet told my father. I wasn't as close to him. He was still the lime coaster in my life, my last family choice.

It was March, and the girls had left their hate letter in my locker. I couldn't hide my social reject status anymore; I felt completely defeated. After dinner, my dad and I were cleaning up the kitchen. Marc had left the room, and it wasn't my mother's "night" to be home, so it was just my dad and me. I screwed up my courage, and I told my father my whole sad tale. I told him I had no friends, and that they had all turned on me. I told him about the hate note. I told him I was being harassed and bullied every day. I told him about my lunches in the school bathroom.

My dad listened attentively, but without surprise. I think someone had already told him about my situation. He asked a couple of questions but was otherwise without comment. I sat on top of the kitchen counter, leaning against the side of the refrigerator, and he listened to me patiently until I was done. I felt unburdened.

He regarded me calmly, his face engaged, his blue eyes sparking. "Well, now that you have shared your secret with me, I would like to share my secret with you."

I looked at him, from my perch on the counter. Sitting up high, I was eye to eye with him, my six-foot-tall father. This was not the reply I had expected. My dad was not the best at comforting words or saying the right thing, I knew that. But I hadn't anticipated some kind of Truth or Dare situation. Still, there was no point in objecting, and I wasn't sure I wanted to. Everybody loves to hear a secret. Maybe he was going to tell me something wonderful, like we were going on a surprise vacation, or he was going to buy me the horse I asked for every Christmas. Curiously, I waited for him to continue.

"I'm bisexual. I like to be with both women and men," he said, confidently. "It's like being gay but I am also straight. I'm both."

"Oh," I said. "Really? Wow."

We fell into silence.

I tried to be open to this conversation, but inside I shut down. My insides were blank and I seemed to have no feelings. I went automatically into my mode of just-get-through-the-moment. It was how I survived many things, like bandage changes and school lunches. My body knew how to stop feeling emotions and just survive the minute.

On the other hand, my father was looking for affirmation and acceptance. For him, this was a moment of great vulnerability. I knew that I should be supportive and open-minded. My job now was to support him. To me, this was one of many moments in a lifetime of emotional mismatch with my father. I had laid out my worst problem for him, looking for support and guidance. Instead, he laid out his worst problem to me. He thought this was a reasonable response, matching vulnerability with vulnerability, which it might have been, had I not been his 13-year-old daughter.

For a while after my parent's separation, my dad dated numerous women simultaneously. Eventually he settled into an apparently committed relationship with one woman, Irene. They stayed together for many years, although they never married or lived together. I liked Irene fine, she was smart and kind and devoted to my dad. She was good to my Memere, better than I managed to be, frequently visiting with her in Glens Falls. Irene was a good companion to my dad, fun and warm and up for adventure.

It was the mid-80s now in New York City. I was in graduate school, my father was with Irene, and my mother and John were together. John's brother Harry, whom I liked a lot, was active in the gay scene in New York. He had been successful in business and now he had a new job, raising money for research. There was a new disease attacking gay men in New York. Nobody understood what was happening. Otherwise healthy young gay men were catching this weird "gay cancer" and dying.

It wasn't long before Harry himself came down with this illness that we now call AIDS. He had been a handsome man, with dark curly hair, friendly brown eyes, slim and well-built. Within months, he wasted away to a sad sack of withered bones, barely able to hold up his own head. He died shockingly quickly. John, already mortally wounded by his daughter Jackie's suicide, fell further into alcoholism and emotional decline.

Then we lost Frank, our old family friend, who had been Dad's student. Frank was the fellow who had taught me how to waltz, many years ago, whirling me around our spacious living room. Frank was the first person my dad had mentioned, when he was teaching me to accept gay people. But Frank, like so many gay musicians and artists, succumbed to the "gay plague" all around us.

It was terrifying to be gay in the 80s and it was terrifying to love gay people in the 80s. I worried about Joe, one of my best friends, the future architect who likened my scars to marble. He was a beautiful young gay man. He assured me that he was careful but his words felt inadequate to the danger. I worried about many other men I knew, my theater and singing friends. I did not worry about my father, because he was with Irene. Also, he assured me that he had been tested and he was fine. He practiced safe sex.

For theater lovers in New York, we watched horrified as revered artists died, one by one. Michael Bennett died of AIDS in 1987. He was a gifted director and choreographer, best known for his iconic production of *A Chorus Line*. Larry Kert died of AIDS in 1991. He was the original Tony in *West Side Story*, blessed with one of the most beautiful tenor voices in American musical history. There were so many deaths of young men, made all the more bitter by lack of support by Ronald Reagan's government.

It was a dark and grim time. Men in the prime of their lives were wasting away, often rejected by their homophobic parents, and dying alone in pain. Gradually, the medical community found some medicines that prolonged life, even if there was no cure. In the beginning, a healthy man could die from AIDS within six months. By the mid-90s, that man might live for two years, with AZT and good medical support.

At the age of 89, my Memere died. She had lived to see her only son's marriage collapse and her only grandson kill himself. She was, to the end, a devout Catholic, going to mass, praying the rosary, and not eating the candy she loved. In the end, I had not been the best granddaughter to her. After my parent's divorce, we no longer took our monthly family trip to see her. I began to be less and less interested in making the trek up to Glens Falls. My father nagged me to visit my Memere, or to write her, or to just call her. I did these things, begrudgingly, and not as often as I should have.

My father, on the other hand, was a good son to his mother until the day she died. He called her weekly and visited her monthly. He took her for dinners, and long drives in the countryside. No one could have been a better son, particularly as he lived hours away. He did his duty, responsibly and cheerfully. And then, after she died, he no longer had to make his Catholic mother happy. In his sixties, for the first time, he was free.

After Memere died, my father came bursting out of the closet. To be sure, he had not been fully in the closet for many years. Many of his friends knew he was gay, or bisexual. I had known since my traumatizing conversation sitting on the kitchen counter. But now, my dad felt fully liberated. He slowly ended his 20-year relationship with Irene. And he found himself a boyfriend.

I wish I could say that I liked James, but I never did. On the surface, you might accuse me of prejudice towards gays, or perhaps towards Blacks, as James was a gay Black man. I hadn't expected my dad to be in a relationship with a man, let alone a much younger Black man who delighted in placing gilded candelabras on our previously dignified Steinway. It was not an easy adjustment for me to make. But my dislike of James extended far beyond my need to be more tolerant. James was not a good person.

James was untruthful. In the beginning, he told my dad that he had won the lottery, and that a huge fortune was headed his way. In the long run, it turned out that he had never won the lottery, and in fact he was quite poor. James also had emotional outbursts which grew increasingly violent. Once, he became so outraged that he poured bleach over his own two Chihuahuas. My father did his best to rescue the little dogs, catching them and dousing them in the sink. My dad wept when he told me this story, so upset that James would hurt his own dogs.

Another time, James hit my dad. My dad ran out of his own country house into the snow, calling the police to come and take James, who was threatening him. James was taken to the local psychiatric unit, ironically the same place where Irene worked. She could hear James, screaming her name down the hall as he was "escorted" forcibly to the unit.

All those behaviors were reprehensible. But here is the reason why I hate James: James killed my dad. He may not have meant to, but he did. When they first got together, my dad and James did what gay men did in the 1990s: they went to get tested for AIDS together. My dad's results were negative; he did not have AIDS. James told my dad that his test results were also negative, and he did not have AIDS. They had both been tested previously to this, and again, both declared that they didn't have AIDS. Thus, being declared negative twice, they safely entered into a supposedly committed, monogamous relationship, which may or may not have involved condoms. But two years later, James had AIDS. And six months after that, so did my father.

My father had many faults but he was not a liar. He would never have lied about something as crucial as AIDS status. And if he promised to be monogamous, I believe he would be monogamous. So my only conclusion is that either James was HIV positive all along, or he cheated on my dad during their relationship. James had already established himself as a liar. Because of him, my father was going to die.

My father was brave in the face of his grim diagnosis. He did not wallow in self-pity or bathe in anger. He was practical in adversity. He began to attend an AIDS support group in New York, he started taking AZT, a medicine that extended the length of life of most AIDS patients, and he started therapy. He traveled to Iceland and went on his usual plentiful road trips to visit friends all over the country.

James died quickly, and I did not mourn him even one minute. My father did mourn him, even though they had broken up well before his death. James was my father's one long-term adult relationship with a male lover. Even though I couldn't stand James, my father was sentimental. I felt sorry for my dad. It was awful that he had finally come out of the closet, into a full gay identity, only to get AIDS, lose his lover to AIDS, and be facing death so quickly himself.

My dad's strength began to fade. He lost weight. He had wanted to lose weight all his life and had always complained about his belly. Still, this was not the way to lose weight. He became skinny and then painfully bony. My dad also began to lose his piano skills. He could still play by ear, but he would forget where he was in the piece. Sometimes he couldn't think of a song at all. He still played some shows for money, but at some point he lost these side jobs. A colleague whispered to me, as delicately as he could, that my dad was no longer able to play professionally, so they had to stop employing him. He didn't want to tell my dad to his face.

I began to worry about my father's driving skills. He lived alone in the middle of the country, in a tiny one-bedroom house. My dad's little historic house lay along a small country road, miles from the nearest town. There was no way for Dad to get anywhere unless he drove. I began to hear stories of him getting lost, not knowing where he was. One day, I got in the car with him and he drove. The car sped along, erratically. I clutched the handle of my passenger door in fright. We entered a traffic circle. My father thought we were in a parking lot, and stopped the car to park, right in the middle of the traffic circle.

"Dad!" I yelled. "Move the car, keep going! You are in a traffic circle; you can't park here!"

When we got back to his house, I explained to him about the traffic circle. He told me he thought he had parked well, and he was aghast that he had been so confused. "Dad, I have to talk to your doctor. You can't drive anymore, you just can't. I'm sorry but you aren't safe."

My dad was compliant with me. As much as he had had a temper all his life, that temper was now gone. In turn, I began to be less afraid of him. I don't know whether his mortality had given him a new perspective on life, making upsetting things seem trivial in comparison. I don't know whether he was just too incredibly fatigued to bother getting angry anymore. But, he became a sweet, compliant, and patient man. When I told him he couldn't drive anymore, he said "OK" and that was that. He didn't yell at me, or fight me, or call me a bitch. He just said "OK" even though it meant the loss of his freedom.

Bill Deguire had been a good friend to many people, and many people now wanted to be there for him. Scores of people offered to help him, any way they could. One of his students was particularly devoted to my dad. I got on the phone with her, and we came up with a system. Every day of the week, someone would drive out to dad's country house to visit, or to take him to appointments. The visitors had a planned rotation. Some came out weekly, and some were on a less frequent rotation. There were so many people who wanted to help my dad that it was a cheerful system, full of supporters who truly wished to be there. So, even though dad could no longer drive, he was never alone for long.

Although we had a great visiting system going, Dad did not last long at home. His medical needs became too serious, and he needed someone with him every day, all the time. I was with my first husband, Mike, and we lived 90 minutes away in Philadelphia. Mike loved my dad too, and he would have done anything for him, but we couldn't live with Dad. Instead, I found an inpatient hospice program, and Dad was moved to this facility.

Dad lived in the hospice program for a month until he died. He had cytomegalovirus, and he had wasted away from 180 pounds to 120. Weakened, he spent his time in a wheelchair or in bed. Although there was a grand piano there, he didn't have the interest or energy to play it. He did enjoy visits, and he got a lot of them. He also got many phone calls. I was there one day when he got a call from an old student. The student said, "Hi Bill, what are you up to?"

My dad croaked out weakly, but with a devilish smile, "Well, I'm dying! How about you?"

I visited Dad as often as I could when he was in hospice. We listened to music and sat together. He talked less and less as time went on but I got to know my dad better, underneath all the anger he had always had. He was a sweet person, underneath all that.

My dad never understood how much his anger had damaged our relationship. He was not inclined to introspection. He shocked me one day, however, with an unexpected apology. My dad never apologized for any of his behaviors, so it came out of the blue.

"I'm sorry about Lionel," he murmured quietly. Lionel, the man who had French kissed me when I was six. Lionel, the man who had forcibly kissed me when I was 15, whom my dad had always defended.

My dad had gotten close to some distant relatives over the previous couple of years. He had learned that they had been sexually abused when they were little. They had told him how damaged they were by the abuse. He had told me their stories. He had never told me that he was reconsidering mine.

"I'm sorry about Lionel," he said softly to me.

"Thanks, Dad. Thanks for saying that. I know," I said. It was a rare moment of vulnerability, and the only apology he ever gave me. It meant the world to me.

It was March of 1996. My cousin Mary, who was devoted to my dad, had heard rumors that there was a new medication coming out which drastically helped with AIDS. But there was no information about the medication in the news, and my dad's country doctor knew nothing about it. Hospice also knew nothing. A week prior, my dad had decided to stop eating. He was dying, but not fast enough for him. Living with end-stage AIDS was awful and he wanted to be done. So, Dad told me and his hospice team that he was going to stop eating.

My cousin, Mary, encouraged me to try to get my dad to eat, because maybe this new medicine could save him. I was exhausted and skeptical. My kind-hearted cousin tended to believe in all possible intervention for her loved ones, and my dad wasn't interested in that. We discussed the mystery medicine. I asked Mary to see if she could find more information about the new medication, other than the vague rumor she had heard.

Mary called the Gay Men's Health Crisis center in New York City, and managed to speak to a doctor there. He was cautious on the phone, and discussed the brand-new medicine, but he was dubious that it could help someone as terminally ill as my father. The doctor said it might help him, but the odds weren't good. My cousin relayed all this information to my dad. Dad weakly considered it, but he concluded that the chance that a new, unreleased medication could be such a miracle was too small. He continued on with his plan, refusing food, and releasing himself to death. I brought him my old stuffed Kitty from my hospital days, long ago. Dad lay with Kitty in his arms, blankets tucked all around his bony frame.

On April 3, 1996, Bill Deguire died. We held a going away party in his room the night before. We played music he loved, and his closest friends came by to wish him bon voyage. He was unresponsive by this time, with his eyes closed, lying in the bed. By all intents and purposes you would think he was completely unconscious, but I noticed something. When anyone would tease him, or say something funny, my dad would twitch in response. It happened again and again, a perfectly timed twitch. It seemed like he was able to hear us, even though he couldn't speak, and that his body was letting us know that he had a funny response to make, even though he couldn't get the words out. Twitch. Twitch.

My husband Mike and I slept in his room that night. Mike woke me up in the middle of the night. "I think your dad is getting ready to go," he said. We turned on the light, and saw that Dad's breathing pattern had changed. He was "actively dying" as they say in hospice. We sat up with him, talking to him. I sat on the bed, holding his hand.

Dying is harder than you think it would be. The body just doesn't seem to want to stop. Again and again, I thought Dad had taken his last breath, only to see his chest rise again, almost in spite of himself. It was agonizing to watch him, unable to stop breathing, unable to let go.

My dad had been raised Catholic, but he had left the church years ago. I knew that the ideas of Catholicism would not be comforting to him now.

But he had embraced the idea of the afterlife, in his own way. He had read the book *Life After Life* years before, in which multiple people reported after-death experiences. Dad believed those stories. He believed that he would be reunited with his loved ones when he died. So, I had an idea of a way to help him stop struggling.

"Go to Marc," I said to my dad. "Marc is waiting for you. Go to him now." The room was silent. He did not breathe.

And then, that minute, my dad died.

My dad died in April of 1996; in June, a new class of drugs was released for the experimental treatment of AIDS called protease inhibitors. With this new medication, many AIDS patients were saved from death. AIDS became a chronic disease, instead of an invariably fatal one. There were stories of men at death's door who took the medication and resumed their lives again. But my father was not one of those stories. My father had already gone.

Now it was just my mother and me left, the last two Deguires. But our bond would break irrevocably, sooner than I ever imagined.

LESSON ELEVEN:

Try to be there for your loved ones when they are dying. In those moments of complete vulnerability, a space of love and forgiveness can unexpectedly open up. Don't be afraid to be there. Hold hands, sing, and sit with your loved ones. These moments may become the treasured memories of your life.

TWELVE

Being a Mom

The best therapy of my life was not with a therapist at all; it happened when I had my children. I had Julia when I was 33, and Anna when I was 35. I always knew I wanted children. Even when I was single for so long, I knew I would have children, regardless of marriage. I would have had a baby on my own, and taken care of it somehow. There was never a question in my mind.

I anticipated a lot about having children, but I didn't know how complete motherhood would make me feel. My girls did not replace my brother in any way. My first family collapsed into a yawning sinkhole, never to be seen again. But, the miracle of childbirth gave me a family of my own again. I no longer felt alone; I felt like I belonged somewhere again.

My girls are extraordinary people. They are different and alike. The most obvious way they are alike is in their appearance. They look so much alike that acquaintances mistake them for each other. Kids in high school used to get them confused. They have been known to share IDs. They share the same blue eyes, arched eyebrows, big smiles, wide cheekbones and thick blonde hair. Their faces sing with beauty.

My girls are also alike in having strong voices. They speak with confidence, freely sharing their thoughts, feelings and opinions. Like me, both of them have gotten into conflicts, fiercely advocating for their strong values, standing up against incompetence, hate or intolerance. The girls also both have wonderful senses of humor. Julia is outrageous, a clown, unafraid of looking foolish. Near the Eiffel tower, she videoed herself dancing alone to "Bad Girl," wearing a black raincoat, hood up, and sunglasses. Anna is sardonically observant; she is a wonderful mimic. She mocks me, noticing how I always blow my nose whenever I pee. They make me laugh and laugh.

I love being a mother. When my girls were babies, I loved holding them in my arms, all wrapped in their blankets. I don't know how anyone could find babies boring. Yes, babies don't do much and yes, they don't say anything. But you can see the light of recognition in their eyes. Every week they do more, understand more, respond more. Julia was an exciting baby. She was hyper-alert from the day of her birth, eyes tracking everything around her, eager and intrigued. Anna was more mellow, and she gave off a deeply peaceful vibe. Holding her as a baby, she would gaze into my eyes with peaceful assurance, as if she were comforting me.

My mother loved her grandchildren. She helped me with Julia when I first brought her home from the hospital, staying overnight to help with feedings. Despite my burned breasts' earnest attempts, I couldn't breastfeed, so it was all hands on deck for bottle feedings. My mom would watch her sometimes when I was sick or when I needed to go out.

One weekend we left Julia with my mother, and Mike and I went away overnight. Julia was about six months old. Mike and I were eager for a quick break. We hoped to have at least one night where we didn't have to get up in the middle of the night with the baby.

When I returned to my mother's house to pick up Julia, my mother declared that they had had a wonderful time. They had even gotten out to see a historic home in the town, which was on display.

"Julia did OK with a historic tour?" I asked. It didn't seem like something she would tolerate, my active, lively baby.

"Oh yes," said my mother, "she was sleeping so I left her in the car."

"You left Julia alone in the car while you went on a tour of a house?" I asked, my voice unsteady. "Was that safe? That doesn't sound safe. What if she were in trouble while you were gone, or someone took her?"

"That wouldn't happen. It's so safe here that I just leave my purse in the car, and the car doors unlocked. She was fine."

I was stunned to realize that my mother had left my six-month-old daughter alone in a car, unsupervised and out of eyeshot for at least 30 minutes, with my mother's purse next to her and the car unlocked. Furthermore, as I asked her about it, my mother showed no sign of recognition that she had put Julia in danger. She gazed at me calmly, but with a quiet criticism, because I was clearly overreacting.

On a deeper level, something deep inside me rumbled and shifted. What kind of mother was this? Who was this woman, so unaffected by concern for her granddaughter's safety? A mother is supposed to care more for her children's safety than perhaps anything else in life. Did my mother actually feel this way? Or did she only seem to?

As my girls grew up, memories of my own childhood flooded back. Things that I had never contemplated, noticed, or analyzed began whispering to me. Old memories flashed in my head, unbidden, with brand new hazard signs blinking. What kind of mother leaves her four-year-old alone in the hospital for most of the time? What kind of mother lets her severely disfigured kidergartener walk alone to school amid taunts and jeers? What kind of mother lets her five-year-old get a contact high from marijuana and finds it funny? What kind of mother leaves her depressed 13-year-old daughter alone in a house every other weekend for five straight years? Decisions that I had taken for granted began to appear starkly different, now that I had children of my own. Behaviors that had flashed as glamorously hip and laissez-faire now revealed themselves to be frank child neglect.

With each passing year, I would involuntarily contrast my young daughters' experiences with my own at the same age. Both girls were toilet trained at the normal age, around two years old. In contrast, I had been toilet trained at six months. My strict Minnesotan grandmother had declared that I was the kind of baby who could be toilet trained early. Thus encouraged, my mother started sticking me on the potty at six months, and I somehow figured out what I was supposed to do, the first Good Girl accomplishment of my life. This was a story of pride in the family, told again and again throughout the years. I was such an unusual baby! So advanced! But now, I understood how abnormal it was to expect and demand that a six-month-old be out of diapers. My entire childhood, every story, began to seem twisted and distorted.

ARRESTINGLY BEAUTIFUL; ARRESTINGLY UGLY

My younger daughter, Anna, was an arresting beauty as a toddler. Out in the grocery store, safely secured in the excitingly high grocery cart, she stopped strangers in their tracks. The sight of her large sea blue eyes, her wide toothless grin, her perfect white skin made strangers slightly breathless. "What a gorgeous baby!" they would sigh. Anna would beam her perfect smile back at them. Time would slow for a moment, the hassles of the day receding into the background. Beauty and the love of beauty overtook time. Baby Anna glowed in her gorgeousness and strangers smiled back at her with instant love, forgetting their troubles for a moment or two.

I, too, used to be an arresting beauty. Then I became an arresting ugly. I, too, can stop people in their tracks. Even today, after years of hospitalizations, surgeries and procedures, I can stop people cold if I'm in a bathing suit. Walking on the beach, sand between my toes, I concentrate on the sound of the waves, and the blue ocean stretched out everywhere. I do not concentrate on the faces of the strangers around me. If I were to, I would see their faces frozen at the sight of me, brows furrowed, eyes wide. Some people look shocked; some people look puzzled; some people look repulsed, children in particular. Little children shrink at the sight of my body.

If I allowed myself to see the looks of repulsion on people's faces, I would never go swimming again. So, I do not look. I look at the children digging in the sand, their little castles growing. I watch the seagulls. I sing songs in my head.

The antidote to the shock of the sight of me is connection. If I want to stop the arresting ugly, I talk to the person. I make clear eye contact with the boy who is staring open mouthed at my body. "Hello," I say cheerfully.

"Um. . . hi," he mumbles back, eyes darting away. He is embarrassed to be caught staring. He suddenly remembers that staring is rude.

"What are you makin'? That's a cool sandcastle."

"Yeah," he looks back at me, still cautious but interested to be actually talking to the scarred woman.

"Those look like great sand toys to build with. How do you use them?"

"Well, I use this one to get the water, and this one to dig with and this one. . ." and off he goes, chatting and showing off his toys. The arresting ugly spell is broken. We are now just two people talking about sand.

The conversation gently reminds the boy that I am a person. I am a burned person, but I am a person just like him. I speak, I have words, I have feelings. The trance of my ugliness fades away and we connect.

I have broken the trance of my ugliness all my life, since I was four. I speak effortlessly to strangers; I can talk to anyone. I have had to learn, otherwise I would always be an Other, always on the outside, humiliated, alone.

All this is horrible. The pain sears me, I weep with the burden. I am exhausted. Don't think it is easy, although I grant you, I make it look easy. I am a trapeze artist, flipping and spinning in the air, effortlessly performing. You can't see my sweat, my exhaustion, my terror. I make it look easy so that people will talk to me and people will like me. But truthfully, the pain is excruciating. Being on the outside, being stared at, and having to be so fucking pleasant about it might just kill me someday. Someday I may fall off the trapeze, arms flailing, plummeting down to the floor. As I fall, I will shout, "Good. I'm so tired of this anyway."

My beautiful adult daughters weep at my words. They see me writing about my scars and my disfigurement, and they weep. They weep with sadness and rage.

"You are not ugly, you are beautiful," exclaims Anna, my sweet girl. In tears, she posts photos of me, with a heartfelt tribute to my face, my eyes, my hair, and my burned skin, which she says smells like ginger.

"Maybe you used to be ugly, but you are beautiful now, partly due to the privileges you have had," chimes Julia, in her low, resonant voice. We sit in a Cuban restaurant, during the intermission of an eight-hour play. "You've had the best medical care; no one would call you ugly now. Many people don't even notice your scars."

"They do if I'm in a bathing suit."

"Everyone feels ugly in a bathing suit," she quips with a wince. She has a point. We share a smirk together and sip our sangria.

Are my scars as bad as I say they are? Are they worse than I can even let myself imagine? The founder of the Phoenix Society, a national organization for burn survivors, once told me that I was the prettiest burned woman he ever met. Two brilliant plastic surgeons have labored over my skin for a half century, suturing, lasering, reconstructing. Although I have had a lifetime of suffering, I have also had a lifetime of care. Thousands of doctors and nurses worked tirelessly to keep me alive and to restore my body. My health insurance company must quake with loathing when my name pops up.

So, after all this care, all this expense, all this first world "privilege," am I ugly or am I beautiful? And if you saw me in a bathing suit, would your answer remain the same?

ACTUAL FLASHBACK ARRESTORS; AND ARRESTING WRONGS

A flashback arrestor is a tiny metal safety device. It looks like a simple cylinder, but the device stops flames or fumes from re-entering a container and setting the container on fire. Flashback arrestors have been in use since the 19th century. They are not new; they are not expensive.

A half-cent flashback arrestor would have saved me from my mother's carelessness. My mother might have doused and re-doused the barbecue, my little body right beside her. She might have carelessly thrown a household solvent onto the grill, saying "Oh, what the hell, I'm starving." In the moment of re-dousing, a lick of flame would have attempted to scurry up the opening of the solvent. At the opening of the can of Solox, however, there would have been the tiny safety device, a flashback arrestor. The arrestor, like the guard at Oz, would have stood mightily at the entrance and proclaimed, "Go away." The tiny flame flicker would have turned back, dejected and rejected. No explosion today. No little girl to devour.

But there was no flashback arrestor in that can of Solox.

My daughters laugh, with a mixture of pride and mortification, at my willingness to confront wrong. I embarrass them. Once, we were in a theater, waiting for a movie to start. A woman came into the theater with her family. The seats were mostly taken; the family was too late. The woman spoke to the man seated in front of us, and asked him if he would move his family down the row to accommodate hers. He glanced down the aisle; she was asking him to move to worse seats, instead of just taking the worse seats herself. The man said no. The woman towered above him, insisting that he move. The man said no again. Their argument escalated, getting louder. Finally, in a stunning move, the standing woman smacked the man right across his face.

I stood up in the theater. I glared at the woman and put my right hand straight out, like a traffic cop. "Stop that!" I bellowed loudly. The woman looked up at me, face blank, shocked. I stood there, with my hand outstretched, fiercely. Everyone in the theater was seated, but I stood and stared at her. I didn't say another word. My daughters rustled next to me. "Mom, sit down!" they whispered in mortification.

The standing woman looked at me, and then glanced away, eyes cast downward. She grabbed her family, and strode to the end of the row, slumping miserably in the undesired spots. The seated man relaxed back into his chair. I sat down too, ignoring my embarrassed daughters. The movie started. Civility reigned again.

I am my own kind of arrestor now. I work to arrest heartbreak and sorrow, self-loathing and hatred, self-recrimination and guilt. I usually work in the warm confines of my office, but my work also carries me well beyond those walls. Sometimes the work lies in a sobbing conversation with a friend. Sometimes I work in protest, joining action groups to combat hate. Sometimes the work literally stands right in front of me, like this inexplicably hostile woman in the movie theater.

I wish I could just stand up and shout "Stop that!" 20 times a day. I don't get to just pull on my super-hero cape and fly about the room. Usually, being an arrestor requires a lot more subtlety and sophistication. Combating hatred, self-loathing and neglect require elegant precision, months of observation, delicate rapport. Arresting the ugliness in life is a calling.

AS A MOTHER, SEEING MY MOTHER

When Julia turned four years old, she became the age I was when I was burned. She was so lovely, vulnerable and needy. Most of my consciousness was preoccupied with my daughters' safety and welfare. I couldn't imagine running away from Julia in a fire and leaving her there to fend for herself. Even worse, I couldn't imagine not visiting her in the hospital. I couldn't imagine leaving my little girl to strangers to see if she would live or die. I couldn't imagine letting her be in the hospital alone for one day, let alone for months and years of post-burn recovery. I began to wonder if my mother was capable of maternal bonding and protectiveness. I started to see the ways in which Marc and I had been left alone, adrift and without parental protection.

I started to get mad.

Every year, as my girls got older, I saw what had seemed like normal behavior through a new lens. Why did my parents leave me home alone, unsupervised for hours at a time, starting when I was five? Why didn't they help me with the constant bullying and verbal abuse I endured? Why did we move so many times, leaving me to fend for myself with new kids every couple of years? Why was I exposed to drugs at five years old? Why did my parents talk to me incessantly about their sex lives when I was a child? The more I could see, through the eyes of my own children, how vulnerable and needy a little girl is, the more outraged I became.

My outrage flared not only on my own behalf. I became outraged for my brother as well. I could see now how young he had been, how troubled, and how little protection had been afforded him. I became convinced that my beloved brother might still be alive, if only a parent had effectively looked after him. Depression was a treatable illness. Suicidality could be managed. Every week, I helped my seriously impaired clients manage their suicidality, and stay alive. But neither of my parents had prioritized my brother's emotional health or his safety. He was left to manage a serious, life threatening illness on his own, and he paid the price for their negligence.

Many times, I tried to talk to my mother about my new feelings, attempting to manage our relationship constructively. These conversations were tense and unproductive. Sometimes she would blame my father for what had happened. Sometimes she would blame my stepfather. Always, she would minimize her own behavior and its effects. She would look at me, green eyes cool and appraising, and I could feel her outrage. "Who are you to criticize me? What is wrong with you, to think such terrible things about me?" her eyes flashed, although she would not say these words aloud. Sometimes, rarely, she would apologize. Even on those few occasions, the apologetic attitude vanished quickly, and it would be as if we never had the conversation. Instead, my mother seemed to feel quite pleased with herself. My questioning of her was ridiculous, in her eyes.

My mother brimmed with pride and self-confidence. There was an unsaid expectation that I should be constantly remarking on her accomplishments. To her, she was a brilliant, cultured master of piano, singing, culinary arts, finances, hiking and stained glass. All these accomplishments were true, but I had entirely different needs from her. I hadn't needed a cultured master, I had needed an actual mother, to nurture and protect me.

It drove me crazy. To me, I now understood that she had been a severely neglectful mother, who had endangered both of her children's lives by her self-absorption. For her, none of this was true or had even happened. Indeed, she felt deserving of unending praise and recognition for her special talents.

And then there was the money. When we won the lawsuit against Solox, the explosive household solvent, both my mother and I were awarded a settlement. The amount I won was considered large at the time, but it was by no means enough to make me rich. Nowadays, the amount would be considered paltry. Because I was seven at the time, and a minor, my mother was put in charge of my settlement.

In many ways, Kathryn was a good choice to put in charge of my money. She was thrifty, never inclined to overspend, raised during the Great Depression. She was the kind of person who put water into a shampoo container to get three extra washes out of the bottle. She was the kind of person who never threw out food, because she accurately purchased only the exact right amount of chicken for each person at the table. She was the kind of person who reused a tissue four times before she threw it away, completely sodden.

The story goes that our attorney, Edward Swartz, told my parents that my settlement money could be used for my expenses. I am not sure what he meant by that, but my thrifty mother took the concept and ran with it. From the age of seven on, I completely paid for myself. My settlement money bought all of my clothes, my activities, my summer camp, my braces. My settlement money was used to pay for one quarter of our grocery bill. And, when my mother and I moved out on our own, she informed me that my settlement money would be used to pay for one half of the mortgage. I was essentially financially emancipated from age seven on.

Once I had children of my own, I was hit by the enormity of this decision. If my little Anna were horribly burned in a fire, I couldn't imagine using her lawsuit compensation to pay for her food and clothes. That money was there to give me some compensation for the lifelong pain and suffering of my injury. We were not a poor family. My mother was a psychologist and my father was a college professor. They could afford to buy my food and to pay their own mortgage. It was just easier not to.

I tried to talk with my mother about my feelings, but these talks were unproductive and futile, often leaving me more upset than I was before the talk. Not only had my mother been neglectful and selfish, she refused to acknowledge that these things had ever happened. Each talk left me more frustrated.

I decided to stop talking, to put my feelings aside, and to be the bigger person. At this point, my mother was in her mid-70s and divorced for the third time. She lived alone, and I was her only living child. I tried to repress my hurt and anger and just be there for her. She needed me.

The effort drained me dry, but I managed for a while. I included her in our little family, and had her over frequently to see Julia and Anna. The hardest part for me was my mother's unending need for recognition and praise, which was exactly the opposite of how I felt. But I tried to be there for her as much as I could.

Then came the final straw.

When my stepfather John killed himself, it was the third suicide in the family. My mother had been passionately devoted to him for decades, prioritizing her relationship with him over me and everyone else in her life. Her explanation was essentially that they had a *great love,* which I should understand took all precedence. She sounded like the teenage Maria in *West*

Side Story, perpetually singing "I Have a Love" to explain why she was leaving her family to be with her new boyfriend.

When John killed himself, my mother took a number of actions that shocked me. Unlike Maria, she did not seem particularly upset by his death. She was, however, deeply gratified to have received his last letter, in which he reaffirmed his love for her. Instead of sadly grieving his suicide, my mother kept talking about this letter, and how good she felt that he still loved her. Her absence of grief creeped me out. It reminded me of what I had said to Doug for years.

"If I die young, my mother will grieve me for three weeks. Then she'll be over it."

"Lise, no. That's not true. She's still your mother."

"I'm telling you. It won't really bother her. Distant friends will be more upset about my death than my own mother. Look at Marc. She never even mentions him. And it's not because it's too painful for her to think of him. She just doesn't think about him."

About five days after my stepfather's death, my mother went to their house, where they had lived before their second divorce. John had killed himself there, on the tiny rickety screen porch, shooting off his head with a gun. He had lain dead for days in his blood, before the police came. My mother went to the house a few days later to get it ready to sell. I called her that afternoon, to see if she was OK.

"How was it? How are you doing?" I asked. "Was it awful?"

"Oh I had a nice day," she said, surprisingly chipper. "It was pretty out and I got a lot done. At lunch, I took a break. I made myself a sandwich, and I sat outside on the porch. The birds were singing and it was so pretty."

"You sat on the porch?" I asked, my voice rising. "You sat on the screen porch and ate? *That* screen porch?"

"Yes, it was such a nice day, the birds were singing, and I had a lovely lunch."

This moment is frozen in time for me. I could not believe that my mother was so emotionally detached, and so unfeeling that she could eat a sandwich on the exact spot where her beloved John had shot his head off only days ago. And yet, I could believe it. I began to fully comprehend that my mother was simply incapable of deep emotional attachment. She felt love when it was convenient and pleasing to feel it. Otherwise, she was empty. Her emotional emptiness went far beyond my father, Marc and me. She just didn't feel bonded. She unconsciously faked it well, but deep down, there was no connection.

I was in agony. I felt an obligation to take care of my mother, as her only living child. Yet, my mother's very presence had become destabilizing to me. Every time I spoke with her, she said something upsetting from which it took me days to recover. One day, she talked about the organist for her chorus, a lovely warm man named Mark. He was a big friendly fellow, they enjoyed music together, and he had begun to invite her over for holidays. Happily, my mother declared, "He's the Marc in my life now!"

I reeled from her words, from the casualness about my brother's death. What kind of mother who loses her son to suicide can have a "new Marc?"

I would cry, ruminating over my old wounds. For her, as long as I met her needs, she was fine. For me, it was like taking care of a scorpion that kept biting me. She was happy, but I was paying a heavy emotional price. It was becoming difficult to take care of myself and my family, as I was so pulled down by the weight of the past.

Drawing on all my forces of detachment, I resolved to pull back, way back. Although I remained in contact with my mother, I called her less, and I was much less available. I became emotionally neutral, offering neither warmth nor conflict. I decided to have as little contact with my mother as I felt was ethically viable.

My mother confronted me, asking what was wrong, and asked to go to therapy with me to resolve our issues. No part of me wished to consent. I had already drawn the painful conclusion that my mother's emotional limitations were more than I could bear to handle. But it seemed only fair to try, one last time, to mend this relationship that had caused so much pain.

On the other hand, it began to seem like my emotional survival rested on remembering the past, without forgiveness or excuses. Sometimes, when I was alone, I would incant her failures aloud, detail after detail. I recited her betrayals again and again, like a rosary. "She abandoned me in a fire," was the first bead. "She wouldn't visit me in the hospital for weeks," went the second. "She isn't even sorry about it," was the third bead. I would move along to the emotional neglect, the financial exploitation, the neglect of my brother. On and on, I incanted the maternal failures.

It was my mother herself who had taught me how to rehearse. The language was piano, and my mother was the master. She sat on a dining room chair next the yellow piano bench. I sat on the bench, fingers curled, wrists held high. I played my scales, my arpeggios, my little pieces. My mother would listen carefully, face impassive, correcting my errors. When the lesson was done, she would write my assignments on a lined piece of paper. Practice D, A and E scales. Practice the Clementi sonata, the Kabalevsky. Practice at least 30 minutes a day, preferably with the metronome.

So, it was my mother who taught me how play the same piece over and over again until I memorized it. She asked for pianistic perfection. I couldn't give that to her. But I did learn how to rehearse. She thought I was learning Bartok. Instead I was learning how to remember what I needed to survive.

I rehearsed her crimes, not out of dark motivation, although remembering the crimes drenched me in bitterness. I recited her crimes to protect myself. In remembering, I could steel my usually warm and forgiving heart from further attack. It was my way of remembering who she really was, not who I wanted her to be, or who she thought herself to be. I had to be on guard so I wouldn't be hurt again. She couldn't help herself, because she was totally unaware of who she was.

There is a story about a frog and a scorpion that are stranded on an island by a flood. The deluge swirls around them, and the waters rise. The frog prepares to leave the island, and to swim across the river to safety. The scorpion pleads with the frog to be allowed to ride on the frog's back to dry land. The frog says, "But you are a scorpion, and you kill frogs. It's not safe for me to help you. I'm sorry, but no."

The scorpion whispers sweetly, "Why would I hurt you? You are my only chance at survival. I would be foolish to attack you and I would be so grateful if you would help me."

The frog, a warm-hearted if cold-blooded fellow, assents. The scorpion hops on the frog's green back, and off they go. The frog swims vigorously, little legs pumping, and the scorpion clings onto his back. They traverse the river, and land is in sight. The frog rejoices, knowing he is saved. In that instant, he feels a sharp sting in his back. The scorpion has just poisoned him.

"Why would you hurt me? I was saving you. Now we will both drown." The frog begins to succumb to the poison. His strong green legs weaken and dangle. The scorpion clings to the frog's back; they are starting to sink.

The scorpion hisses, "I am a scorpion, it is who I am. This is what I do." The frog and the scorpion drift down into the flood waters, drowning together.

My mother was a Scorpio. Her birthday was November 16. Her nature was what it was, and she couldn't help herself. I had been a good frog for her all my life, forgiving her and seeing the best in her. The only way to protect myself from her was to keep reminding myself, again and again, she is a scorpion. She is a scorpion. Do not let her on your back. She will hurt you. She can't help it.

My brother first tried to jump off the MIT building on September 16, but the roof door was locked and he went back to his dorm. He then lived one more month, exactly, until October 16th. On that day, he went to the 16th floor of the same building, and threw himself out the window. 16, 16 and 16. For years I wondered, what is with the 16s? I will never know for sure; dead brothers tell no tales. However, I did realize, years later, that my mother's birthday was on November 16. September 16, October 16, 16th floor, and then the next month it would be her birthday.

Marc was not a haphazard fellow. The 16s meant something. He was also a kind fellow. He would not blatantly blame anyone for his misery. But he might leave a clue or two, perhaps a clue for me to follow. A clue to say, *Lise, watch out.*

LESSON TWELVE:

Just because a person has the title of "parent" doesn't mean that they are able to function as a parent. Some people are not emotionally built to be parents. They may harm you tremendously, even if they don't mean to. See the parents you have for who they actually are and not for who you hope them to be.

FLASHBACK GIRL

An Animal Attachment Fable

There is a famous study on emotional attachment done by Harry Harlow in the 1950s. He separated infant baby monkeys from their mothers a few hours after their birth. In absence of their real mothers, Harlow created wire frames in the shape of mother monkeys, to use for studying infant emotional attachment. Some of the wire "mothers" had a milk bottle attached to them. The other wire mothers did not have a bottle, but were covered over with soft terry cloth. The orphaned infant monkeys all preferred the cloth mothers. They clung to the cloth mothers for comfort. They would only go to the wire mothers for food when they had to; otherwise, they hung on the cloth mothers. The baby monkeys all craved a soft touch more than they craved sustenance.

When I was a baby monkey, I thought I had a cloth mother. I certainly had a mother who told me, for many years, that she was a great cloth mother. But I found when I clung to her, that wires hurt my hands. I thought there would be cloth to hold, but somehow I snagged myself on wire instead. Probably it was my fault.

Sometimes I would try to cling to her, and wrap my baby tail around her, but she would be gone. She would go away and I didn't know why. Other times, she was too busy to notice me there. She would say, "Oh, you are such a needy little monkey," and I would hang my furry head in shame.

One day, the lights came on in the lab. Instead of the usual dim light, spotlights blasted. Colors were clearer, shadows disappeared. Everything looked different in the bright light. That day, to my shock, I saw that my cloth mother wasn't a cloth monkey. I was in the monkey lab, but my mother wasn't a monkey, not even a wire monkey. I realized that she was cold blooded; she was really an alligator. She was programed to lay eggs, and then she was programed to leave.

Stunned, I wept for my mother-who-was-an-alligator. "Mommy, Mommy!" but my alligator mother looked at me blandly. "What's the matter with you?" she hissed. The lights began to dim. My mother morphed back into being a cloth mother, it seemed. I could feel her cloth under my hands, even though the cloth now seemed stiff and scaly to me. Still, I clung to her, and fell asleep, knowing it was just a dream. I was such a silly baby monkey.

Another day, I was playing with my little monkey friends. We were swinging from the lights with our tails, catching each other in midair. We chattered with excitement. One of my monkey friends didn't catch me. He meant to, but he missed, and I fell to the ground. "Mommy!" I cried, scampering off to her. I found my mommy and clung on fiercely. Suddenly the lights came on again, and there was my monkey mommy, an alligator. "Oh Mommy!" I shrieked.

"What?" snarled the alligator. "What is the matter with you?"

"You're an alligator again!"

"I'm not. I'm not an alligator. I'm a soft cloth monkey, and you are a very critical, demanding and difficult baby monkey." The lights began to dim. I could kind of see my cloth mommy again, if I squinted. I felt bad that I had upset her. I am a needy and demanding little monkey. I was lucky to have my mommy at all, given how difficult I was. I clung to her, even though her scales cut me a bit. Maybe she wasn't the best cloth mommy, but she was mine and I loved her.

One day, my mommy left the lab. She left me often, so I was used to it. I swung from the lights with the other baby monkeys. I sat and picked bugs off my best friend, Susan, and Susan picked bugs off me. Because I was alone, Susan let me cuddle on her cloth mommy with her. Susan and I wrapped our tails around her mommy. Her mommy was so soft; I could bury my head into her. Susan slid her monkey hand over mine, so warm and gentle. We clung together forever. I felt the warmth and softness all over my baby monkey body. I drank it in, again and again. Soft, warm, gentle. Drink, drink, drink.

Hours, days, or years later, my mommy came back to the lab. The lights were low, but I saw her slithering in. She was dark green and low to the ground. Her cold eyes flashed at mine. "Hello, baby monkey, I'm back. Come to Mommy."

"No," I said. "I see you, Mommy. You are not a monkey. You are definitely an alligator. You don't feel soft to me. You don't feel like these other mommy monkeys."

"I am a very special mommy. I am fast and strong. Everyone knows how unique and wonderful I am. I don't know how you can be so critical of me after all I have done for you, taking care of you."

I looked at my mommy carefully. She seemed to look sad, but I didn't think she was. Alligator tears dripped down her face, but her eyes were cold.

"You are my baby. I will be a better mommy, although, truth be told, I think I have been a fantastic mommy."

I looked at the ground. She was the only mommy I would ever have. If I didn't have her, I would be on my own. How would I survive without a mommy?

Then I looked over at Susan. She was watching me, sleepy-eyed, hanging onto her mommy. She grinned. I smiled back, a little. I noticed all my other baby monkey friends. We were together. We could swing, we could play, we could pick bugs off each other. I had them; they loved me.

"I'm sorry Mommy, but I can't be your baby. You hurt me when I cling to you. Then, when I need you, you go away. Even when you are here, you are not who you say you are. You are a reptile. You aren't able to take care of me. It's not your fault. You just don't know how."

"What an ungrateful, crazy little baby monkey you are. How dare you criticize me, when I am such a special mommy. I'm out of here. I'm going to Switzerland." My alligator mommy slithered out the door. She left without looking back.

I stood on my back legs, my tail up. I cocked my head, and watched her go. I felt sad to say goodbye to the only mommy I would ever have. Was I sad? My heart thumped a little. Yes, I was sad. But my chest felt open, and I took a deep breath. I was also not sad. I felt safe. I felt free.

"Come over here," called Susan. "Stay with us, there's room for you."

I climbed up to Susan and her cloth mommy. Susan wrapped her tail around me. She whispered, "You are a good and brave baby monkey. Don't worry. We will make it through together. We have each other and we will be fine."

I looked at Susan. Her round brown eyes smiled into mine. I felt her mother's terry cloth softness underneath me. All around, the other baby monkeys cuddled and slept peacefully. I was a baby monkey without a mommy, but I was not alone. And I was safer than I had ever been.

We all lived happily ever after.

End of Fable

FLASHBACK GIRL

THIRTEEN

My Last Therapist

My mother found a family therapist named Cecily. She had a degree from an excellent local program, and seemed experienced and well-qualified. Before our first session, I spoke with Cecily on the phone. Most family therapists are gung-ho about keeping families together, understandably. That is usually what is best for a family. In my circumstances, though, I no longer thought this would be healthy for me.

I called her warily. "Is it your position that families should be in close relationship no matter what?" I asked her. "Because I have worked hard to pull back emotionally to protect myself. I'm not sure that it is healthy for me to be close to my mother. I don't know if it is possible."

"I understand," she said, kindly. "Sometimes it's like that. Let's see what happens."

My mother and I met with Cecily in her warm office in the countryside. She was small and thin, with long thick brown hair. Her couches burst with orange and brown pillows. I sat as far away from my mother as possible. Kathryn sat erect on the couch, her short gray hair neatly feathered back, wearing her silver glasses. She looked like any ordinary older mother, slim in her jeans and purple sweater.

I felt like a complete wreck.

Earlier, I had written my mother a letter, detailing my issues with our relationship and our history. I didn't want to inflict pain, but I had to give my mother the scope of our therapeutic impasse. In the letter, I asked my mother if she thought therapy was worth trying, given the bleakness of my perceptions about our relationship. I asked that we not go to therapy, unless she truly felt open to my feelings.

My mother found this letter to be objectionable nonsense, as far as I could tell. I think she thought the letter proved how disturbed and unreasonable I was. At any rate, we brought the letter in to show Cecily what some of the many issues were. Cecily tried her best to help us over several weeks' time. But, we could never get past the first issue: the fire.

My mother accepted no accountability for the fire. We couldn't stop discussing it, because we got nowhere, week after week. I couldn't move on to the myriad of other issues I had with my mother, because we couldn't reach accord on this first tragedy in our relationship. Finally, at the end of one session, my mother asked me in a calm but incredulous voice, "Do you really think I'm at fault for the fire?"

I stopped, breathed a bit, and thought a long time. Slowly, I answered, "I do not hold you responsible for the lighter fluid which was defectively canned, which caused the explosion." (At this point, I didn't know that it wasn't even lighter fluid that she used.) "I do hold you responsible for three things. You did not use proper fire safety, by pouring lighter fluid again on coals that you had already tried to light. You also started this fire unsafely with your four-year-old standing right next to you. And when the explosion happened, you abandoned me there to save yourself."

My mother looked at me, tense but calm. There was no emotion on her face.

"OK," said Cecily, calmly. "It's the end of our time today. We will meet next week. In the meantime, Kathryn, please contemplate Lise's response to your question. I want to get right back to this next week." I went home, drained but hopeful that I had clearly articulated my issues around this first tragedy. I hoped my mother would understand my points, voice true empathy, and perhaps even apologize.

At our next session, my mother came prepared. She had clearly remembered and thought about each one of my points. She seemed eager to respond. We sat down on the couches together. I picked up an orange pillow for protection. I placed the pillow over my heart, if it could block any pain that might be coming. After the opening pleasantries, we began.

"I have thought a lot about what you said. I want to respond to you. So, to your first point, I thought I was using proper fire safety but I obviously wasn't." That was the end of the first point.

OK, I thought to myself. That was kind of brief but let's keep going. She's not done.

"Second, I have never thought about the fact that I lit that fire with you standing right next to me."

Hmm. So, in the last 45 years, she hadn't once considered that starting fires is something one should avoid doing next to a tiny child? Most mothers would be overwhelmed with guilt and remorse for not being more protective. She didn't ever second guess that decision after the fire? Not once? I started to feel squirmy inside. This didn't feel right.

Now, she leaned into me. Calmly and deliberately, without warmth or remorse, her words came. "Third, in terms of leaving you in the fire, I'm sorry I hurt your feelings." She sat back into her chair. That was it; she was done.

I'm sorry I hurt your feelings.

At this moment, I collapsed. I burst into tears, clutching the pillow to my chest. I hunched over, bending over my knees and hyperventilating. I tried to breathe. I had never anticipated that her response to me would be so cool, so calculated, and so blind to everything that I had endured, because of her. I heaved with sobs. My mother went to touch my leg.

"Don't touch her," Cecily said quickly, with sharpness in her voice. My mother instantly sat back.

They waited until I got myself together. Gradually, I gathered myself, wiping my eyes and blowing my nose. Voice low, I said, "I just can't do this anymore. I can't deal with these sessions. I can't keep explaining the ways you have hurt me, and have you minimize and deny them. It isn't healthy for me."

I stopped, and breathed a bit more, looking around the room to ground myself. "This is what I think we should do. Mom, I think you should continue to work with Cecily. The two of you can work on these issues without me here. She can help you understand my perspective, so I don't have to keep explaining my feelings again and again. When Cecily feels like you are ready to talk to with me again, I will come back. We can work on it later. But I can't continue like this. It is just too traumatizing. It's too much."

My mother looked at me. After a while, she said, "I think if I have to look at myself the way you look at me, I won't survive it."

There was silence in the room. I understood what she meant. Her self-image was so grandiose and yet so brittle, based on so much unconscious falseness. Understanding who she really was and what she had really done to me, and to all of her family, might emotionally destroy her. I looked at her, trying to be as gentle as I could. "Then don't do it," I said. "It's OK. I understand. Don't do it. But, I need to protect myself and I can't be close to you. That is how it will have to be."

The room was still. I was crying again; my mother looked composed but angry. Things weren't turning out the way she wanted.

Through my tears, I said, "I'm sorry I am not able to be the daughter you wanted." Kathryn looked at me, as I cried and cried. Other than my tears, there was silence.

Cecily stepped in. She looked at my mother, and said, "And you are sorry that. . ."

My mother stared at her. There was a brief pause. Woodenly, Kathryn followed along. "I'm sorry that I can't be the mother you wanted." She said the words, but without feeling or intent. They were just the words that kind-hearted Cecily knew I needed to hear.

That was my last session with my mother.

* * *

A week later, I went to see Cecily one more time, this time with my husband Doug. Doug had always tried to help me keep a relationship with my mother. He is a family man, loyal and true. He was disturbed by the rift with my mother, and he kept hoping that I might find a way to manage it better emotionally, even though he knew full well that my mother wasn't capable of change.

Cecily sat down with us and heard his concerns. She helped us work out a plan that perhaps Doug could assist my mother more, when she needed something. She also assured Doug that we had done everything we could to try to fix this relationship, but it could not be fixed. "Your mother is a very limited person," she said, looking at me, "You did everything you could."

I asked if my mother had made arrangements to continue in therapy with her. "No," she said, "I don't expect I will ever hear from her. It didn't turn out the way she wanted and she will be mad at me now."

We sat with that for a while. Cecily looked kindly at me, and then at Doug. "It's OK. Your wife did a magnificent job. But it's done." I could have kissed her. After all the hurt and pain, the explanations, the therapy, the accommodations, for the first time ever, I felt released.

I was free. Or was I?

LESSON THIRTEEN:

If a relationship does you deep damage, repeatedly, and you have done all that you can do to fix it, it is OK to walk away, even if others don't understand. If a person can't stop hurting you, you have an obligation to protect yourself from damage. Sometimes, that is the only way you can be healthy. Not all relationships can work; not all relationships should last.

FOURTEEN

Flashback Girl Meets a Mighty Laser

I endured countless plastic surgeries as a girl and on into my twenties. My dear Dr. Constable, with his refined accent and earnest foot holding, took painstaking care of me. Nevertheless, each operation was extremely difficult. The pain seared me, the recovery process dragged on, and the surgical results were diminishing. Only so much could be done to help me look "normal," and Dr. Constable had done what he could. Yes, there were possible tweaks here and there, but the results weren't worth what I had to endure to get there. So, in my late twenties, I stopped having operations.

After that, I had minimal connection to the burn world. I had all my surgeries in Boston with Dr. Constable, but now I lived near Philadelphia, so I didn't have an ongoing relationship with burn services. There was an organization for burn survivors called The Phoenix Society. I don't remember joining them, but somehow they found me. I began to receive their periodic publication called *Burn Support News*. I received the newsletter, but I hardly ever read it. I put that time of my life behind me.

It was Christmas time, 2014, and I had taken some days off from my psychology practice. I was kicking around the house, looking for something to do, and I half-heartedly picked up my latest, unread issue of *Burn Support News*. I didn't feel like reading it, but I thought I should glance at it before throwing it out, like I always did. I began to leaf through the magazine.

Halfway inside, an article stopped me cold. It was entitled, "Lasers and Burn Scars: An Exciting New Era in Burn Reconstruction" by Dr. Pirko Maguina. Dr. Maguina described a new laser procedure which dramatically improved the appearance of burn scars, even scars which were decades old.

Fractional laser treatment began to be used around 2008 for burn scars. The laser makes thousands of tiny columns of new controlled burns in the scar, reaching all the way down to the deepest layer of the skin tissue. The skin then re-heals itself. The skin remains scar tissue; once you have a third-degree burn, you will always have scar tissue. But, because the skin has been re-wounded in an orderly grid pattern by the laser, when the scar heals, it does so in a more even fashion. As a result, the burn scar grows back flatter and softer. The procedure itself is done on an outpatient basis. It involves little pain afterwards and no donor sites.

I read Dr. Maguina's article with astonishment. No one had ever claimed they could make old burn scars improve in appearance so dramatically and without hospitalization or tremendous pain. I put the article down. "Hmm," I thought. I read the article again, and saw that Dr. Maguina practiced in California. "Well, that's that," I sniffed. "I'm not going to California for burn care. I have a psychology practice and two daughters to care for."

Still, I couldn't bring myself to toss the magazine, the way I always did. I kept the issue on my bedside table for weeks, contemplating it in the back of my mind. After a while, I thought about contacting Dr. Maguina. I searched online but couldn't find an email address for him. "Hmm," I thought. "Well, that's that." But I couldn't put the article out of my mind.

One day, weeks later, I mentioned the article to Doug. We stood in our bright kitchen, overlooking the oak trees, starting our day. I explained about the new laser treatment, and the doctor all the way in California, and my inability to email him. "You could write him a letter, you know," he said. I stopped short. I had somehow never conceived of writing an actual letter.

With minimal expectation, I sat down to write Dr. Maguina. It seemed to me unlikely that he would help. What doctor has the time to write to someone about a treatment when that person won't even be your patient? All the doctors I knew were too busy to give their time that selflessly. I wrote Dr. Maguina just the same. I told him about my injury, which was then 47 years ago, and asked if this laser procedure might be able to help me. I asked if he knew anyone near me who was trained in the new fractional laser intervention. I sent my letter off, assuming I would never hear back from Dr. Maguina.

Two weeks later, Dr. Maguina responded. Yes, this procedure might really be able to help, he said. He gave me the name of an esteemed colleague, Dr. Sigrid Blome-Eberwein, at Lehigh Valley Hospital in Pennsylvania. He emailed her my name in advance, so she would be aware that I might be contacting her. I emailed this new doctor and she responded to me within the hour. A consultation was arranged, and I was in.

I was nervous going to see Dr. Eberwein. I had never worked with any other surgeon than my dear Dr. Constable, who had always made me feel so safe and loved. Dr. Eberwein strode into the consultation room with quiet serious confidence. She was from Germany, so she spoke with a slight accent, but her English was as perfect as could be. She wore her straight long blonde hair pulled back in a loose ponytail. She was pretty, with blue eyes and high cheekbones. She stood slim, looking like she hit the gym every day at 4 AM.

There is something inherently humiliating about being assessed as a burn patient. Sooner or later, after discussion and consultation, there is a moment when you have to get completely naked and have a stranger (the doctor) appraise every part of you carefully. Dr. Eberwein looked me all over, asking me to raise my arms and turn my neck to both sides. She did not seem impressed with my state. I had always thought I had had very best burn care. I still think that was true at the time, in the late 1960s. Now, it seemed that science had advanced, and perhaps I was not the state of the art burn survivor I thought I was. "We will start with the laser," she declared.

Lehigh Valley Burn Center is located in Allentown, PA, a small city in the Pocono Mountains. You would not think that this hospital would be the place for the very best burn care, but in fact, Lehigh Valley has a fine reputation.

The care starts with the receptionist, Rachael. She checks me in, greeting me warmly, and teasing me about something or another. She has a stash of special socks that she stores and gives away as presents. In my sock drawer, I have garish pairs of Valentine socks and Christmas socks from her. Perhaps if she had another job, Rachael would have a bountiful candy jar at her desk, giving away treats. But many burned people checking in with her are about to have surgery, and they can't eat a bite. So, she gives away her festive socks instead.

The nurses in the outpatient area are uniformly wonderful as well. Some of them are warm and sweet. Some of them are more matter-of-fact, getting their job done. But, regardless of their level of emotional accessibility, they are all kind, well-meaning and sensitive to trauma. After I get changed into the hospital gown, it is always too cold in the exam room. The nurses will wrap me up in a blanket. Often they will run out and get an extra warm blanket straight out of the dryer. They will wrap the toasty blanket around my shoulders and look at me, with a little smile of satisfaction.

I am in my fifties now, but when I go for a laser treatment, I can easily become a scared four-year-old. It isn't hard to make me regress. Certain smells strike dread in my heart: the smell of an alcohol swab, or the dreaded rubber gas mask. The sight of the operating room, with its sterile metallic coldness, sets my spine on edge. Getting an IV put in is always a painful drama. My veins are old and tired and probably all scarred up on the inside. Sometimes, it takes five tries to get an IV in. Each attempt is excruciating, the needle jabbing against my veins again and again, stabbing.

Each time I go into the operating room, I am filled with dread. This is despite the fact that the burn team truly couldn't be nicer. But the sights, the smells, the approaching IV insertion, all these things fill me with fear. I look like a normal middle-aged woman, but inside I quake like a frightened little girl all over again. And no one holds my foot.

Still, the burn team is so good to me. One time, I waited in the operating room, ready to get started with the laser. The burn team stood all around me, masked and gowned up, but they had their backs to me. The anesthesiologist was checking the equipment, the nurse was preparing my bandages for later, and two other people were buzzing about, but no one was in my line of sight, and no one was looking at me.

Inside my old panic began to grow. "I don't know these people and they don't know me. If I have anesthesia, they won't know me and they won't bring me back. I am going to die." Silently I started to cry, tears streaming down my face. No one noticed, because they were all busy working. Still, I felt I could say something. "I'm scared!" I piped up, with a child's voice.

Instantly, the four people in the OR rushed to the operating table. "You are scared? Why are you scared?" they asked. I could only see half of each face, because they all had their masks on. Still, I could see the looks in their eyes. From face to face, I saw deep, genuine concern.

"I don't know," I said. "I don't have any reason to be upset. You are all so nice. I shouldn't be upset."

One nurse took my hand and held it gently. Over the top of her mask, I could see her deep brown eyes, looking earnestly at me. "I'm sure you have had many reasons to be upset and scared. I'm sure that you have been through so much. But we will take good care of you. We will all be here, taking good care of you."

That moment was one of the most healing, compassionate moments of my life. No one in that room minimized my feelings. They all understood, somehow, the weight of everything I had gone through. No one minimized my trauma. I didn't feel brushed off. I felt that the staff were taking me seriously and that my feelings were important. No one questioned my terror. They validated my fears and reassured me that they would take excellent care of me. They made me feel completely safe.

Another time in the OR, they were trying and trying to get the dreaded IV into my veins. They worked all over my right arm. My left arm is burned so badly that it is tough to get IVs through the skin, so my right arm has to do double duty. The nurse was trying to get the IV into me. Every time, it hurt terribly. I was crying. Another nurse was holding my left hand, and we were talking, both of us trying to get my attention onto something other than the pain. Finally, the nurse got the IV into me and we all breathed a sigh of relief.

The nurse anesthetist came over to me, and talked about how she was going to give me some sedation. At the same time, the anesthesiologist behind me reached over my head, and began to place the dreaded rubber mask over my mouth.

"NO!" I shouted, and I shoved his arm away. We all looked at each other, astonished. I felt out of my body, shocked at my own aggression, which I witnessed as if someone else had done it. I felt embarrassed for my outburst. "I'm sorry!" I said. "The gas mask scares me. I'm so sorry. I didn't mean to push you. It just happened."

"It's OK," said the anesthesiologist behind me. "No mask. No mask." A few days after this incident, I got a phone call from the nurse anesthesiologist who works with the burn team. "This is Jill," she said. "I want to make sure that getting anesthesia is like a big nothing for you from here on. I want to understand everything that is hard for you, and to fix it, so that you never have to feel scared when you come to us."

We spent a long time talking on the phone. I told her about my crappy veins, and how hard it is to get an IV inserted. I explained how the gas mask petrifies me. She listened attentively, took notes, and came up with a plan for me, which would involve numbing my skin prior to the IV, and the whole team being informed of my anxieties. She gave me her cell number and asked me to call her one week prior to each surgery, so she could have the team prepared. "Don't worry. I am going to make it so that getting anesthesia feels like just going for a dental checkup."

Jill was as good as her word, and that's exactly what happened the next surgery. My next laser treatment was calm, pain-free, with no sign of a gas mask in sight.

I don't know Dr. Eberwein the way I knew Dr. Constable. She didn't care for me as a child, save my life, and maintain a lifelong written correspondence with me. It's a different relationship. Initially, I wasn't sure how connected I would feel to her. Dr. Eberwein is cerebral, practical, efficient. I didn't know if I could feel more connected, but I do. I smile wide every time she enters the room. She is as smart as they come, with a lively sense of humor and a sincere kindness in her eyes. I don't have the decades-long child/doctor connection to her, but I have an adult/adult connection to her. I know she knows me as a person, not just a patient, and that she gets who I am. And I think she is a genius.

All the staff at Lehigh Valley sing Dr. Eberwein's praises. The word "artist" comes up repeatedly when people describe her work. Dr. Eberwein seems to have a special magic with scars; they speak to her; she knows how to soothe them. Although third-degree burn scars will never go away, she has the ability to modulate the scars, making their appearance better and better. She is constantly working on new techniques and suggesting various interventions to help my scars improve.

Setting aside my disfigurement, the worst problem I have with being burned is about heat. On a more practical level, being burned is uncomfortable. Scarred skin cannot sweat. So, when it is hot and humid out, I become dangerously overheated, quickly. I once fainted at an outdoor concert from the heat. I get lightheaded. If you touch my scarred skin on a hot day, you can feel that it is a different temperature from my unscarred skin. The scars feel much hotter to the touch. They band around me, tightly, holding in the heat.

At the same time, because many layers of fat tissue were burned away, I also grow cold quickly. In particular, I lost the layers of subcutaneous fat around my torso, burned away and permanently lost. Subcutaneous fat is one of the things that protects our organs from the cold and helps to regulate body temperature. So, I also get chilled quite rapidly. Add menopause to the mix and I am a thermostatic disaster.

I used to carpool with a friend to a singing group. Our ride was about an hour long. Frequently, I would adjust the vents, making the air hotter, then colder, then hotter again. I turned the fan speed up and down. I fiddled with the temperature every five minutes. I did this on every drive. One day as I changed the temperature yet again, my friend turned to me, her face gentle and her tone warm. She said, in the kindest way possible, "You have a narrow band of comfort."

Indeed.

Dr. Eberwein can't fix my problems with heat, but in her hands, my appearance has changed dramatically. I have had fourteen laser treatments by now, with many more to go. It is a long, slow process, and it is not easy. Each time, I take a week off from my practice, unable to work with my clients. Each time, I am weak and befuddled from the anesthesia for days. My lasered skin is hot, dry and itchy for weeks afterwards. While not in frank pain, I am terribly uncomfortable.

The results, though, are splendid. My facial scars are lying much flatter, and the lasered skin is softer. If I am wearing the right outfit, and have a little makeup on, there are times a stranger would never notice I had been burned at all.

A laser's results emerge like a flower bud opens. If you watch a flower bud, it may seem like it will never open, and that nothing is happening. But, if you glance at the flower repeatedly, over the course of a few days, you can see the bud gradually opening, spreading and transforming into a full flower. A laser treatment is like that. Initially, it may seem like nothing has changed. But over the course of days, weeks and months, scars transform into smoother, softer versions of themselves. About two weeks after a laser treatment, it becomes fun to look in the mirror in the morning.

I wake up to find that I look better than I did, just since I went to bed the night before.

For years, when I was little, I would go to bed at night with my own personal prayer. I hadn't been raised in any religion, so prayer was not part of our family routine. We didn't pray at meals, and we didn't pray at bedtime. I didn't really believe in God, but I also didn't *not* believe in God. I didn't know what to think about God.

I had my own bedtime routine. My mother would tuck me into bed at night. I had 15 stuffed animals that I placed around me, each in its own assigned spot on the bed. My brown dog belonged at my right side, next to the white dog. My stuffed bear belonged near my feet. They watched over me at night. I would lie under the covers, holding my favorite stuffed bunny in my arms. Alone, I would pray, "Please God, let me wake up in the morning and not be burned." Every morning, I would wake up burned as usual, and get on with my day.

It is 50 years later, and I am still burned. But, thanks to my laser treatments, I actually do wake up less burned than I was when I went to sleep.

Medical science is a miracle. And it turns out that my burn care will be a forever job.

LESSON FOURTEEN:
You never know what might come along to help you. Never count on a miracle. Plan for the worst but hope for the best. You have to make the most of your current situation, but remain open to the possibility that a miracle could happen.

FIFTEEN

Switzerland

THE FOURTH OF FOUR

For many years, my mother complained of word-finding difficulties. It started in her fifties, but never seemed that significant. She would begin a sentence, and have trouble finding the right word to say. She would point to the object in question, or perhaps describe the item, in a circular fashion. "The object into which one puts water," she would say. John or I would guess the word for her. "Glass?" I would suggest. "Tea kettle?" John would say. We all laughed at these incidents and found them endearing. My mother would be a little unsettled when she couldn't find the right word, but she saw the humor as well. She was an intelligent woman, widely read, with a broad vocabulary. Still, word finding difficulties are not unusual as a person ages.

Benign as they seemed, I remembered these incidents many years later, when my mother was diagnosed with a rare speech disorder called primary progressive aphasia. Her speech became more and more halting and her ability to recall and speak words became impaired. She saw many doctors, who had difficulty diagnosing her. She sounded like she had had a stroke, but her brain imaging did not show evidence of infarcts. Instead, the speech areas of her brain were withering away in a rare sort of dementia process. Her memory was mostly intact, as well as the rest of her cognitive functions. But her verbal fluency was vanishing.

It struck me as fittingly ironic that my mother would lose her verbal adroitness. All my life, she had used words to paint a certain sanitized picture of herself. She presented her own versions of reality in which she was often a blameless victim, and others were bitterly at fault. Her words had often bewildered, manipulated or hurt me. Now, she was having trouble speaking. It struck me as odd that she should lose the one capacity that had caused me such confusion.

It would be hard for anyone to lose the capacity for speech, but for my mother, it was devastating. She had always needed a lot of positive attention, the former self-declared Miss Mankato. Conversations had often revolved around ways in which she was special. Now, she was unable to use words to focus the limelight on herself. Other older people might have settled into being an appreciative member of the audience. They might have enjoyed listening to other people talk, and gotten happiness simply by being present for social gatherings. However, my mother often needed the attention to be on her and her accomplishments. So, even with her aphasia, she tried to dominate in conversation. Talking to her became a tedious exercise in waiting for her to say everything she needed to say about herself.

Kathryn and I had settled into a relationship which was connected but not close. I rarely called her and she didn't call me. We emailed each other weekly, though. I dutifully invited her to Julia and Anna's school activities. So, I saw her regularly at Anna's band concerts and Julia's dramas. I also made sure that we celebrated birthdays, Mother's Day and Christmas together, sometime around the holiday.

My guiding principal was to not cause her additional pain or social embarrassment, but to also keep tight limits on seeing her, because she invariably said or did something painful. It was a difficult seesaw between not inflicting more pain on her, and not putting myself in a position that she would inflict pain on me. Always, there were conflicting questions: what do I want to be able to say when she dies? Will I feel guilty if I don't do this? On the other hand, how could this hurt me? How can I protect myself?

My mother, always adept at getting her needs met, had seemingly moved on from our relationship. Just as I had predicted to Doug, she detached quickly from my absence in her daily life. She settled into a beautiful adult continuing care community, which was a blessing. She now lived in a safe, beautiful environment, with services, great food and social opportunities. I was released from providing the level of care a daughter might be expected to provide. She sang in a chorus and spent time with friends. As much as I felt guilty, she seemed content enough.

Although I tried to make sensitive ethical choices around my mother, I often felt defensive. Everyone I knew had a good or at least civil relationship with their mother. I had friends who were entirely devoted to caring for their mothers and did so with great kindness and generosity. I barely spoke to mine. One of my favorite cousins once asked breezily if I wasn't done with all that stuff with my mother yet. Another cousin said that he really couldn't understand how I felt. My aunt would call me to ask about my mother, assuming I would know things about her that I no longer knew. Some newer friends would look at me a little warily when I discussed the distance between me and my mother.

It was hard to explain why I couldn't be closer to my mother without it causing me great pain. There was no easy label to put on her. My mother wasn't alcoholic, or physically abusive. My issues with her would take hours to convey, which was tedious and painful each time. I also didn't want to criticize my mother to her own family, so I had to rely on vague wording, and hope that my relatives trusted my character enough to have faith in me and my decisions, even if they didn't understand them.

My very closest friends had heard my stories about my mother for decades. They formed a loving and fiercely protective phalanx of support around me. I didn't have to convince any of them that I shouldn't see my mother much. They all knew that each time I saw her I was emotionally unraveled for days, weepy and agitated. They knew because they each spent a fair amount of time talking me through each incident, patching me back together with love, humor and care.

My mother attempted to maintain close relationships with her granddaughters, but it was challenging. Around the same time that I distanced myself from her, Julia was entering adolescence, so she wasn't particularly interested in spending much time with her grandmother anymore anyway. Little Anna spent more time with her. She occasionally slept over at my mother's new apartment in her elegant continuing care community.

Initially Anna really enjoyed these visits. My mother would show her the stained glass she was working on, and they would go swimming in the pool. Over time, Anna also grew up, and was not as interested in spending time with her grandmother. My mother was not a warm, relaxed, comfy grandmother. My mother was usually focused on what appealed to her; she couldn't enjoy or appreciate children's interests. It wasn't easy for the girls, and their social interactions with their grandmother became more stilted over time.

I invited my mother to see the girls in school performances. Julia was active in the choral department in high school, as she was an excellent singer. Our high school had an award-winning music department, both in band and chorus, and my girls thrived there. As my mother was devoted to her own chorus, I kept hoping she would come to one of Julia's choral concerts, which were truly impressive. The high school chorus performed on Wednesdays, which was the same night my mother had her own chorus meetings. Through four years of high school, I invited my mother to every choral concert, but she always said she had a conflict and couldn't come.

It was Julia's senior year, and her final concert at the school was a week away. I invited my mother, for her last opportunity to hear Julia's chorus. Julia told my mother that she herself didn't really like the piece they were singing, but the chorus did a good job, so she hoped my mother would enjoy it. This time, my mother agreed to attend. We listened to the young chorale sing, and they did a magnificent job with a difficult classical music piece. At the end, we all stood, waiting for Julia to come off the stage.

Eventually Julia found us. She trotted up in her long black choral gown, with her blond hair pulled back, and a big smile on her face when she saw us.

"Grandma!" Julia said. "You made it! What did you think?"

My mother leaned in to hug Julia. She held Julia by her shoulders, and looked at her earnestly, her face serious. "I. . . (long pause). . . didn't. . . (long pause). . . like. . . (long pause). . . it!"

We all stared at my mother in shock. No one said a word. I wasn't sure what my daughter would say or do. Julia looked hard at my mother, tossed her head back, and laughed wholeheartedly. I sighed with appreciation, watching my 17-year-old daughter muster more social aplomb then her 81-year-old grandmother.

Over time, my mother's aphasia got worse and worse. She also began to have short periods of confusion and increasing headaches. Her ability to problem-solve was deteriorating as well. She was 84 years old, and she could feel the gradual deterioration from the aphasia. On the other hand, physically, she was well. She was thin and well-muscled, exercised daily, and could walk miles with no pain or problem. Her mind was deteriorating but her body was fit as a fiddle.

It was winter, 2017, when my mother invited Doug and me over to her apartment for an important meeting, as she needed to discuss something. After a quick hello and a glass of water, my mother unceremoniously presented us with documents she was completing, toward the goal of legally taking her life. In the documents, she wrote that she had Alzheimer's, could no longer converse, and that she wanted to die. She mentioned me as her daughter, to whom she was "not close," and mentioned her two granddaughters, whom she loved dearly. She wanted to end her life, due to her increasing cognitive limitations.

Impassively, my mother watched me read these documents, and asked me what I thought.

I thought so many different things; it was hard to have words myself. My mind went blank and I had trouble breathing. On the one hand, I intellectually understood assisted suicide as an ethical choice if a person had a fatal illness, or was in intractable, intense pain. I could understand assisted suicide in those circumstances. My own father had hastened his death from AIDS by refusing food. At the time, I had supported his choice. He was dying anyway, it was inevitable, and his life was not joyful.

On the other hand, my mother did not have a fatal disease, and she was in no physical pain at all. She did not, in fact, have Alzheimer's, although she did have a progressive dementia. I could see not wanting to live with dementia. But she lived in a gorgeous place, with good food, friends all around, fun activities, and she wanted for nothing.

On a deeper level, I puffed with outrage that she would allow herself to consider suicide at all. I had endured three family suicides, in addition to my father's death. It seemed to me the height of selfishness that she would contemplate that path, knowing what I had been through. I was further incensed that she would inflict this suicide wound on her granddaughters, whom she claimed to love so much. But a scorpion is a scorpion.

I didn't say any of those things to my mother. Instead, Doug and I encouraged her to try to enjoy her life. We discussed the many wonderful things in life that did not require speech. We reminded her about her love of nature, music, beauty and food. We encouraged her to go to concerts, to plant flowers, to play croquet, and to focus on the positive aspects of her life. Kathryn listened to us with skepticism, her face furrowed in disappointment. Reluctantly, she agreed to try to be positive for the next three months, and then she would revisit her decision.

Three months later, on the dot, Kathryn declared that she was definitely going to pursue assisted suicide. Her decision was final. It was not possible for her to legally take her life in the United States. The few states that allowed assisted suicide required state residency to qualify for the "service." She had found an agency that would provide assisted-suicide services.

It was in Switzerland.

In the meantime, I was awash in conflicting, contradictory feelings. To be frank, I knew my mother's death might be a relief. My relationship with her had been deeply painful for years. Interacting with her was fraught, and she often hurt me. I felt guilty that I wasn't taking better care of her, but I felt outraged that I should even have to, after how poorly she had taken care of me and Marc.

If my mother died, I wouldn't have to second-guess myself. I wouldn't have to keep wondering if I had done enough for her, or did I truly need to keep such distance? As soon as I posed those questions, my inner dialogue would flip into self-justification. Of course I needed distance from her! I would remind myself of all the ways that she had failed to care for or protect me. Then I would question myself again. It was relentless. On and on it went, like a grim, joyless merry-go-round from hell, playing the same theme again and again in my head.

If she died, I would be free of that.

On the other hand, I was aghast at the thought of having a fourth suicide in our family history, for myself and for my daughters. Anyone who has lived through a family suicide knows that people never really get over them. Suicides leave an unending wake of guilt, sadness, anger and grief. I had never recovered from my brother Marc's death.

Gingerly, I tried to convey the situation to my daughters. Julia was away at college, and Anna was a senior in high school. They understood that their grandmother had a non-curable speech problem, and that it was getting worse. They had an intellectual grasp of right-to-die issues and were not unsympathetic. Yet, the questions came. "Why would she do this?" "Doesn't she want to see us grow up?"

Doug, Anna and I went to visit my mother together in June. We sat tensely in my mother's small living room, Anna and I huddled close together on the tan loveseat. My mother perched erectly on a dining room chair, peering at us stony faced through her triple lens glasses. We chatted about Anna's senior year, and her multiple acceptances into prestigious pre-occupational therapy programs. We gave her the date for Anna's graduation party at our house. Slowly the conversation turned to my mother's planned suicide.

Anna, 18 years old, looked at Kathryn. Anna's long thick blonde hair was up in a ponytail, and her luminous blue eyes were full of emotion. "Aren't you going to miss us?" she asked her grandmother. "I'm going to college soon. You won't see me graduate. I'm going to get my master's degree in occupational therapy and you won't be there. Julia will be graduating college. She will be going to New York and getting roles as an actress. You won't be there to see her perform. Someday, we will get married. You won't be there for any of that. Aren't you going to miss us?"

My mother looked at Anna, listening carefully, implacable. "Y-e-s," she said, very slowly. "Y-e-s but. . ." Kathryn pointed to her own head, and made a face. "But. . . ." And that was her answer.

Anna's face fell. My heart flooded with love for my daughter, watching how little impact her impassioned words had on her grandmother.

During her summer break, Julia went to have her last visit with my mother. They had a similar conversation, in which Julia confronted her grandmother on the implications of her suicide, with minimal response. The last time my daughters saw their grandmother was at Anna's graduation party in August.

We live in a gracious four-bedroom colonial in a lovely development in Bucks County, PA. Our house is beautiful but not unique; it's a standard nice house. The special aspects of our home are its large wooded backyard, which give us space and privacy, and a lovely screened porch, which we built.

The vaulted airy porch is the size of two rooms, and it looks invitingly onto our yard, full of tall oak trees. This outdoor space is a wonderful setting for family celebrations and parties.

The house was already full of good food and good friends when my mother arrived at the party. Before I even saw my mother, several friends alerted me that she had arrived. "Your mother is here. You should see her dress. You won't believe it." My mother arrived at the summer garden party wearing a long completely black dress, as if in mourning for herself. In addition, she arrived with four scrapbooks (all about her), a lamp for Julia and a necklace for Anna. These were not gifts, but rather personal bequests that she was efficiently passing along, in advance of her death. All this was happening in the midst of Anna's high school graduation party.

My friends did their best to keep the party going. They took turns sitting with my funeral-dressed mother and keeping her company, and we carried on with the day. Anna, blessedly, was focused on her party, and not paying much attention to the drama of her grandmother's arrival. Several people tried to talk to my mother about her intentions, including my ex-husband, encouraging her to change her mind. Kathryn remained resolute.

The Swiss agency which does legal assisted suicide required many screenings before approving my mother's case. She had to provide documentation of her illness, and her identity. She also had to provide documentation from a psychiatrist that she was not clinically depressed, and that she was legally competent to make this decision. My mother gradually passed through all these hurdles, and was approved for the "green light," signaling that she could come to Switzerland for the grim procedure.

Doug and I went to see her the week before she died. Julia and Anna were now both at college, Anna just starting her freshman orientation. Doug and I drove to the retirement community, passing through the beautiful gardens, under the gracious trees, and over the small lake. We arrived at her apartment, full of tension and trepidation. How do you knowingly have a last visit with your mother, who is about to kill herself?

She hugged us but did not offer us so much as a glass of water. Ahead of time, I had decided that I would end my relationship with her with as much kindness, warmth and appreciation as I could muster. I brought her some fresh strawberries, along with peach muffins from a farm stand that she loved, but could no longer drive to. She thanked me, and put the strawberries and muffins away, to eat later by herself.

We sank down in her little living room, the three of us, gazing at each other. The silent moment ached with tension.

My mother said that she was anxious.

"Why are you anxious? Are you having second thoughts?" I asked, hoping for and also dreading that response.

"N-o."

"Are you worried about the assisted suicide procedure?" asked Doug.

"N-o." said my mother slowly. It turned out that she was worried about getting to Switzerland without a hitch, despite the fact that she had four people who had agreed to accompany her there. One of these people was an old friend, who, prior to that, had been a patient of my mother's. Thus, my mother's former psychotherapy patient was scheduled to fly to Switzerland to witness her old psychologist kill herself. (The clinical inappropriateness of this plan boggles the mind.) Regardless, we assured Kathryn that her travel plans would go smoothly, and that her travel companions would get her there safely.

I pulled out some photographs of Julia and Anna, now back at school, to show my mother. She pulled out her checkbook and financial statements, and showed me where to find her will. I asked her a question about my dad.

"Do you ever miss him?" I asked.

"N-o. Ra-re-ly."

"Whom do you miss?" I asked, hoping she would say her son, Marc, whom she rarely mentioned. There were no photos of Marc in her apartment. There were no photos of me there either.

"Jo-hn," she said. John, her ex-husband, whom she had divorced twice. John's photo sat in her bedroom.

The conversation, my last with my mother, focused entirely on her. It was our final visit. I didn't imagine that she would have nice last words or parting thoughts for me, her last living child. But, although I didn't expect anything different, it still hurt.

Ahead of time, I had prepared myself. I wanted to end our relationship as kindly and generously as I could manage. I wanted express gratitude for the gifts that she had given me, and not be focused on my litany of disappointments. So, I told my mother that I had prepared a thank-you list for her. Eyes brightening, she sat down next to me on the love seat. I pulled out my list.

Thank you for:

1. *Teaching me about music, which has enriched my life.*
2. *Teaching me how to play the piano and read music.*
3. *Enriching me culturally with museums, restaurants and concerts.*
4. *Giving me the love of travel.*
5. *Listening to my problems.*
6. *Loving my girls and being a nice grandmother to them.*
7. *Helping me with babysitting and caring for them when they were little.*
8. *Reading to me and helping me develop a love of books.*
9. *Helping to pay for my first wedding.*
10. *Teaching me practical things like money management, being responsible, etc.*
11. *Telling me I could accomplish anything I wanted.*
12. *Always loving me.*

By the time I was done reading this list, I could barely breathe through my tears. My mother did not cry, but she was touched by my words.

She leaned over and gave me a long hug. I calmed down and gathered myself together. We looked at each other. I wondered what she would say now, in response.

Very slowly, and with great effort, she said, "I wish I had something to say to you, but I don't remember." She gazed at me matter-of-factly. There was no warmth in her face.

Although I had expected nothing more from my mother, the moment still shattered me. She seemed to have put as much thought into our last meeting as she would in making a bank deposit. There was no emotion or sentimentality on her part, no final words, or benediction.

That was it for me; I was done. Quickly, I pulled myself together. I said we should go, and I stood up to leave. She seemed ready for us to go, too. We walked to the doorway, and she hugged Doug and me. "I lo-ve y-ou," she warbled.

"I love you, too," I said, although I wasn't sure that I did.

We met up with friends of my mother's afterwards for a drink. They were about to say goodbye to her, too. I told them the story of my thank-you list, and Kathryn's lack of response, and their faces darkened. "What a nice thing you did. We will try to get her to make a response to you. We will work on it with her tonight." I felt encouraged.

The next day, I received an email from my mother. It was entitled "Twelve Wishes." I smiled when I read the title. Our friends had gotten through to her! They had managed to focus my mother on wishes that she had for me and my family. Eagerly, I opened up the email, to see what my mother had written, her final blessings for me.

> Was only 10 wishes. I did not remembered! I would to remember through this last week of my life of that wishes. Nothing comes but for "music." Could I fill out the reminder? Could I ask one last favor? I love you, Mother.

Translation: I don't remember how many wishes there were. I would like to remember the list that you wrote me for the last week of my life. I don't remember them in detail, other than that you said "music." Can you please write them down for me as one last favor? I love you, Mother.

My eyes filled with tears. This was my mother's final list for me. Instead of it being a response about me, wishing me well or thanking me for being her daughter, her last wish list was, inevitably, entirely about *herself* and her own need to feel special. First, I felt devastated. Then, fury rose inside me.

I sat down to email her, fingers flying in rage. I diligently wrote out every appreciation I had previously said to her, in full detail. I assumed that she would be showing this list to all of her friends, proving that she had indeed been a good mother to me, all this time, despite my coldness. So, I thought carefully how to make my experience transparent, should anyone else read it.

I wrote, "After I read this to you, you said you couldn't remember anything to say to me. Given this was our last meeting, I was surprised that you didn't have anything to say to me, or what you would want for me. Now that you have had time, have you thought of anything? Love, Lise."

Her response came a few days later:

> I can't remember what I said last remembering. It was a pleasant meeting, more then, a memorable meeting. I hope the laser surgery goes well. Thank you for your remembrances. I will hold them dear to me. My words come less and less. I will always love thru eternity. I love you, Mom.

On August 29, 2017, Kathryn self-administered a lethal dose of medication, fully competent, and under the care of a Swiss physician. She died peacefully, with loving friends nearby, including her ex-patient. I was not there. I was home, recovering from another laser procedure, to treat the scars from my life with my mother.

I was fully prepared for her death. I am embarrassed to admit that a part of me even looked forward to it. Yet, when the news came, my body reacted as if it weren't attached to my mind. At some point, I began to hyperventilate. I had a panic attack. My body held the trauma of the loss of my mother, the only mother I would ever have, even as my mind was saying I didn't care.

* * *

I don't miss my mother. It's been decades since our peaceful evenings together on the paper clip palace's couch. The times when we were close ended long ago, and I have gotten used to not having a relationship with her. Her death doesn't feel much different.

There are times, however, when I think of her and cry. Those times are always involve music. Music was my mother's best language, in which she seemed to express full emotion and true connection. Sometimes, I hear a classical music piece that we both loved, and I am overwhelmed with sadness. I sobbed through Kathryn's memorial service, overwhelmed with the beauty of her chorus, which sang so kindly in her honor.

Another time, I heard a Ravel piano duet that she and my dad played, most memorably, at my first wedding. The piece is from the *Mother Goose Suite,* and it is sweet, sentimental, and ends in jubilation. That piece brings me back. I can see my parents sitting together in the church. They sit side by side on the piano bench, just like they used to when I was little. They had been divorced for years at this point, but they came together just once to play this duet for their daughter's wedding. I can see them playing the *Mother Goose Suite* together, earnestly concentrating as one, to make the most beautiful performance they could. They were perfect. There wasn't a dry eye in the church.

Months after her death, I went alone to a concert of the Brahms' Requiem. I knew it would be emotional for me. I had listened to the Requiem many times around my father's death, and it was a great comfort. Now,

I wanted to hear it as I came to terms with my mother's death. I sat regrettably near the front of the auditorium and wept uncontrollably through the entire piece. I did my best to contain my sobs and prolific nose blowing, but I was a sight.

I used to love my mother very much.

LOOK AROUND

I planned my mother's memorial service, along with her friends. It was a beautiful ceremony, made stunning by the performance of her chorus. Julia and Anna came home from college. Anna had only been at Juniata College for three weeks, but she made the trip. Julia flew up from North Carolina School of the Arts. My girls had talked and they had a plan. They informed me that they would both be speaking at their grandmother's funeral.

"You don't have to. It's not an obligation."

"We want to. You won't be saying anything, and so we want to. She's our grandmother."

They were right. I did not say a single word at my mother's funeral. This was uncharacteristic of me. I spoke spontaneously at Marc's funeral, although I don't remember a word of it. I sang at Jackie's funeral. I spoke at my father's funeral. I even said a few words at John's funeral. But I couldn't figure out anything to say for my mother's funeral. I had no words for my feelings, and nothing to say that seemed appropriate.

"I can't stand my mother, but I used to adore her."

"My mother is the most selfish person I know."

"If you think she's a good person, then you just don't know her well enough."

Instead, I sat, in the foremost pew, silently sobbing throughout the ceremony.

Julia stood up and recounted her years as her grandmother's reluctant piano student. She made the story humorous and sweet, describing my mother's patience with Julia's lack of diligent practice. Anna stood up and described her many visits to her grandmother's home, and the little gifts my mother would give her. She brought show and tell props from her visits years ago, pink hair ties, purses, sparkly necklaces. Both of my girls stood erect, voices projecting, smiling and holding the small audience in their hands. My heart burst with pride.

Behind me, and around me, sat my friends. Susan was there with her family, whom I had known all my life. Caryn and Brad were there, up from Maryland. Karen, my best friend from eighth grade was there. Our dear friends Jeff and Nancy were there. Celeste, my best friend from my first job, was there. The church was not full, but it was full of love.

After the ceremony, we all went back to my house for a reception on the screen porch, looking out into the stately oak trees. I put on an old recording that my mother had made, many years ago, her one professional record. Thus, Kathryn, former child prodigy, played the piano at her own funeral reception. I put out the scrapbooks she had given me at Anna's graduation party. The scrapbooks were full of local newspaper clippings about my mother when she was little, and old programs from her many recitals. I chatted with everyone there. Eventually I sank down on the sunny deck, exhausted.

Susan sat down next to me. Then Nancy was there, and Celeste, too. I had known each of these women for decades, and they knew everything about me. We talked about the service and my mother's death. We talked about the girls, and how wonderful they had been. I talked about the trauma of the last month, and the traumas of the past many years. I talked about my grief, my exhaustion and my relief too. My friends' faces were all turned toward me, full of kindness, open, attuned.

"Yes, all that is true, and you have been through so much," said my dear friend, Nancy. "It's amazing what you have been through, I don't even know how you have done it. There is no explanation for it. But, look at everything that you have built. Look at all of it." Nancy gestured around her. Her gestures guided my eyes to Doug, and to my amazing daughters. Her gestures guided my eyes to the lovely gracious home we had made together, the yard, the trees, our sweet dog, and the welcoming porch. Her gestures guided my eyes to the friends all around me, loving friends who were more family than friend now, always there, always loving.

"Look at what you have made. Look at everything you have built."

With these words, I felt released into the Present. Relief filled my chest. The Present was glimmering, shining with love and hope. The dark Past, full of loss and despair seemed to slip away, like an alligator descending into a river at night. I could release the sadness of my mother's suicide, and everything my mother was, or wasn't, to me. My focus was fully on the day I was having, and the marvels of my life as it has turned out. I started this book.

I have felt released ever since.

LESSON FIFTEEN:
You can't pick your family. You can pick your friends. Choose wisely, and care for them as deeply as you care for your family. They may turn out to be the best family you ever have.

The Last Deguire

It hurts to write about the good in my family, because the good is all lost. It is easier to remember the bad, and then say, "Thank God that is over. What a relief." Remembering the good sears me with grief. The good lasted 12 years, if even that long, too short for me, too short for Marc. But, once upon a time, we were a happy Deguire family, or so it seemed.

Our house sang with music. The Steinway grand sat majestically by the entrance of our spacious Glen Ridge home. My mother played it like an angel; my father played it like an entertainer; I played it like a student. My brother, forsaking the piano, played his drums athletically, arms akimbo, drumsticks flying so fast they were a blur. When none of us were playing, there were records spinning: Gregorian chants, *Aida, The White Album, Cinderella,* Debussy. Every genre of music was played enthusiastically by one of us. Music sang everywhere, lifting the mood, raising our spirits, making us smile.

Together, my parents could function like parents. Together, they had the strength to provide regular meals, definitive bedtimes, interesting vacations, cultural excursions. We drove to New York City regularly, speeding down the winding helix into the dark beige tunnel, emerging into the city in a burst of light. We saw Broadway shows, we visited art museums, we traversed the length of the Bronx zoo. We would walk the city, block after block. When it got boring, my father would declare a game. "Tag, you're it!" he would yell at my brother. We would chase each other down the block, suddenly energetic, indifferent to the glances of strangers.

Our family vacations sparkled from ambitious planning. Both of my parents had their summers free; my father was a professor and my mother was a student. So off we would go, driving in every direction. We took three cross-country trips: one to the north, one to the south and the one straight across the center of the country. By the time my family disintegrated, I had been to 42 of the 50 states.

The trips took a month at a time. Our daily world became confined to the beige interior of the sedan. I sat in the back next to Marc, behind my father as he drove. I read for hours, book after book that I stowed in my bag under my feet. My parents sat up front, listening to NPR on the radio, or searching for the local classical music station. Marc sat straight backed next to me. We argued occasionally about the small space we shared. He would glare at me indignantly, instructing me to keep my ever-expanding collection of stuffed animals on *my side*. We might devolve into a kick fight now and then, feet flying in fury. Every fight ended with my father, turning around to glare at us, his blue eyes hard and steely, "Do you want me to stop this car?" Our fight would immediately cease. No one wanted to know what would actually happen if my volatile father stopped the car.

Mostly, though, Marc and I shared our space serenely. Every afternoon, I would nap, whiling away the many hours of a cross-country drive. I would lay my pillow down on Marc's lap. Although a child himself, he would never complain. He would sit, perfectly still, while I lay on my side, my head on his lap, napping away the long afternoon.

All of this to say, I used to have a family. I was a part of this family, the Deguires. We were quirky, we were creative, we were smart. I was the littlest one, the least gifted, the one to whom everything had to be explained. But, I felt a part of something; I belonged.

My family had Christmas traditions and family dinners. We energetically sang "The Bear Went Over The Mountain." In a more refined mood, we would sing "Frere Jacques" in French, in a perfect four-part round. We saw the New York Philharmonic, with me, bored and restless, willing myself to sit still. We saw the beautiful countryside and soaring mountains of almost every state. We camped; we swam; we ate; we laughed. I loved them so.

We visited historical sites along the way. We went to Jamestown, Saratoga, The Alamo. As he drove there, my father would recount the history that happened at the site. "Let me tell you about the Battle of Bunker Hill!" he would start, enthusiastically beginning the tale. We listened, rapt. Later, I would arrive at the site, as excited as if I were going to Disneyland, bounding out of the car to see the actual site of my latest history lesson.

We were an imperfect family. My father yelled. My brother talked about killing himself. My mother was emotionally detached. I was traumatized. Still, we all belonged together. Then, this glass snow globe — containing a whole family, precious and quirky—this snow globe smashed to the ground, glass on concrete, shards and white beads everywhere, splattered, irreplaceable, irretrievable.

When my parents split up, neither functioned well. It turns out, as much as they struggled together, they could not manage as parents apart. My mother lost her interest in parenting altogether. My father still tried, but his energy was limited and his temper remained a forest fire. My father needed my mother to keep him calm, to create a sense of safety from his fearful erratic rage. My mother needed my father to provide energy and focus on parenting. They worked off each other well enough. She was calm; he was fun. He had adventurous ideas; she was a good planner. There were still major problems, but, together, they functioned. Apart, the snow globe shattered.

Sadness overwhelms me. The loss, the pain. I loved my family. I loved being the littlest Deguire. We were happy once. Or maybe it was just me.

My father seemed happy but he was a closeted gay man. My mother seemed happy but later she seethed with resentment over my father, my brother, and me. My brother rarely seemed happy, but he loved us. So maybe it was just me who was happy.

Inside the snow globe, there is a stately Glen Ridge home and a maroon Mercedes. The mother sits calmly, if silently, resentful. The father restlessly paces, hands curiously feminine. The son lies on his bed alone, reading. The daughter smiles defensively with her crooked mouth, playing with her stuffed animals. The beginnings of a yellow superhero cape flap around her sides. Or maybe they all sit together at their kitchen table in front of the beautiful bay window, eating their perfectly balanced meal at six o'clock. Or maybe the mother is weeping in front of the stereo, imagining a different life with a romantic, attentive lover. Or maybe the father is sneaking out to go to the city alone, to find a gay bar where he can be himself. But still, they are a family, contained, protected, belonging together.

When my mother left my father, the snow globe shattered on the ground, smashing a million pieces of glass far and wide. My brother lost his one true home where he felt safe and wanted. My father wheeled off into a spiral of sexual conquests, trying to prove himself lovable, forgetting to raise his children. My mother found John, and fell forever into a romantic fantasy, in which her children had no role to play. No one remembered to watch me. No one remembered to watch Marc. I forged on, already schooled in the art of survival.

Released from the snow globe, Marc flew like Icarus, too proud, unchecked. He spun between friends, places, schools, homes. Eventually, there came a second explosion of glass. Glass shattered 16 stories up and fell in tiny pieces through the Cambridge night sky. For years, I could go to the spot on the MIT campus, and find tiny shards of light green glass, the glass that fell with my brother, dropping like a gentle rain shower all around his sprawled body, so quickly turned corpse.

Inside me now, little pieces of bone, like glass, are growing. This is the truth; I am growing tiny bone fragments inside my thighs, and no one knows why. Dr. Eberwein, my brilliant surgeon, has dug five bony shards out of me, huffing with the exertion. My skin is growing tiny bone fragments, perpendicular to my skin. The entire burn team is stumped; why would my body do this? They are writing a paper on my bone fragments; I will be Case Number One again, because they have never seen this phenomenon. I have a new boney shard growing inside my skin now. The sharpness of it abrades me from inside; it hurts when I walk.

Tiny sharp fragments everywhere, outside and within. Maybe my body is still trying to knit the sharp pieces of the snow globe back together. One little piece here, one little piece there, growing next to each other inside the burned skin of my thighs. Maybe my body is trying to take all the shards of the broken glass from my family, incorporate them into myself, and create a new whole. Or maybe it's a new superpower. Like Wolverine, who has claws that grow out of his hand, Flashback Girl has bones that grow out of her skin. It doesn't seem to be a useful superpower; it causes me nothing but pain. Truthfully, no one knows why my body is doing this.

Or maybe now that I have written about all the sharp pieces, all the tiny lovely lost fragments, my skin will stop spontaneously generating them. Maybe now I can rest.

An African Postscript

After my mother died, she left me her estate. She didn't have to. Other mothers, bitter in their daughter's rejection, might have left their money to someone else. My cousin Mary was fully deserving of Kathryn's money. She had been a loving, attentive companion to my mother in her old age, driving her, entertaining her, assisting her. My mother might also have left her estate directly to her granddaughters, bypassing me altogether, permanently cementing her grievance against me. She could have even bequeathed her estate to her choral group, which had given her so much joy. She left her money to me.

In most ways, her decision was right and fair. Although our relationship was strained at the end, we had been close for 45 years, and still understood each other. In the depths of her aphasia, I was the one who understood her garbled speech the best. I had shown up for her when she absolutely needed me; skulking anxiously in the hospital when she had her surgeries. I was still there for her, albeit in a reluctant and tense way. So, in the end, I agreed with my mother. I thought it was fair and just for her money to come to me, regardless of the limitations of our relationship.

In the face of this small but not inconsequential windfall, Doug asked me, "What do you want to do?"

"African safari," I responded immediately, grinning broadly.

"Right," he said.

For 30 years, I had dreamed of going on safari. Perhaps it was seeing *Out of Africa* in the 1980s, with its beautiful vistas. Perhaps it was my lifelong adoration of *Born Free,* the story of the Kenyan lion cub Elsa, with its haunting theme song. For decades I had longed to see these African savannas and windswept plains. But the trip is long and expensive, and always seemed too far out of reach. Now, we could use my mother's money, and I could finally get to Africa.

A year later, we embarked on a safari through Tanzania, Doug, me and our guide Willy. The protected lands of Tanzania spread out around me, the grasslands extending in every direction, as far as the eye could see. Standing up in the jeep, with the top popped open, I turned a slow circle. Everywhere I looked, golden grasses waved in the fields, with the occasional small tree stretching into the sky. Doug stood behind me, equally transfixed by the endless golden shimmer. The air smelled of dust and earth, clean and dry.

Off in the distance, over to the east, there were flames, low to the ground. "Willy, what's that?" I asked, with some alarm. "There's a forest fire?"

Willy turned to me, his brown arm resting on the seat next to him, his intelligent face calm. In his lilting English, he responded, "No, it's not a problem. They set these fires. They set them all the time. The rangers set the fires to help the animals."

"I don't understand."

"It helps with the soil. The soil here can become bad. Maybe it gets worn out, and it doesn't have the nutrients the animals need any more. You have seen the elephants with only one tusk, because they don't get the minerals they need for strong teeth, yes? So, they set the fires. It turns everything black, yes? But in a month, the grasses all grow back again. And under the grass, the earth is stronger. The minerals come back because of the fire. The soil is made better by the fire, and then the animals are stronger again. Yes?"

Mile after mile, we drove slowly through the Serengeti. We gazed at the elephants who stood close to our jeep, regarding us without fear. The zebra grazed around us, swatting their tails against the flies. The wildebeests grunted and ran in an endless procession toward the northern waters. Many places, there were small controlled fires, blackening the landscape, enriching the soil.

I stood in the jeep, transfixed by the sights, wondering. Fire enriches the soil. From the red-hot flames, flickering around the savannah, nutrients reappeared, which these gorgeous animals ate, from which they grew strong and sturdy.

I wondered. I thought.

In my mind, I am like the burned African savanna. All around me, golden grasses wave in the wind, soft and silky. I am the burned part, charred and blackened. I have no soft gold grass; I lie lumpy and hardened, covered with gray ash. The sleek cheetah and noble elephant have left me. They graze nearby, eying my desolation. I lie alone, darkened and abandoned. I lie alone, days and nights going by.

Days go by, years go by, decades go by. Above me, the Southern Cross glitters at night. Rainy seasons come and go. Slowly inside my charred skin, I begin to regrow, bountiful and rich. Tiny green shoots sprout, building a soft light green carpet of life. From the devastating fire grows new soil, rich with the nutrients of wisdom, patience and compassion. In the ashy wake, I grow the emotional strength that can only come from devastation.

Now the elephants flock to me. Their huge feet walk slowly through me, trunks reaching for the enriched grass that only charred plains like me can provide. The elephants reach out for kindness in their grief, compassion for their pain. The elephants never forget, but they can learn to live with their loss. The zebras come too, looking for lessons in companionship and connection. They need each other to keep watch for the lions. They have to be able to work together to survive. The shy leopard slinks in, wanting to know how to be braver at parties. The lion struts in, wanting help to be less aggressive, so he doesn't scare away his little cubs.

From the charred remains of my life, I have grown these nutrients for others. I didn't mean to; I didn't choose it. Someone else set me ablaze, I didn't ask for this. But here I am, just the same, making the best of things, as best I can.

If my suffering helps other lonely elephants, zebras, leopards, and lions, I am glad. If my story helps other people, I am glad. I am gladdest of all to live in peace, stretching out endlessly into the horizon, my newly golden grasses waving in the breeze, surrounded by the hairy, warm, majestic animals of the earth.

Photo Gallery

A: *The photo of Lise, 1967, which appears in the Senate record.*

B: *Lise, January 1969. One and a half years after the fire.*

C: *Lise and Marc*

D: *Bill Deguire*

E: *The Deguires*

F: *Kathryn Deguire*

G: *Lise, in elementary school*

H: *Lise, Bill, Marc and the Mercedes*

I: *Lise and Kathryn's last visit before Switzerland*

J: *Lise, present day*

K: *Anna, age 5 and Julia, age 7*

L: *Anna, Lise, Doug, Frankie, and Julia*

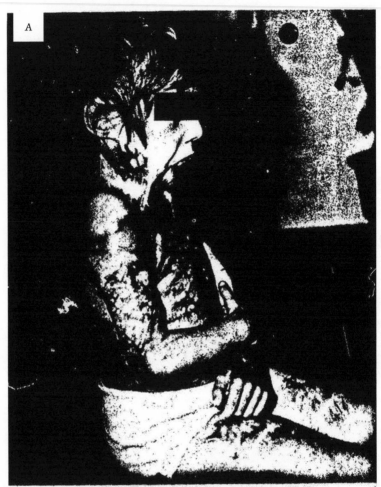

AN INEXPENSIVE PLASTIC FLASH-BACK ARRESTOR (IN USE BY OTHER MANUFACTURERS) ON A CAN OF CHARCOAL STARTER FLUID WOULD HAVE PREVENTED THE TERRIBLE RESULT DEPICTED HERE. BOTH BEFORE AND AFTER THIS OCCURRENCE, OTHER CHILDREN AND ADULTS HAVE BEEN INJURED AND KILLED BY THE SAME PRODUCT IN SIMILAR FASHION. THE CARNAGE CONTINUES DESPITE THE FACT THAT THE FLASH-BACK ARRESTOR IS 100% EFFECTIVE TO PREVENT THIS KIND OF EXPLOSION. EXHIBIT PRESENTED AS PART OF AUTHOR AND ATTORNEY EDWARD M. SWARTZ' TESTIMONY ON PRODUCT HAZARDS BEFORE THE SENATE COMMERCE COMMITTEE ON JULY 28, 1971.

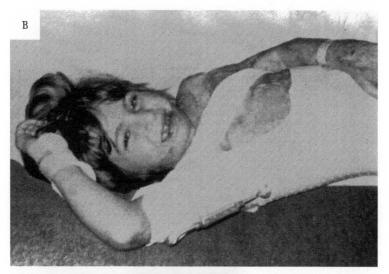

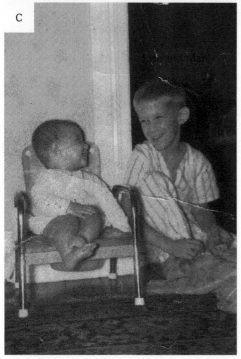

G

J

Acknowledgements

An inexperienced author, I wrote this book in one year. I benefited from all the wonderful memoirs I have read by other people, sharing their lives and entrancing me along the way. My expert help all came to me via loved ones. My friend Nancy Harrison practically besieged me, imploring me again and again to attend the Harvard Writers Conference for Healthcare Professionals, despite my practical concerns about money and travel. Thanks to her cheerful advocacy, I did attend the conference, which was indeed invaluable.

My husband Doug connected me to his former writing instructor, Miri Jaffe, who provided expert assistance in deepening my writing, reworking and reorganizing the material into a better piece of work. Miri's expertise was invaluable, and her support and encouragement helped me to move confidently forward. Thanks to Linda Konner and John Hanc (we tried!). Thanks so much to Martha Murphy, whose skilled editing and advice pulled *Flashback Girl* to completion.

As has always been the case in my life, unexpected helpers showed up, volunteering their expertise, guidance, connections and assistance. Thanks to Karen Sedlak Schultz, who connected me to Beth Schulman. Thanks to Kathy Seid, an early cheerleading reader, who connected me to Samantha Verant, who helped tighten up the book and the title. Thanks to Miriam Albert, Gary

Merken, and Sabrina Sacks Mann. Thanks to Lisa Gage, who held my hand and helped immeasurably with marketing. Thanks to Celeste Montgomery, my generous final editor with a focused eagle eye. Thanks especially to my dear nephew, Austin Alphonse, for his generous, loving spirit, and his brilliant art designs for *Flashback Girl*.

I would not be here without my beloved Dr. Constable and The Shriners Burns Institutes. I would not look like I do now without Dr. Eberwein and the burn team at Lehigh Valley. I am eternally grateful to all the doctors, nurses and therapists who worked with me over the years, helping me to heal physically and emotionally.

I thank every best friend I have ever had. I wasn't able to write about everyone by name, but I am grateful for the love and friendship so many people have given me. In chronological order of appearance in my life, I thank Michael Lennox, Melissa Stubis Virrill, Karen Sedlak Schultz, Kirsten Smith Navin, Cindy Carter, Nancy Caciola, Arlene O'Leary, Joe Rispo, Susan Algieri-Reiss, Cindy Lewis, Caryn and Brad Anthony, Celeste Montgomery, Kathy Seid, and Nancy and Jeff Harrison. Every one of you sparkles like a gem. You saved my heart so many times.

I thank my first family. I thank my Memere and Pepere, Emile and Viola Deguire. I thank my Aunt Betty Silber and my cousins, particularly Mary Deal. I thank my mother, Kathryn Deguire, for the lessons she taught me. I thank my father, Bill Deguire, for rescuing me from the fire, saving my life, and giving me show music, which I still adore.

I thank my brother, the best Batman, Marc-Emile Deguire, for being everything to me. "God only knows what I'd be without you."

I thank my second family. I thank my Behan family. Thank you to my little dog Frankie, who slumbered supportively by my side while I wrote this book. Thank you to my beloved daughters Julia and Anna Sismour, for bringing such joy into my life again. Thank you to my husband, friend and partner, Doug Behan, for everything you do and for always being there for me. I am so happy to have a family again, and I love you all so much.

REFERENCES

Consumer Product Safety Act of 1971: Hearings before the Committee on Commerce, U.S. Senate, 92nd Cong. 421-431 (1971).

Harry Harlow. https://en.wikipedia.org/wiki/Harry_Harlow

Larry Kert. https://en.wikipedia.org/wiki/Larry_Kert

Michael Bennett. https://en.wikipedia.org/wiki/Michael_Bennett_(theater)

Maguina, P. (2014). Lasers and Burn Scars: An Exciting New Era in Burn Reconstruction. *Burn Support Magazine.*

Ravage, B. (2004). *Burn unit: Saving lives after the flames.* Cambridge MA, Da Capo Press.

Scorpion and the Frog. https://en.wikipedia.org/wiki/The_Scorpion_and_the_Frog

Solox Denatured Alcohol Solvent. National Distillers and Chemical Corporation. New York, NY. www.ebay.com/itm/Vintage-Oil-Advertising-Tin-Solox-Denatured-Alcohol-Shellac-Fuel-Gas-Solvent-/262892819489

(1971). Wife, Daughter of City Native, Awarded. Glens Falls News.

Lise Deguire, Psy.D

Dr. Lise Deguire is a clinical psychologist in private practice. She grew up all over New Jersey and Long Island, the lone surviving child of unsettled and iconoclastic parents. After being severely burned at the age of four, she spent most of her childhood in the hospital, undergoing countless surgical procedures.

Dr. Deguire attended Tufts University, graduating in 1985, summa cum laude, Phi Beta Kappa. She earned her doctorate in clinical psychology from Hahnemann/Widener University in 1990. For the past twenty years she has maintained a solo practice in Pennington, New Jersey. In addition to her private practice, she is a keynote speaker. She has appeared on television, on the radio, and has been published in the Trenton Times, GrownandFlown.com, and Medium.com as well as her own blog.

She has waited 50 years to write her life story.

Dr. Deguire is married and is the mother of two daughters.

Made in the USA
Monee, IL
13 March 2023